P9-DDN-856

HOW I LEARNED TO COOK

HOW I LEARNED TO COOK

Culinary Educations from the World's Greatest Chefs

Edited by Kimberly Witherspoon
and Peter Meehan

BLOOMSBURY

Copyright © 2006 by Inkwell Management

All rights reserved. No part of this book may be used or
reproduced in any manner whatsoever without written permission
from the publisher except in the case of brief quotations embodied
in critical articles or reviews. For information address
Bloomsbury USA, 175 Fifth Avenue, New York, NY 10010.

Published by Bloomsbury USA, New York
Distributed to the trade by Holtzbrinck Publishers

All papers used by Bloomsbury USA are natural,
recyclable products made from wood grown in well-managed
forests. The manufacturing processes conform to the
environmental regulations of the country of origin.

"The Swim Club" is adapted from *Think Like a Chef* by Tom Colicchio.
"That's Entertainment" is adapted from *The Minimalist Entertains*
by Mark Bittman.

Lyrics from "I'm Your Captain": Words and music by Grand Funk
Railroad. © 1970 by Grand Funk Railroad. All rights controlled and
administered by Storybook Music. All rights reserved. International
copyright secured. Used by permission.

Library of Congress Cataloging-in-Publication Data has been applied for.

ISBN 1-59691-247-2
ISBN-13 978-1-59691-247-2

First U.S. Edition 2006

1 3 5 7 9 10 8 6 4 2

Typeset by Westchester Book Group
Printed in the United States of America by RR Donnelley, Harrisonburg

As always, to Summer and Paul

—K.W.

To Hannah

—P.F.M

CONTENTS

CONTENTS

Introduction

I F THE TITLE of this book has captured your attention, we'd wager the chances are good that you have your own story, if not several, about how you learned to cook.

We'd also wager that you will hear your story echoed by at least one of the forty essays presented in this volume. Not because all cooks come to the kitchen by the same route—far from it. No, any similarity to your own experience is a consequence of just the opposite virtue: diversity. The world-renowned chefs who generously took the time to reflect on the question, how did *you* learn to cook? recount here a delightful array of inspirations. From childhood creations to memories of tastes that brought enlightenment, from grueling apprenticeships in legendary kitchens to comic catastrophes brought on by ill-conceived experimentation, these professionals have come across it all. And in witnessing the great breadth and depth of these culinary experiences, the home cook cannot help but share, on occasion, a reassuring sense of familiarity and recognition.

What all of these very different chefs ultimately have in

common is best expressed in the aphorism "Cooking, like love, is best entered into with abandon, or not at all." Regardless of their styles and histories, it is this passion that distinguishes them—and that frequently leads them in over their heads. And it is the climb back to safety from the precipice of disaster that often makes for such a satisfying journey.

There are also gentler revelations to be shared, like youthful discoveries of Julia Child and Jacques Pepin, mentors unearthed in a treasured book. There are stories that anyone reading this collection will find hard to resist, magical instances when eyes were opened to possibilities that await anyone in the kitchen: an elaborate twenty-four-hour recipe at last turns out right; a nervous newlywed succeeds in delighting her food-obsessed husband.

Other lessons are less enchanting but demonstrate that electrocution, near-asphyxiation, and scalding airborne oil can be very instructive and that death threats, packs of dogs, and crack pipes can all play unexpected roles in a chef's rise to the top.

Throughout the book these chefs also share practical wisdom gained from their experiences, and for that we are grateful because, as one chef has learned from his relationship with the inimitable Madeleine Kamman, learning to cook is not a process—or a story—that is ever truly finished.

KIMBERLY WITHERSPOON
PETER MEEHAN

The Big Red Book, or El Práctico
FERRÁN ADRIÀ

Ferrán Adrià began his celebrated culinary career washing dishes at a restaurant in the town of Castelldefels, Spain. He went on to work at various restaurants before serving in the Spanish military at the naval base of Cartagena. In 1984, at the age of twenty-two, he joined the kitchen staff of El Bulli. Only eighteen months later, he became head chef of the restaurant—which went on to receive its third Michelin star in 1997. Adrià's gift for combining unexpected contrasts of flavor, temperature, and texture has won him global acclaim as one of the most creative and inventive culinary geniuses in the world; Gourmet *magazine has hailed him as "the Salvador Dali of the kitchen."*

I CAME TO COOKING purely by chance; it was not, by any means, a vocation. It unfolded gradually, and rather surprisingly, over several years. It was never a search, a mission, a holy grail.

To begin with, I was not one of those children who, at age six or seven, discovers an enthusiasm for baking cookies. I did not watch, ablaze with curiosity, as my grandmother stirred the family broth. The kitchen in the home where I grew up in Barcelona was a place that delivered regular, honest, solid, un-complicated meat-and-potato meals. Growing up, as a child and as an adolescent, the goings-on over the kitchen stove were as uninteresting to me as they were incomprehensible.

What did interest me, and keenly, as I ventured deeper into adolescence, was soccer. And parties. And, above all, girls. High school, on the other hand, held no charm for me at all. I was not a bad student. I actually got good grades, especially in economics, the subject it was supposed that I would study in college. But it was in my final year of high school that I realized economics held no appeal for me either. In fact, I was fed up with studying altogether. I didn't see much future in it—not for me. At the age of seventeen what I most wanted to do in the world was to spend the summer in Ibiza. This was 1980. Ibiza, a small Mediterranean island half an hour's flight south and east of Barcelona, was then the party capital of the world. It's still a mecca for party animals. But it was even more so then. It was *the* fiesta spot, par excellence.

So I quit school and set myself the heroic quest of spending a summer vacation in Ibiza. My dad, who was a plasterer by trade and had high hopes for me, was not too impressed with my decision. On the other hand, neither did he try to dissuade me. He said, "Fine. No problem. Go ahead. But don't expect one penny from me. You do this, by all means. But you're on your own."

Well, I wasn't entirely on my own. My father did lend a help-ing hand. I needed a job to raise the money to get to Ibiza, and he put me in touch with a friend of his, a cook named Miguel Moy. Miguel gave me a job at his kitchen in a hotel in Castellde-fels, a beach resort twenty minutes south of Barcelona. Now don't imagine for one moment that this was a prospect that excited me. It was purely a means to an end. I might just as well have got a job in a factory or as a gardener or an assistant garage mechanic. As it turned out, I was a junior assistant cook. Translated, that meant "dishwasher."

This was no dive, though. Miguel's kitchen cooked classic cuisine. Tournedo Rossini, paella—that sort of thing. And Miguel was a taskmaster. After a while he got me to help out with the cooking basics, but he was always mightily demanding—of himself as well as everybody else. I've never come across a chef who shouted so much or who was angrier more often. The slightest deviation from what he considered the accepted way of doing things provided a loud and fearsome bark. He demanded absolute punctuality. You were five minutes late and you knew about it! It's from Miguel that I learned the value of punctuality, of doing things on time. It is a lesson I have never forgotten and for which I am deeply grateful to him.

In retrospect, that is. Just as I am grateful to him for having given me a big fat book five hundred pages long to read and learn. A book of classic recipes, sixty-five hundred of them, a mix of traditional Spanish cooking and dishes heavily influenced by French cuisine. Miguel said I had to learn all the dishes by heart. So I began copying them down on pieces of paper, each and every one of them. I would do it in my spare time, usually before work in the morning. I still have the book. It has a red hardback cover. It is called *El Práctico*. The pages are frayed. The spine is cracked. But I have it in a prominent place, always at hand, in my laboratory workshop in Barcelona.

The first dish I learned to make was a potato stew. Miguel did not trust me at this stage to cook for the clientele. This was the food for the staff of the hotel, which was where I lived for the nine months I worked there. I still preserved my dream of going to Ibiza but, as it turned out, Castelldefels served very nicely in the meantime. My one regret was that I wasn't able to play soccer on Saturdays and Sundays, because of my work commitments. But otherwise it was a lot of fun. Nonstop parties and lots of girls. It was very unusual for me to go to bed before dawn. I remember Miguel came out with us one night. He was a guy at who partied hard, too! He drank all of us under the table. One Cuba libre after another.

Little by little I learned to cook. I never loved it. Not at that stage. It was not what turned me on. It was just a job, like any other. I learned how to make the regular, popular dishes people asked for at the restaurant. Rice dishes and also, for example, *fideuá*—a Catalan favorite, like paella but with noodles. It was a good period of my life. I was having a lot of fun. I was being taught a useful trade and being paid for it. And, above all, I was free. For a boy aged seventeen or eighteen to be living on his own, away from his parents, was very unusual in Spain in those days. And I was reveling in it.

But the notion that I might dedicate the rest of my life to this business—impossible! It was entirely out of the question. Besides, deep down somewhere I was ambitious, and cooking was not something that you did in Spain in those days if you dreamed of being a success in life. The notion that a Spanish chef might operate at a world-class level was absolutely implausible, nonsensical. Gastronomy: that was what the French did. We just cooked. The mom and pop stuff our parents had grown up with, and their parents before them.

I finally left Castelldefels in April 1981. And, yes, I achieved my dream. I made it to Ibiza. With the added advantage that I was now employable and could stay there, practically, for as long as I liked. I got a job at a place called Club Cala Leña. It was a condominium vacation club with its own restaurant.

What I most remember from that phase was, naturally, the parties again. It was like Castelldefels, only multiplied by three. Every night. It was relentless!

But my cooking improved, too. I had brought *El Práctico*, my big red recipe book, along with me, and I continued to study it. This was the alpha and the omega of cuisine in Spain. You learned that and you'd learned it all. I was in a smaller kitchen now, just four or five of us, and that was great for developing my basic skills. Being so few, each person had much more responsibility, had to cook more things. There was less specialization. I broadened my repertoire. I made gazpacho, sole *meunière*, those sorts of things. It was another wonderful experience. I worked hard and played hard.

Four months later the vacation club went bankrupt and we were all out on the street. But I had saved some money, so I stayed a month longer—now the *only* thing I did was party— and then headed back home to Barcelona. Here I flitted from one job to another, two months here, two months there. But always, without quite realizing it (this was why I say my career has been the product of pure chance, never a search) I was working my way up. I worked at a tapas bar in the center of the city; I worked at a place called el Suquet—where I really learned how to make suquet, a soupy fish stew very popular in Catalonia. I also worked at a restaurant where the kitchen staff were not a happy bunch, because they wouldn't pay us, so we took our revenge by quitting en masse on December 31.

Wherever I went, it was still basically the same food. It was all out of *El Práctico*. Always. Until one day early in 1982 I got a job at a place called Finisterre. I remember my surprise upon entering the kitchen. It wasn't so much because of the food, which did have an air of nouvelle cuisine about it and was decidedly different from what I had been used to; it was more because of the vastness and the organized operation of the kitchen. For the first time I learned what it was to work in brigades. I was still very much an assistant cook, but, there was no doubt about it, it was a step up. Until then the best I had known was a Mercedes Benz. This was a Ferrari.

I was certainly learning now. And yet it still wasn't a vocation. In fact during those days I often thought of chucking it all. Not because I didn't like cooking, but because it didn't grab me. I was eager to try something else.

As it turned out, the next step I took had nothing to do with my own free will. I was called up for military service, as all young men were in those days in Spain, and assigned to the navy, in the port of Cartagena. But never once did I board a ship! Instead I was made to work in the kitchens. It was far from the glamour of Finisterre, believe me. I was part of a vast team of anonymous cooks charged with feeding three thousand troops. The challenge had nothing to do with the food itself: fried eggs, soups, potato omelettes—what the sailors wanted. It was a challenge in terms of cooking for such a large number of people. The organization required to feed all those mouths at the same time was of an order different from anything I had experienced.

And then I caught another break, without realizing at the time just how valuable an apprenticeship I was serving. I got a job working in the kitchen of the Captain General, the main man in the navy detachment of Cartagena, the admiral. I cooked in the kitchen of the mansion where he lived. There were just four or five of us, and whereas the emphasis at the base had been on quantity, quality was now the paramount objective. We would often have to cook for visiting dignitaries, ministers, even for the king! Soon I became head of the kitchen and the buck suddenly, for the first time in my life, stopped with me! I not only learned to lead and to organize, I also learned another very valuable skill: how to go shopping—to buy the food on my own, every single day.

I also began to expand my repertoire. Never before had I branched out in my reading beyond my trusty *El Práctico*. But now I read Robert Lafont, author of what was then the bible of nouvelle cuisine. And, as I had done with *El Práctico*, I copied down the recipes, intrigued because somewhere I think I was beginning to understand that this was revolutionary stuff, changing the course of gastronomy. But it was still a trade, not a passion. I still hadn't caught the bug.

It was then, however, that I had my first truly serious encounter with nouvelle cuisine, thanks to Fermí Puig, who today runs the excellent restaurant Drolma, at the Majestic Hotel in Barcelona. He came to work in the captain general's kitchen for a while, after I had been in charge for three or four months, but he was already an employee at El Bulli. There was no established professional route to success in cooking then, the way there is now. It was all a question of getting the breaks, of who you chanced to meet. Meeting Fermí was a huge, random, fateful moment, in my life, though again I had no idea that was the case at the time.

He proposed that I come and work at El Bulli for a month in August that year, 1983. I did, and they seemed to like what they saw because they offered me a job for when I finished my military service that December. I accepted, acknowledging a deep debt of gratitude to the Spanish navy. It was very rare for anyone, in any line of business, to derive much long-term benefit from their military service. In my case I was the exception to the rule—in, of all things, cookery!

I was about to take a big step. El Bulli was already a two-star Michelin restaurant. There were no three-star restaurants in

Spain, and only one other two-star—Arzak in San Sebastian. I began at El Bulli in earnest, and in March 1984 I was put in charge of the fish section, with three or four assistants under me. In October that same year I made the grade. At the age of twenty-two I was offered the job of head chef by the owner, and today my partner, Juli Soler. I would be joint head chef, he stressed, with Christian Lutaud. That was just fine with me. The truth is I wouldn't have said yes if it had been me on my own. I wouldn't have dared take on so much responsibility.

It was at this point that I finally began to understand that maybe, just maybe, this was the road I was destined to take in life. It hadn't quite sunk in. Nearly, but not yet. And this was perhaps because the truth remained that, technically proficient as I might have become by now, I was not truly producing my own dishes. I was still copying the work of other chefs. I was still getting my inspiration from books and magazines. After all, it was what all of us Spanish chefs were doing, so why should I have been any different?

The decisive step came in 1985 when I went to spend a month at the magnificent Pic Restaurant in Valence, France. I sat at the feet of the head chef, Georges Blanc, who was absolutely one of the top chefs in the world. That month was a time of continual amazement and awe. The kitchen was vast, with thirty chefs, but the quality was stupendous. This was no longer a Ferrari. This was a Formula One. And it was here that I learned to really cook at the highest level. It was here that I picked up the critical know-how.

In October of 1986 Christian Lutaud left and I was now completely in charge of El Bulli. That same month Juli and I went to attend a course in Cannes under another truly great chef, Jacques Maximin. There was one thing he said to us that has always stayed with me. Someone asked him, "What is creativity?" And he replied, "Creativity is not copying." So simple and so obvious, I suppose, yet that was a key moment for me, the final turning point. Until then I had always copied—but from that moment on everything changed. I understood something I had never understood before. I evolved, at last, and went from technician to creator.

From 1987 on I knew that this was my life. Like most people, I had always worked to live. Now I lived to work. At El Bulli we went on to redefine, to reinvent Spanish cuisine. I have a stack of books, totaling six thousand pages of pictures and text, that trace the evolution of our cooking from then to this day.

The thing to emphasize, though, is how gradual, how circumstantial a process I underwent in the business of learning how to cook. It was not, I repeat, a magical moment of revelation with my grandmother when I was six years old. I was like any young boy in my attitude to food. I found it, at best, a necessary evil. But I am glad that was how I felt. For I believe that had I learned from my family, I would have been far less creative in my adult life. The creativity would, I believe, have been smothered from the start, smothered under the weight of tradition. It was fortunate, from my point of view, to have started with a clean slate. That way I had the imaginative breadth to allow me to do the truly important thing in cooking, which is not to make one dish, but to invent a technique that allows you to produce a thousand dishes.

That is why it's not true when people say that their mother's or their grandmother's cooking is the best in the world. It's not true! Okay, in a sentimental sense, maybe. But technically, categorically it is not! In fact, the difference today between home cooking and restaurant cooking is wider than it ever has been. In the old days, even as recently as when I began to cook, the amateur was nearly at the level of the professional. That's all changed massively. Now the difference in difficulty between cooking done at home and haute cuisine is on a scale of one to hundred. And what that means—and this is the beauty of it all—is that in truth you never stop learning to cook. I myself never stop learning. There is a surprise, a new lesson, every single day.

(translated from the Spanish and co-written with John Carlin)

Boiling Point
JOSÉ ANDRÉS

*José Andrés was born in Nieres, Spain, and attended Escola de
Restauracio i Hostalatge of Barcelona, apprenticing at restaurant El Bulli under celebrated master chef and mentor Ferrán
Adrià. In 1990 Andrés moved to New York City to work for
the Barcelona-based restaurant El Dorado Petit. In 1993 he
moved to Washington, D.C., to become head chef and partner
at Jaleo, a Spanish restaurant there. He has since opened two
more Jaleo locations and serves as executive chef-partner at
Café Atlantico, Oyamel, Zaytinya, and the six-seat minibar
within Café Atlantico, one of the premiere destinations for
avant-garde cooking in the United States. In 2003 the James
Beard Foundation named Andrés Best Chef: Mid-Atlantic Region, and in 2004 Bon Appetit named him Chef of the Year. He
published his first cookbook,* Tapas: A Taste of Spain in America, *in 2005. José is also the host of the wildy popular* Vamos a
cocinar, *a daily food program on Television Española (TVE),
Spanish national television.*

I LEARNED A LOT of what I know about cooking, especially traditional Catalan cooking, from my mother. She was a working mom, but she cooked for us every night. My father, on the other hand, confined his cooking to the weekends, as do many men in northern Spain and, as I've learned, here in America.

My father's Sunday cookouts were kind of like American weekend barbecues, when the men are out in the backyard with their friends, beers in their hands, gathered around the grill poking at hamburgers, except that his were grander in scale than the run-of-the-mill barbecue.

His specialty, the dish that he used to make every other Sunday for the entire time I was growing up, was paella. Paella is a Spanish classic, a rice dish prepared in a broad, shallow, two-handled pan called a *paella*. He cooked tremendous paellas, paellas that could feed a hundred people. He used a gorgeous copper paella pan that was giant—a meter and a half across—big and beautiful. It seemed impossibly huge to me when I was a child, the size of the moon.

One of the first paellas I remember my father cooking was at a fund-raiser for my school, in Santa Coloma de Cervelló, when I was six or seven years old. It was during the spring, and the cherry trees were in full blossom. Sometimes I think that I feel so at home here in Washington, D.C., because the first time I visited, the cherry trees were flowering, like they did every spring in the rural town I grew up in Cataluña.

By the time I was eleven or twelve, I was old enough and eager enough to start helping my father with his Sunday meals. But while he agreed to let me assist him, to my disappointment he never let me participate in the physical act of cooking, the sautéing, simmering, stirring: the glory work. That was always for him and his adult friends. There were other tasks for me to look after.

As instructed, early Sunday mornings I would commandeer the other young kids from the neighboring houses to start the preparations. There were dozens of things to be done until the paella was ready in the early afternoon. We would put the tables together and set them. We would open bottles of wine that the adults would drink later in the day. We would gather bunches of wildflowers to decorate the tables.

And then there was the fire to be dealt with. An all-day fire for a giant copper pot requires a *lot* of fuel. Initially, I would just go out with the other kids to gather wood from the countryside. When I got a little older and a little more savvy, however, my father revealed to me how the fire under the paella pan needed to work: in the beginning, when you are sautéing the meat or the seafood or the shellfish, you need a moderate to high fire; at the stage when you add everything to the pan—the rice, water or broth, the saffron and pimentos—you need huge boiling, amazing boiling, supernatural boiling. This is the moment of truth, and the fire must not fail you. The flame needs to be very, very strong for a few minutes—and then suddenly die down, so that the paella steadily simmers and doesn't overcook.

My father explained how all the different woods we were gathering would burn. Cherrywood burns differently from oak and different still from olive. I learned that wood is a whole world of knowledge unto itself: some wood burns hot and fast and dies after three or four minutes—that's what you need for the crucial boiling; some burns slow and steady, which is the kind of wood you need for before and after. Over time I became adept at making and managing the fire under the paella. But, oh, do I still remember how much I would sweat. It was the heat of the fire, certainly, but also in part from worrying whether or not I had it right.

It took a few months—not that we ever lost a paella on account of the fire—before I eventually mastered it. But I'm a guy who's always asking myself, What's next? I think it's important to be curious if you're going to be a chef, to always be searching, to not sit around and be satisfied with what you're doing. Maybe I am that way today because I was always curious as a kid, always impatient, always wanting to know what came next.

I was thirteen or fourteen by the time I was put completely in charge of the fire, just the time in your life when you really start questioning everything: Why does this happen? Why do I cry when I cut up onions? Why do you add things in a certain order? Why don't you stir the paella after a certain point? Everything. It's also when you stop being satisfied with grown-ups just letting you hang around and you actually want to be dealt with like a person.

Every couple of weeks I'd think, *This* will be the week when I get to cook the paella. I'd finally get to stir, to stand around with the men, to be one of the cooks. And every Sunday I was back down there sweating, hand in the fire, burning myself. My temper grew as hot as the cherrywood flame. I was headed toward a confrontation with my father.

One week I couldn't stand it anymore and I blew up at him in front of everyone: "When am I going to get to cook the paella? It's always fire, fire, fire. I want to cook!" I was pissed off, with all the indignant rage that only a teenager can muster. My father, a jovial guy, always with a little bit of something to eat in one hand and a smile on his face, turned serious for a second. "José," he said. "We are cooking right now. We will talk about this later, my boy." And he went back to tending to his paella. I stormed off, fuming.

He found me later in the day, when our neighbors had all gone home. "Son, I would have thought you were smarter. The fire is the most important job! Don't you see that everything begins and ends with the fire? Without the fire there wouldn't *be* a paella." He grinned and placed his hand on my shoulder, directing my gaze toward our backyard, the scene of countless festivities. "And if there wasn't wine to drink, tables to sit at, and neighbors to eat with, there would be no point in making the paella at all. The cooking? The cooking is the easy part. The truth is that every step is important."

How simple he made it seem. How hard it was for me to accept. Though I continued to help make the fire every other Sunday until I went off to cooking school at fifteen, I never woke up one morning and thought, "My dad was right."

Now that I'm a grown man, I know that he was. I've been cooking—not just making the fire—for twenty years, and I understand that every inglorious step, from the most rudimentary chopping and prepping to cleaning up at the end of the night, is important. And that in order to reach the point where you get to be the one stirring the paella, you've got to master each step along the way.

Country Living
MARIO BATALI

Mario Batali believes that olive oil is as precious as gold, shorts are acceptable attire for every season, and food, like most things, is best when left to its own simple beauty. Batali is the chef and co-owner of a quintet of restaurants that have redefined Italian dining for New Yorkers over the past decade: Babbo, Lupa, Esca, Otto, and Del Posto. Among his many accolades, in 1999 GQ magazine named Mario Man of the Year in the chef category. In 2002 he won the James Beard Foundation's Best Chef: New York City award; in 2005 the foundation named Mario Outstanding Chef of the Year; and in 2006 he took home the Foundation's award for best international cookbook for his book Molto Italiano.

W HEN I WAS in my early twenties, I worked for the Four Seasons in a couple of their West Coast hotels: first in San Francisco and then in Santa Barbara.

Like most hotel chefs, I was too smart for my own good. I had way too much to say. I had all kinds of ideas, and I tended to combine as many of them as possible on every plate. If one ingredient was good, three would be better. It was the double kick pedal, fingertapping, wretchedly excessive style of the 1980s. It was loud cooking.

But it went over well enough with my employers that the company offered me a gig that I'm sure plenty of chefs would have jumped at: a job developing their restaurant concepts at a new property in Hawaii.

The offer, while generous, didn't sit right with me. My food cost was going to be astronomical in a place where you have to import everything other than milk and pineapples. There would not be a large pool of cooks to draw from. And it was just too much of a backwater—too cut off from everything else.

While I was tempted by the stunning tropical locale—Who wouldn't be?—I knew that ultimately it wasn't a move I wanted to make. I talked over my situation on the phone with my dad, a career engineer for Boeing, and he proposed a plan. He'd chat with his contacts at the manufacturers in Europe that Boeing sourced plane parts from and see if they'd approach the restaurants where they did their corporate entertaining on my behalf. Maybe one of them would be amenable to taking a young American cook under their wing.

He made the calls, his friends wrote the letters. And, out of the ten restaurants to which my services were offered, only Trattoria La Volta responded, saying that they'd take me. That certainly made choosing easy.

I negotiated a start date with the voice on the other end of the line, halfway around the world, and they said they'd have someone meet me at the train station at an appointed time.

For the next few weeks, I planned the trip. It was tougher than I had initially anticipated. First off, I couldn't find Borgo Capanne, the town where the trattoria was located, in any of the guidebooks I bought. Or even in any of the remaining volumes on the shelves of the book store (when I returned in desperation). I thought I'd get smart and just locate it in an atlas, to give me a rough idea, but after an exhaustive study of the Rand-McNally provided me with nothing, I was a little nervous.

Finally I found mention of the town and the restaurant in Faith Willinger's *Eating in Italy,* which also happened to note that it was one of the best places for fresh pasta in all of Italy. Perched on the border of Emilia-Romagna and Tuscany, the trattoria was situated out in the country. Deep in the country.

I flew into London, took a train to Torino in Piedmont, and another to the station nearest the town. Watching the city, then the suburbs, fall away as we started up and into the Apennine, I was positively giddy. It was the scenery from *The Sound of Music* unfolding just outside my train window.

Hours later, we pulled into the mountainside town. I climbed out of the train car, glad to stretch my legs, and strode onto the platform. All around me were elegant Italians trying not to stare at me like I was some kind of Hungarian circus freak. When you're the only guy with a long red ponytail sporting brightly patterned weightlifting pants and a tank top, a bag of golf clubs slung over one shoulder and a knife roll in the other, you stick out. To be fair, I was checking them out a little intently, too, since I had no idea who I was meeting at the station. As the crowd thinned and then gradually disappeared, I figured it out: no one. There had been a miscommunication somewhere along the line.

After a few minutes of very diligent but entirely unproductive fiddling with a phone at the train station—I didn't know which numbers to dial and which to omit, since I had everything written down with international dialing and country codes intact—a kindly gentleman helped me out by dialing the restaurant. Unfortunately, because it was a Monday, the restaurant was closed. So I had to press him into dialing assistance again: I chased down my father's acquaintance at the airplane parts factory, and he helped me arrange a ride to the restaurant.

As soon as I arrived, Gianni and Betta, the owners, set me up in my room, a cozy space with a big window that looked down into a valley dotted with stands of chestnut trees and up onto a ridge from where tall Tuscan pines shot up skyward like spires. If I had any qualms about passing on Hawaii and coming to the trattoria, the view from my room's window dispeled them.

And they were quashed entirely at dinner that night. I ate with the family down in the dining room of the twenty-five-seat restaurant: we polished off a magnum of an excellent wine, I tasted the best pasta I had ever encountered, and, as it was the beginning of truffle season, there was a snowstorm of shaved white truffles over half of everything I was served. That dinner gave me a glimpse of the unimaginable greatness of the place where I'd be working.

My immersion into that greatness began the next morning, after a fitful night's sleep. (I had two espressos after dinner like everyone else, but I wasn't calibrated to that speed of life yet.) I reported to the kitchen at eight a.m., like I would have back at the hotel and . . . nothing. Nine and ten o'clock came and went. I looked around the kitchen a little bit, getting to know the space, but I didn't want to get caught poking around when someone finally showed up, so mostly I kept to myself.

Finally, at around eleven a.m., Betta breezed into the kitchen and the deprogramming started. I eagerly asked where the *mise en place* was so we could start cooking. She looked at me funny, her head cocked, and then led me over to the refrigerator, where there were whole onions in the vegetable drawer and a whole veal loin on the shelf above it. At Trattoria La Volta, they cooked with ingredients, not with *mise en place*.

We'd start with the pasta, she told me. She shaped a mound of flour on a wooden cutting board, burrowed out a well in the middle, and cracked ten eggs into it. As she was kneading the dough, I asked Betta where the pasta machine was, figuring I'd set it up while she finished her little demonstration on how to mix the flour and eggs together. She looked over at me and said, straight-faced, "If I go into a restaurant and see one of those rollers, I leave."

She rolled the pasta out with a worn wooden rolling pin on a big wooden board. I'd later come to learn that if you want that incomparable cat's-tongue-rough texture that really holds on to the sauce, you need to make pasta the way Betta does. There are no shortcuts.

In an attempt to get to know her new charge better, she asked me what kind of *minestra* I made. *Minestra*, in textbook Italian, means soup, but in the Bolognese dialect, it refers to pasta, soups, and rice dishes—she was essentially asking me to describe my cooking style or name a dish that typified it.

It didn't matter that I misunderstood her and answered the question like it was about soup: nothing I was cooking at the time would have impressed her. I told her about a raw tomato-zucchini gazpacho with poached lobster we'd been running at the hotel in Santa Barbara. She had a look on her face like I had just told her I liked cooking dog.

Later in the day, I overheard her telling someone at the restaurant about my "*minestra*" in an incredulous, disbelieving tone, naming each of ingredients in the soup like she was reading the counts of an indictment: cooked lobster, raw tomato, raw zucchini. She found the combination preposterous. She must have feared that I'd never come to understand what they were doing at La Volta.

But, over the course of nearly three years, I did.

The landscape taught me things: one morning I woke up to find the trees outside my windows strung with orange balls, dozens if not hundreds of them. When I went outside to take a closer look, I saw that they weren't a prank and they weren't orange balls—they were persimmons.

You only have to see how quickly a persimmon tree is flooded with fruit once in your life to immediately understand why persimmon recipes always make passing reference to dealing with an abundance of them. And when I picked a plump orange persimmon off the tree, polished it on my jacket, and took what turned out to be an acidic, sour, painful bite, I learned that persimmons need time to ripen before they're ready to eat.

What wasn't broadcast to me in bright orange lights was taken care of by Betta's father, Quintillio. Quintillio, who had the best truffle dog in the area, helped me get in touch with the forager's spirit. I'd accompany him on his daily hikes: he was the kind of guy who liked to walk around in the woods for three hours at a stretch. I'd go mushroom foraging with him, and while I'd be hoping to stumble onto a patch of mushrooms before he would, he'd sagaciously redirect my attention to a patch of wild dandelions (called in Italian *striccapugne,* close your fist, because it closed its flower at night) that I, in my single-minded focus, had just bypassed.

And back at the restaurant, Betta would show me how to cook, whether it was those freshly gathered *striccapugne* (it took an hour of hard boiling to get them ready for the table), or a simple pasta dish. She taught me in clear, direct pronouncements, like her restrictive qualification for fresh pasta in a restaurant, or by quiet example, ignoring my exuberant enthusiasm for dishes crowded with ingredients, while demonstrating how to make perfect papardelle with peas: papardelle and peas. That was all.

And over time, I didn't so much as come around to Betta's way of cooking as I let go of the baggage I brought with me. Helping her cook there in the mountains of Emilia-Romagna, I learned that adding one or two or six extra ingredients to a dish didn't make it more intense—it muddied it up. She made me filter the white noise out of my cooking, but she didn't turn the volume down: she taught me how to get across what I wanted louder and clearer than ever before.

Sweet Child O' Mine
RICK BAYLESS

Chef-restaurateur, cookbook author, and television personality, Rick Bayless is from the fourth generation of an Oklahoma family of restaurateurs and grocers. After studying Spanish and Latin American studies as an undergraduate and doing doctoral work in anthropological linguistics at the University of Michigan, Rick spent six years in Mexico with his wife, Deann, and wrote Authentic Mexican: Regional Cooking from the Heart of Mexico *in 1986. The book was hailed by the* New York Times's *legendary Craig Claiborne as the "greatest contribution to the Mexican table imaginable." In 1987 Rick moved to Chicago and opened the hugely successful Frontera Grill, which specializes in contemporary regional Mexican cooking. In 1989, on the heels of Frontera Grill's success, Rick opened the elegant Topolobampo, one of the only fine-dining Mexican restaurants in the United States. In 1991 the James Beard Foundation named him Best Chef: Midwest and in 1995 as Chef of the Year. That same year he was chosen Chef of the Year by the International Association of Culinary Professionals. In 1996 Rick started a line of prepared foods, including salsas, chips, and grilling rubs, bearing the Frontera Foods label. He is the author of six cookbooks, including* Mexican Everyday, *which was nominated for a James Beard Book Award in 2006.*

I DISCOVERED JULIA IN 1963. Her first television program, *The French Chef,* had just hit the airwaves of public television and I eagerly tuned in. I was transfixed.

By ten years old, I'd already become a kid who threw myself headlong into projects, coming up for air only after months— sometimes years—of total absorption. My older brother, Skip, played practically every sport with great success, but I never could throw myself into sports the way he did. I came from a more creative mold, and cooking had always held a certain fascination. Julia was about to fan the embers of that fascination into a raging fire.

I grew up in my parents' barbecue restaurant in Oklahoma, and I'd always felt totally at home playing around in the kitchen there, being immersed in the flavors and smells of the place, and watching the cooks work over the open fire. *The French Chef,* however, opened the door to a world I didn't know existed: Julia exposed me to a more complex and varied side of cooking and, over the course of a few shows, demonstrated that it was a sophisticated discipline. At that time barbecue and simple home cooking were all I knew.

The first television my family owned was a steel-cased black-and-white Admiral that could be carried from room to room. On the night that Julia chirped her "bon appétit" over the airwaves, I would lug the set into my room and stare at the little gray screen and dream about duplicating her exotic, miraculous dishes. Julia's world of French cooking, where a culture-wide reverence for food seemed like the most natural thing, felt so far off from where I was. But I knew that someday I'd have to get there.

That fall of my tenth year, when football season started and my brother had to get fitted for his gear, I lobbied my parents for an equal expenditure, the must-have gear for my passion. I wanted them to buy me a copy of *Mastering the Art of French Cooking*, Julia Child's first cookbook. It had been published a year or two earlier and I had pored over it at the bookstore on numerous occasions. I had cradled it in my arms, sensing that it was a masterful tome.

My parents listened to my urgent pleas with bewilderment; football helmets and baseball bats are what ten-year-old boys want, not cookbooks. Still, they decided to support me, to buy me the book, perhaps just to end my persistent campaign of pestering. When they saw the price tag on *Mastering the Art*, however, they were ready to change their minds. But I knew what the cost of football gear was, so I made my case: I didn't ask for any pricey sporting equipment, and now they needed to *get me that book*. I stood my ground and I got my copy.

For the next year, I read that book everywhere I went. On the couch, in the car, sitting in the backyard—I studied recipe after recipe, trying to taste everything those words meant. And once a week, I absconded with the Admiral, sequestered myself in my room, and dutifully wrote down everything Julia said in a big red notebook filled with newsprint pages and the picture of a Native American in full headdress on the front cover.

I cooked a lot of the recipes scribbled down as notes from episodes of *The French Chef* and from my now well-worn copy of *Mastering the Art* during the years that followed. Every couple of months I announced that I was going to cook a formal meal for my family, which would give me the chance to try out more of Julia's recipes. I'm not sure exactly what they thought of it all—I doubt they were necessarily looking forward to a preteen's amateurish attempts at a complicated cuisine they knew nothing about. Undercooking the green beans and "continental" fare carried little weight at a dining table that permanently smelled of smoky ribs and barbecue sauce.

The food fixation took hold of me even tighter. I, for some inexplicable reason, decided the only way for me to become a complete human being was to cook lamb chops. Suspecting that my mother wouldn't let me buy them, since I couldn't recall us ever eating lamb while I was growing up, I telephoned the one grocery store in town that delivered and, in my most adult voice, I ordered lamb chops to be sent to "the Bayless residence." I charged the chops to my mother's account and hung up, thrilled with the delicious possibilities that now lay within my reach.

That night, I found out why I had been denied the epicurean indulgence of lamb for my entire life: when my father was serving in World War II he had been fed so much mutton that he couldn't stand the thought of lamb, much less the smell of it cooking. I'm not sure if it was my father's reaction to the idea of me cooking lamb or the aghast look on my mother's face when she caught sight of the grocery bill, realizing I'd spent most of that week's grocery money on a single night's dinner, but there were a lot of tears shed before that night was over. There's little I remember about my first taste of lamb chops (except their teary saltiness), though I'm sure I must have cooked them à la Julia and forced myself to swallow every bite. My family still talks about the time that Rick ordered the lamb chops . . .

Many, many years later, after I'd become an established chef with several cookbooks and two successful restaurants here in

Chicago, Julia, through her producers, invited me to tape an episode of her show *In Julia's Kitchen with Master Chefs*.

The offer sparked all kinds of emotions for me, everything from exhilaration to fear to gratitude—but most of all, a deep and powerful anxiety at the thought of meeting Julia in person. I honestly didn't know if I wanted to get that close. She had come to our restaurant once or twice, and I had been careful to be warm and gracious, but not too familiar. I made sure her food was perfect, of course, but she was like the queen to me, and I felt the need to be formal and respectful. I couldn't imagine ever plopping down next to her and gossiping about cookbook authors or deploring the sad state of American home cooking. She and I already had a profound, decades-long "professional" relationship; she just didn't know anything about it. As a consequence, I had no idea how to act around her.

The show was being taped right in Julia's kitchen at her home in Cambridge, Massachusetts, to me one of the holiest shrines in American gastronomy. (Since her passing, they've literally removed and reconstructed the kitchen in the Smithsonian in Washington, D.C.) Even though I'd never set foot in that kitchen, I had come to know it intimately through the photos and diagrams in her book *In Julia's Kitchen*, which was published in the seventies, when I was in graduate school. (During those student days, I'd developed a group of friends who loved to eat. None of us had any money to go *out* to eat, so we all cooked for each other. We'd go months and months between visits to restaurants, but we still managed to eat a lot of great meals. Part of that was thanks to Julia's book; I cooked every single recipe out of *In Julia's Kitchen* while I was in graduate school.)

There was a whole section in the book about how Julia organized her kitchen, and I had spent so many hours reading it, absorbing all the information, that I knew the kitchen's layout perfectly. I knew which pans were hanging on which walls. I knew her gadgets. I knew her pantry. Yet it felt strange to think about going there—to this place that had been part of my fantasy life—and actually cooking in that kitchen with Julia standing beside me . . . But it was an impossible invitation to turn down.

On the summer afternoon that I arrived at her home it was all business. We were to tape our episode the following day, and I was led to the basement, where I stood by the washer and dryer and was briefed by some of the production staff. Afterward, during a break in the episode they were shooting that day, I went upstairs and walked into Julia's kitchen for the first time. It was as though an electric shock pulsed through my body as I crossed the threshold: here was all that stuff I knew, that I'd known about for years. It was like walking into my own family's home in some ways, except that I'd never actually stood in it before.

Julia, someone told me, was not around at the moment, but she'd be downstairs shortly. I asked if she was upstairs resting. This was the day before her eighty-second birthday, and television is hard work, no matter what age you are, so I figured she was sneaking in a well-deserved nap. But as soon as everyone stopped chuckling, they told me she wasn't resting. "Julia doesn't rest," one of the production staff explained. "She's writing the companion book to go with the show and she wants to capture everything while it's fresh in her mind. So she runs upstairs to her computer after we shoot each recipe."

After my preparations were set for the shoot the following day, I packed up my things, ready to head over to Boston's Logan Airport to pick up my wife, Deann, who was flying in that night. I looked forward to sharing with her the power of my initial impressions, which, hopefully, would help me process the whole thing. I wanted to mull it all over, think about what it meant to be on Julia's new television series, a television series that a kid somewhere in Oklahoma City could happen across on a Sunday afternoon in 1994 while flipping through the channels, and see a whole world of cooking that he might not know is out there. With one foot out the door, I was caught off guard. Julia called out to me, "Why don't you come back with your wife and we'll all sit down and have dinner?"

Emotionally, her invitation just opened the floodgates for me. I couldn't imagine what it would be like. It was enough to do something professionally with Julia, but a casual, un-scripted dinner with her and a few of her friends—that was entirely different. I couldn't turn down the invitation, but I accepted it knowing full well that the evening would be filled with a host of emotions, none of which I could really share with Julia.

There was a big fish left over from the day's shoot, which another chef baked very simply, with herbs, and served with some lemon. It was a casual affair. We sat around, drank a little wine, and chatted about topics that ranged from Asian history to politics—never food. And what a brilliant and vital force Julia proved to be. I learned that night why I had loved her for all those years without knowing her.

I came back early the next day to shoot my episode. When I arrived, someone on the set instructed me to go up to Julia's bedroom for makeup, which in anyone's universe, I think, would have seemed a little odd. But I did as I was told and shortly found myself seated square in front of Julia's vanity.

Sitting quietly, patiently there in Julia's bedroom while the makeup artist did her thing, I noticed an odd-looking box. Trying to quell my nervousness with idle chatter, I asked the makeup artist about the box.

She told me that one day, when she was ironing a blouse for Julia, that same box was sitting on the ironing board and she'd asked Julia if it could be put somewhere else. As Julia reached over to move it, the makeup artist inquired about what was inside. In that inimitable, always matter-of-fact warble, Julia replied, "Oh, that's just Paul's ashes. Haven't found the right place for them yet. So here they sit." Paul, of course, was Julia's husband of many years, who'd died the year before.

So, not only was it a near out-of-body experience to visit Julia's kitchen, not only was I being given the professional honor of working with one of my icons, not only had I been invited to an intimate dinner at Mrs. Child's table, but now I was being made up for television at a vanity inches away from Julia's husband's ashes. It was perhaps the most surreal moment of my life—and that's from a guy who's seen a lot of surreal stuff in Mexico.

It was time to shoot the show. The segments were tough work. Julia was a pro, but she had gotten to the age where she couldn't really do the cooking anymore, couldn't move quickly. When you cook on television you have to be right up against the person you are cooking with, and, though she was stooped a little in her later years, at six foot two Julia was a formidable physical presence in the kitchen. Still, we made it work. Once the episode had been shot, we had to do some station promos together. I botched a few of them, but she got every last one perfect. Her mind worked fast, even if her feet didn't.

Then, as quickly as it had started, my day with Julia was over. Television shoots are like that: long, grueling days spent waiting to squeeze 200 percent of your energy into a few minutes, trying to remember what you're supposed to be saying, and then, suddenly, the cameras go off and it's all over. For me, though, it was anything but another day at work.

One Fish, Two Fish
MICHELLE BERNSTEIN

*A graduate of Johnson & Wales University, Michelle Bernstein
began her culinary career at Red Fish Grill and Christy's in
Coral Gables, and Tantra in Miami Beach. She trained with
Jean-Louis Palladin, and honed her skills at Alison on Do-
minick Street and Le Bernardin in New York. She then became
executive chef and co-owner of the Strand, before drawing national attention as executive chef at Azul at the Mandarin Ori-
ental hotel in Miami, and then chef at MB at the Aqua Hotel in
Cancún. In 2005, the Miami native opened her namesake
restaurant, Michy's, located in the new upper east side of Miami, and in early 2006 she partnered with restaurateur Jeffrey
Chodorow to open Social Sagamore in South Beach and Social
Hollywood in Los Angeles. For two years, she cohosted the
Food Network's* Melting Pot. *Bernstein was nominated for the
2004 James Beard Foundation Award Best Chef: Southeast.*

TO BE HONEST, I was a little ignorant as to who Jean-
Louis Palladin was when I went to work for him. I'd seen

his books before, of course. And my old chef had talked about him a lot, always in hallowed tones. But until I arrived at his restaurant, Jean-Louis at the Watergate, in the Watergate Hotel in Washington, D.C., I didn't realize he was a genius.

He was tall and lithe, wore his curly hair long, and he had a craggy, expressive face. He was irrepressibly creative: I'd get to work at one in the afternoon and he'd be sitting with a glass of wine in his hand and a cigarette in his mouth, instructing the staff on how to execute the dishes he had just conjured up. New dishes, new ways of approaching unloved or just plain odd ingredients—his food was something else entirely. The things that came out of his head, and the way he loved to play with people's expectations—no one's ever going to be like that again. When Jean-Louis passed away in 2001, we lost one of the most important chefs we've ever had in this country.

As a person, he could be absolutely terrifying. I saw him make grown men cry. But when he embraced you or when he acknowledged *anything* you did, from the way you peeled asparagus to the way that you sautéed a fish, you walked a little bit lighter for days. He was just that magnetic, that big of a personality: you needed to please him because he was the chef; you wanted to please him because of who he was.

I had been working at Jean-Louis at the Watergate for about three months when Jean-Louis announced that he was doing an event at the James Beard Foundation and would be bringing some of our staff up to New York to help present the dinner. Since I've admitted that I didn't know what a demigod Jean-Louis was when I went to work for him, it probably won't surprise anyone to learn that I didn't know exactly what a James Beard dinner was, but, judging by the tone with which Jean-Louis talked about it, I could tell it was a big deal.

I both wanted and didn't want to go. As a twenty-three-year-old intern, I knew exactly how inexperienced I was and the last thing I wanted was to fail Jean-Louis—especially at a crucial moment. But I wanted Jean-Louis to pick me because, even if I was the runtiest of the kitchen runts, I needed him to think of me as someone who he could count on. Every veteran crew needs a runt, some new kid to take care of the heavy lifting and the simple cooking, and I was hoping that I'd be that runt.

Lucky for me, I was.

A few of the upper-echelon chefs flew to New York with Jean-Louis. My job was to carefully load everything—all our meat, fish, sauce, and prep—into his truck and keep the pastry chef company on the drive from D.C. As silly as it sounds, I was excited about even riding in Jean-Louis's big stick-shift Range Rover. The drive to New York went by fast, so fast I didn't even have time to get nervous about dinner service that night.

We drove straight to the Beard House and unloaded everything. As far as sauces and emulsions and vinaigrettes and things like that were concerned, everything was more or less already done. D.C. was only a few hours from New York and it was easier to have prepped it all in our in home kitchen than it would have been to prep in the tiny kitchen at the Beard House. Whatever serious work remained was being taken care of by Jean-Louis' right-hand guys, the more experienced cooks. As for me, I was given somewhat minimal tasks.

I was assigned two courses out of the many that made up Jean-Louis's menu that night. One course was a kind of baby perch-looking fish that was to be poached in a beautiful bouillabaisse fumet that Jean-Louis had made himself. The other was a fish that looked a little bit like monkfish, but it was tiny—Maybe it was whiting?—and it was to be tempura fried and served with a beautiful emulsion.

Since the fumet and the emulsion were made back in D.C., all I had to do was poach one fish, and flour, batter, and fry the other, then plate the dishes. While really not all that demanding a task, in the cramped kitchen at the Beard House, it managed to take up the couple of hours we had before dinner. Especially when, in the middle of it, people suddenly started filing through the kitchen. I looked up from the perch in utter confusion— Who were all these civilians? And what were they doing here?

It turned out that this is how it works at the James Beard Foundation. The kitchen is open and after guests arrive they are given a glass of champagne, then they mingle and chat with the folks working in the kitchen. Eventually, they are seated in the upstairs dining room. Along with the many chefs, the kitchen was full of reporters, critics, and photographers, asking questions and taking pictures. Amid the flurry of activity, everyone wanted attention from Jean-Louis. At one point he called me away from my prep and I posed for a picture with him, putting my hand into the live baby eel container with the baby eels coming up my arm. It was madness. It was fabulous. Jean-Louis was actually talking to me, and for the first time, I felt like I was part of the kitchen. I was one of the guys. I thought that maybe I'd truly have a career at this sort of thing. Finally, the guests filed out the kitchen and we got back to cooking.

The baby eels went out first; then cotechino, a traditional Italian sausage, followed. We were humming along spectacularly. Next up were my two fish preps—one poached, one fried. I spun into action: all the plates were laid out, the sauces were being put down, and Jean-Louis told me to bring over the fish. I did, and began arranging them on the plates. I felt him staring at me.

"Michelle, what is this? What is this shit?" he demanded in his deeply French-inflected English.

"What do you mean, Jean-Louis? I did exactly as I was instructed," I said, with a sheet pan of perfectly fried fish in one hand and delicately poached fish in the other.

"You stupid girl. You have poached the fish for frying, and you have fried the fish for poaching. Please tell me that you only started doing a couple of them as you were instructed." I looked down. I started to cry.

I choked my confession through my tears: "No, chef, I cooked all of them."

All of a sudden the sheet pan flew across the kitchen. Fish exploded in the air and landed on the floor as if they had been dynamited out of a river.

My memory of the next few minutes is a blur: a blur of his screaming, him beating the walls, and oh, his voice. I'll never forget the voice: guttural, deep, intense.

I figured, okay, my career is finished, it's done with, yeah, I'm quitting, I'm never going back to D.C., I'm going to take a flight home from New York to Miami and find something else to do with my life. I wanted to disappear. All the other cooks were staring at me, and I felt like I was the bellybutton of the universe.

And then it was over. We had a dinner to prepare. So we put the pieces back together. We pretended that the fish I had fried was supposed to be fried and the fish I had poached was supposed to be poached, plated it and sent it up. Service rolled on. No one complained. But, of course, to me life was finished. A career in the kitchen was gone for me. Miserable and humiliated, I tried to stay as far out of the way as possible.

When dinner was wrapping up, Jean-Louis opened a few bottles of wine for the kitchen crew and himself. Guests started meandering down from dinner, to the kitchen, to tell Jean-Louis what a genius he was and compliment those of us working in the kitchen on how lovely the meal had been. No one commented on the fish—I naïvely thought everyone in the kitchen had forgotten about it.

Jean-Louis left for dinner, and when we had finished wrapping up our work, we were invited to join him. That's when I noticed that something had appeared at my station. It was a note saying, *Here are my keys, this*—a couple of illegible road numbers—*is how you get back to D.C. If you can manage to get everything back in one piece, then maybe you'll have a job waiting for you. Good luck.*

So Jean-Louis hadn't forgotten. And it looked like I wasn't going out on the town that night. I went to the hotel, got a good night's rest, and in the morning loaded up Jean-Louis' Range Rover. I hadn't driven a stick in years, and this was a hulking beast of a car to navigate alone through the tight streets of New York City and the warren of roads crisscrossing eastern New Jersey. But I knew that the drive represented my whole career. If the car survived and the ride home was without mishap, and I knew that I would actually cook again.

And I did. When I made it back to the Watergate and work resumed as usual, my fish mix-up was never spoken of. Of course, it was something that we all remembered—especially me—and something that *he* knew I'd never forget.

But never in our friendship afterward—and he did become a mentor and good friend to me—never once did he bring it up. He gave me that drive home to think about my carelessness—it's funny how quick the ride up seemed and how the drive back dragged on—but that was it. He knew how to teach you a lesson.

There is a postscript to this story: years and years later, I presented my first dinner at the James Beard Foundation, when

I was the chef at the Strand in Miami Beach, Florida. I had brought up a skeleton crew, a couple of my best cooks and this young guy who had just started in my kitchen. Sometimes you just need extra hands at an event, you don't need skills. This kid—who was clearly talented, but had very little experience— fit the bill.

I made sure he didn't have any responsibilities he couldn't handle—his main job was going to be to warm up a sauce, a nage, for my first course, Sauté of Skate Wing with Provençal Fish Nage and Peruvian Purple Potato-Osetra Caviar Hash. I had put maybe five hundred dollars' worth of seafood into that Provençal fish nage. It was a thing of beauty that would be next to impossible for him to ruin.

So the event started, the guests filtered through the kitchen and my nerves were a little frayed—Jean-Louis had cooked a million dinners like the one at the Beard House, so he knew how to ham it up with the public, but this was my first time presenting a dinner there and I wanted to get everything right.

When it was time to serve my first course—the skate dish—I turned my attention back to the kitchen and found that the kid had left the sauce over too high a flame without paying any attention to it.

It was scorched. Unusable. I wanted to scream. I wanted to pound on the walls. I wanted to grab a sheet pan and throw fish everywhere and then scream some more. I knew, right then, exactly what Jean-Louis must have felt years before, when I was standing on the other side of that same counter, holding the wrong fishes cooked the wrong way, crying.

But instead I smiled a tiny smile, realizing in some small way that my career had come full circle. I thought about my mentor and friend Jean-Louis for a second, before I told my crew that we would plow ahead sans sauce. The dinner was a smash success. No one commented on the missing sauce. And it was only for a fleeting moment that I wished I had a Range Rover parked down the block so I could make the kid drive back to Miami Beach.

Digging in the Dirt
CHRIS BIANCO

Pizzeria Bianco, Chris Bianco's restaurant in Phoenix, Arizona, is widely considered to serve the best pizza in America. He works the pizza oven five nights a week; makes fresh mozzarella every morning; and is a tireless advocate of local, organic, and seasonal ingredients. Bianco has been celebrated in both in the local Phoenix press and in national publications like Gourmet *and* Travel+Leisure. *Peter Reinhart included an entire chapter on Bianco in his book* American Pie: My Search for the Perfect Pizza *and he was similarly singled out in Ed Levine's* Pizza: A Slice of Heaven. *Bianco was named Best Chef: Southwest by the James Beard Foundation in 2003, and is the chef and co-owner of a second restaurant in Phoenix, Arizona:* Pane Bianco.

I HAD TO LEARN how to eat before I could learn how to cook.

That is not to say I didn't eat well growing up: my mother and my great-aunt, who lived in a small apartment below ours in the Bronx, were both great cooks. Food was omnipresent, but it wasn't all that important to me back then. Led Zeppelin was important. Food was, well, food.

Still, when you grow up in an Italian-American family it's hard not to know at least something about food—as a kid I used to help my great-aunt make cavatelli. It was part of our lives. And it was impossible not to have an opinion about it— you only have to hear so many adults say that Mrs. Annuziata's baked ziti is the best before you're saying the same thing.

But as much as cooking connected my aunt and mom to a sense of their heritage, cooking was work. It was a chore— even if it was one they didn't mind. The object of cooking for my mom and my aunt was to put a meal on the table for the family.

When I was thirteen and started working after school in a neighborhood pizza parlor, the object of cooking was putting money in my pocket. A grilled cheese on white bread, wrapped in tinfoil, and cooked with an iron was about as involved as I'd get if I had to feed myself. When I had a little extra cash, I'd take myself out for chicken parmesan sandwiches from down the block. Understanding then that man does not live on pizza alone.

I wish I could say I fell in love with pizza and cooking then and there at that first pizzeria, that the pizza man saw me as his successor, the torchbearer. But that's not the way it went down. I was the help. I'd lug up bags of flour for the pizza maker and help him dump them in the mixer, then he'd send me back downstairs to grate pounds and pounds of cheese and lug that upstairs. I was an Italian gofer. It was not glamorous work. There was no romance of the kitchen for me to discover there, just the inevitable realities: that cooking is demanding physical labor.

But I didn't mind hard work. In fact, I preferred it to school, so I dropped out at sixteen and split my time between the pizzeria and a tire shop. Most of my friends preferred working and hanging out to being in school. That was just the way it was in the neighborhood.

Just after my eighteenth birthday, my father invited me on a trip to Italy to go visit our relatives. I was excited: I hadn't been to Italy since I was very little. And a week away from slinging pies and rotating tires sounded great.

We landed in Rome, greeted by my cousin Anna, and spent the night at her apartment a stone's throw from Castel Sant' Angelo. From there, we took off for Friuli, in northeastern Italy, where Armando and Annamaria, my uncle and aunt, lived.

I had never been to the north before. This was back in 1980, before regional Italian cooking was a big thing here in the States. (It was new to me, anyway.) So I knew nothing about what we were about to encounter: a part of Italy where food has a strong Slavic and Germanic influence.

On the first night we were there, we went to a local trattoria for dinner, and I was shocked to see goulash and braised spareribs with sauerkraut on the menu. They were totally foreign dishes to me as an Italian-American kid, and they were especially surprising to see in a real Italian restaurant. The food of Puglia, where most of my family is from, was recognizably Italian to me: lots of tomatoes, pasta, and cheese. But this stuff in Friuli was weird.

I had pumpkin gnocchi that night. Gnocchi made out of pumpkin? They called this Italian food? But it was good. In fact, it was really good. It only took one meal for my initial trauma to start giving way to a cautious sense of wonder.

The next afternoon my uncle drove us around the area near Udine, where he and my aunt lived. One of our first stops was at a little bar in the town of San Daniele, where he ordered us a round of local white wine—Tocai Friulano, produced there in Friuli—and handed each of us slices of prosciutto San Daniele wrapped around slender, just-baked, crisp grissini.

He started waxing poetic about how prosciutto from Parma—the only prosciutto I knew to exist before we walked into this bar—is fine, but that San Daniele is what they ate up in Friuli. He talked about how it was butchered, about how it was aged, about how if you had a prosciutto-wrapped grissini in one hand and a glass of Tocai in the other, you could then understand the food of Friuli.

My revelation started in that bar. I was teetering on the edge of getting it. I thought there was something strange, but really cool, about how serious my uncle—and most of the people I met on that trip—were about food. But not just in the "my mother makes the best . . ." way that most Americans I knew were. They wanted me to know the story of the pig before I ate the prosciutto. They needed to point out the window in the direction of the wine country just a few miles away and say that *this* is where this wine is from.

There was an unmistakable sincerity in the way that they spoke about this stuff. I might not have known a tenth of what I thought I knew at the time, but I could recognize that there was something special about how the guy behind the bar methodically operated the meat slicer and delicately swaddled the grissini in prosciutto. The deli man I knew in New York did not approach his job with the same sense of reverence.

After the stop at the bar, we took off to visit a friend of my uncle's. He had an asparagus farm, my uncle told us, and would be cooking a lunch in our honor. I sat in silence in the backseat of the car, staring out the window, watching the Friulian countryside whiz by on the way to the farm. It was a crisp late-April day, still a snap of winter to the air, and the sky was a late-spring blue. Excitedly I imagined the incredible spread that would be waiting for us when we arrived: a long table covered with half a dozen dishes, maybe even a roast goose. It would be a celebratory meal cooked in our honor, the kind of no-holds-barred meal my family would prepare during the holidays when company was coming.

So I was a little surprised that instead of the lavish feast I had envisioned, there was just a bare, timeworn picnic table next to a propane-fueled single burner minding a large pot of boiling water. Near the table there were a couple of loose chickens pecking around that took little notice of our arrival.

My uncle's friend, our host, greeted us warmly and said he'd walk us around the farm before we sat down to lunch. He told us he grew asparagi bianchi—white asparagus—and took us over to the field and showed us how they "blanch" the asparagus, huddling dirt up around the tender young shoots to keep the sun from turning them green. I had never seen white asparagus before then—I had never even heard of them. But they were asparagi bianchi and my last name is Bianco, so I thought it was pretty cool. That's how the eighteen-year-old mind tends to classify things: cool or not cool.

We unearthed and brushed clean enough asparagus to make a hefty bundle, which my uncle's friend tied together with butcher's twine. He tied the end of the twine to a rock, and plunged the bundle into the boiling water.

Then he disappeared into the barn only to reemerge with a half dozen or so eggs, brown and speckled, cradled in his hands. I'd seen chickens and I'd seen eggs, but I had never seen chickens and their eggs at the same time. He blew an errant strand of hay off one of the eggs and plunged them into the boiling water along with the asparagus. His wife laid down a large ceramic platter on the table and, after the asparagus had cooked a good long while, snatched the bundle of it out of the pot. She snipped the twine and let the thick, milky white asparagus tumble helter skelter across the platter. She and her husband fished out the eggs, perfectly boiled, peeled them, and scattered them over the asparagus. They doused everything with a few glugs of vibrant green oil from an unlabeled green glass wine bottle, flung some grains of course sea salt, almost as big as the salt we spread on the sidewalks in New York, over it, and finished the dish with a few turns of black pepper from an old wooden peppermill. We dug in.

It blew my mind. You know the way a beautiful woman can roll out of bed and throw on a T-shirt and look unbelievable, and the way a beautiful woman can spend nine hours putting on makeup for a night on the town and look too "tweaked"? This meal was the beautiful woman in the T-shirt.

At the table, there was an unassuming sense of pride in what we shared and our hosts' role in that gift. I am eternally grateful for the meal they served me because that's when it happened: everything about food made sense to me for the first time. I thought, "There's the dirt, there's what's pushing out of the dirt, there's what's harvested from the dirt, and here is how you celebrate what comes from the dirt." That was how you were supposed to eat.

There was an undeniable honesty and directness to it all, to this process of taking what is local and seasonal and treating it simply and with dignity. Eating this meal, without pretense, I knew there was nothing that could be better than food so simply and honestly prepared. I might experience a similar bliss, but nothing could be better.

I also learned that eating wasn't always about looking for another meal to top it: nobody was talking about this other time they ate asparagus at this one person's farm and oh, *that* was *really* good. There was no competition, just animated appreciation. We ate and talked and were in sync with the countryside around us and with each other as family and friends.

That meal opened my eyes to cooking not being about the singular sense of chefdom that has been the archetype—toques and intimidating menus—for so long. I respect the need for squirt bottles, embroidered chef jackets and all that as much as the next guy. But I was not going to be dressing the plate with a spray of raspberry coulis just because it could use a pop of color. Brown food is brown, and brown is beautiful.

I left Italy motivated by an inkling of what I wanted to do with my life, an unfamiliar feeling for me back then. I just knew that I wanted to cook food that people would respond to on a visceral level. I wanted to cook honest, unpretentious food. I wanted to seek out quality ingredients and to respect and revere food the way they did in Italy. And when I got back home, suddenly inspired and accountable, I set out on the path to do just that.

That's Entertainment
MARK BITTMAN

*Mark Bittman is one of the country's best-known food writers.
His best-selling cookbook* How to Cook Everything *was cho-
sen best general cookbook by both the International Associa-
tion of Culinary Professionals (the Julia Child Award) and the
James Beard Foundation in 1998. In 2005 he published* The
Best Recipes in the World: More Than 1000 International
Dishes to Cook at Home, *his sequel to* How to Cook Every-
thing. *Bittman has collaborated with the internationally cele-
brated chef Jean-Georges Vongerichten on two cookbooks,*
Jean-Georges: Cooking at Home with a Four-Star Chef *and*
Simple to Spectacular. *He is the creator of the weekly column
"The Minimalist" in the* New York Times *and the author of the
award-winning Minimalist Cookbook series, which includes*
The Minimalist Cooks at Home, The Minimalist Cooks Din-
ner, *and* The Minimalist Entertains.

E NTERTAINING" CAN BE an awesome responsibility or
a pleasure. Until a few years ago, I came down hard on the

side of responsibility. Only people like Fred Astaire and Martha Stewart entertained, I believed. It was *my* lot, when periodically seized by obligation, altruism, or guilt (and often all three), to gather my wit, strength, and slightly above-average cooking skills and joylessly stumble through putting together a dinner party. Leave pleasure to the masters.

On those rare occasions, I worried about everything, from my flimsy stainless steel to my unmatched chairs. When it came to the food, I was even worse; I could become downright hysterical if I couldn't find rascasse for a bouillabaisse or live shrimp for a special stir-fry—which was pretty much always the case when I was living in suburban Connecticut.

The result—and this, I have since found out, is common— was that I worked harder than I had to, toiling obsessively for even the most casual affairs, as I attempted to make the food incredible.

Of course this meant never, ever scheduling a dinner party for a weeknight, including Friday (or Sunday, really, since I was usually a wreck afterward), because I needed at least a day or two to cook without the distractions of real life. It meant shopping on Thursday, prepping and cooking on Friday, and cooking and performing last-minute tasks (like driving twenty miles to find some "absolutely essential" ingredient) all day Saturday, until the fateful hour—by which time I was at least partially anesthetized with rosé and, like just about everyone else who cooks, nervous and exhausted.

Need I say that these were difficult, overly ambitious affairs?

There had to be a better way, I came to think, and my discovery of this happened by accident, as things often do. The turning point was the scariest dinner party I ever held, one at which I finally realized that it was my own standards, and not those of

my guests, that made me work like a fiend and worry neuroti-
cally. This revelation changed the way I entertain forever.

I had recently reached an agreement with a friend's friend,
an architect, that he would redesign my office and in exchange
I would cook dinner for him and five guests of his choosing at
my house. He dispatched the task of redesigning with ease: a
little ergonomic hardware here, a simple wood desk to hide all
the office-y looking stuff there, and it was done. I was happy
and we set a date for the dinner that was my end of the bar-
gain.

When that day rolled around I was having a pretty ideal Sunday: I had enjoyed a lazy breakfast with the newspaper,
watched a little football, and, sometime before a phone call
woke me up at four thirty, dozed off on the couch.

It was the architect who interrupted my midafternoon slum-
ber, asking what time he and his party should arrive. I first
caught my breath—I had completely forgotten about the
dinner—blurted out "six thirty" (we eat early in the suburbs),
and then quickly changed that to eight. I hung up and, still
dazed, lumbered over to the refrigerator to survey my options.
I was pessimistic, to say the least.

As I quickly discovered, my pessimism was well founded.
The refrigerator was near barren: there was the lone chicken I
had planned on rather unceremoniously stewing in vinegar for
dinner that night, some mesclun that was destined for the salad
bowl, and not much else to work with.

Obviously this wasn't going to cut it. I'd been cooking
steadily for twenty-five years at the time of this dinner, and I
had just written *How to Cook Everything*, so people thought I
was a fabulous cook (which is why the architect had agreed to
the trade). On any given night I could stroll into the kitchen

and make dinner for my family, but when people came over I still felt like I had to perform.

What was I going to do? For a moment, I thought about calling back and postponing, but then swiftly dismissed the idea. After all, we had an agreement—and he had invited friends. No, postponing wasn't the solution. Somehow, and I didn't know how exactly, but somehow I needed to have a dinner that I wasn't horribly embarrassed about on the table in a matter of hours.

I headed to the supermarket, thinking furiously. I tried to recall any successful dinner parties I had thrown that hadn't been much work and that I might be able to duplicate, but came up empty. If only there was time . . . but, of course, there *was* no time. No time to pore through cookbooks looking for new recipes, no time for research, no time to ask friends for suggestions—no time for anything but a simple weeknight dinner on a slightly grander scale.

The details of my self-rescue are not that impressive: I had originally been planning to prepare chicken with vinegar, a simple salad, and the pan-crisped potato cubes my family adores. I decided to build on this menu, adding some kind of starter, a bread, and finally a dessert as a desperate attempt to provide not only some festivity but the suggestion that I had actually given the whole thing a great deal of consideration.

By the time I arrived at the supermarket, my job was pretty easy: I bought more chicken, more salad greens, and some cream. In what has since become my typical fashion, I bought three kinds of olives, a dry salami, and a couple of loaves of peasant bread.

Back at home, I immediately began to marinate the olives. I knew how much some fresh herbs, a little lemon juice, and a heavy dose of good olive oil could do for ho-hum store-bought olives, so I was confident that they would be okay. Would the architect's guests be expecting something more elaborate, a delicately composed canapé waiting for them at the house of cookbook author Mark Bittman? Maybe, but I didn't have time to worry about that. I had to get something on the table so I didn't look like a fraud. I sliced the bread, cut up the salami, and poured myself a glass of wine. Then I got to cooking.

Since I was pressed for time, I knew any overly involved dessert was out of the question. A friend had recently shared a chocolate mousse recipe with me, one in which you fold together chocolate ganache and whipped cream; she swore by it, and it was certainly easier and faster than my more old-fashioned version using eggs. It seemed simple enough.

I made the chocolate mousse first, so it could chill, and almost instantly I could see that I'd be disappointed. Maybe I had done something wrong. (Isn't that always our first thought? Yet sometimes recipes just don't work.) The ganache made the mousse far stiffer than what I liked. It looked like volcanic rock, but it was too late to do anything about that. I added it to my list of worries and thanked myself for the foresight that led me to buy enough cream to whip and pile on top of the mousse. At least its appearance wasn't going to be an issue. I ferreted out a couple of extra bottles of wine from my basement just to make sure that everyone would be very relaxed by the time we got to that petrified chocolate mousse.

The chicken with vinegar, a classic French peasant dish popularized by the great French chef Paul Bocuse, was not a dish I would usually have prepared for company—it just didn't seem grand enough—but it was a standby in my repertory because it is plain and simple good eating. It's a four-ingredient braise—chicken, shallots, red wine vinegar, and butter—that takes forty-five minutes from start to finish; I upped the butter from my usually modest few tablespoons to the few sticks that Bocuse calls for in his recipe to elevate the dish to the occasion. And that way I wasn't just serving stewed chicken, I told myself, I was serving stewed chicken the way Paul Bocuse did!

When eight o'clock arrived, I nervously went to greet my guests. I was sure that everyone was immediately going to see right through my ruse. But that wasn't, miraculously, the case. They happily began to drink wine while nibbling salami and devouring the olives, which, it turned out, were symbolic of what made the entire event a success—they tasted good and, though simple, were unusual.

In fact, the dinner was a *smashing* success, with my guests raving about the same food that on any given night of the year my children might have complained about. Although everything was imperfect (according to my judgment; my guests seemed to think everything was splendid, including the ultraordinary salad), and far from restaurant-quality, who says that we have to prepare food that's either near perfect or that costs a hundred dollars a person?

So while the meal may not have shouted "I killed myself for you people," it was honest and good and home cooked. And when my nerves finally calmed down, it hit me that no one expected me to cook like a chef; they were just happy to be at someone's house, eating a nice dinner, and enjoying all the relaxed goodness that a meal at a restaurant can never offer. It's comfort and hospitality—not perfection—that home entertaining is really all about.

This was a lesson I never forgot, one that changed my life, not for the near disaster that I feared but for the one that did not happen. In the intervening years, I have yet to develop a foolproof method of getting all dates into my calendar—and have still, I'll admit, been abruptly reminded of a dinner I'd promised—but I have learned that dinner parties need not take days of work. Now I limit my hysteria to only the last couple of hours before the guests arrive, and I also limit most of the work to that time, too. It may not be Martha, but it usually requires only a little bit of volunteer help, it looks pretty good, and the food tastes great.

Extra, Extra!
RAYMOND BLANC

Born in Besancon, France, in 1949, Raymond Blanc opened his first restaurant at the age of twenty-eight. After just one year, it was named Egon Ronay Restaurant of the Year. A Michelin star followed the year after that, and a second star two years after the first. In 1984, Blanc created a hotel and restaurant in harmony when he opened Le Manoir aux Quat'Saisons in Great Milton, Oxford, the only country house hotel in the United Kingdom to achieve and sustain two Michelin stars and the Relais & Chateaux Purple Shield. Le Manoir aux Quat'Saisons is further distinguished by its extensive organic herb and vegetable garden. In 1991 Blanc established the Raymond Blanc Cookery School, welcoming both enthusiastic amateurs and children to the kitchen, and in 1996 he opened the first four Le Petit Blanc brasseries, the only brasseries in the United Kingdom to achieve the Michelin Bib Gourmand. Blanc appears regularly on television and is a member of Slow Food and the Soil Association. He has written many best sellers, including Cooking for Friends, A Blanc Christmas, Recipes from Le Manoir aux Quat'Saisons, Blanc Vite, *and* Foolproof French Cookery.

I HATE WHEN THINGS go wrong for me in public.

Maybe it is because I am French. Maybe it is because I have a sense of pride about what I do. But if there are a thousand things I've learned during my thirty years as a professional chef, there is one thing I know to be certain: there will *always* be an audience when something goes awry for me in the kitchen.

Day to day or cooking at home, I rarely have anything go wrong. Take a simple mistake, like cutting yourself with a knife. When you chop and slice and cut as much as a professional does, you're bound to cut yourself every once in a while. But for me, it is very unusual.

One of the last times it happened was—of course—when I was taping a live cooking segment for a morning television show. I was there in the studio, humming along, getting my ingredients together to do my demonstration.

On television sets, there are always people running around counting down how long it will be until this or that segment starts. Soon, someone rushed by my table and told me I had two minutes until I went on. No problem. I figured I'd cut up a bit extra of the herb I was finishing my dish with to fill up the time. That's when a gaggle of beautiful Moroccan belly dancers started warming up in another corner of the space. I sneaked a glance or two over at the belly-dancing troupe. It would have been hard not to pay some attention to them.

My chopping grew more and more furious and then—in a split second—I realized that the blade of the knife had sunk in most of the way through the tip of my finger. Blood was gushing everywhere. In that moment, I figured I had botched the appearance and would have to reschedule: an inconvenience for the producers of the show and for me, but it has to happen from time to time.

Then someone from the crew rushed up to me, assessed that the cut was nasty (the tip of my finger was gone almost to the bone) but that it wasn't particularly serious, and—as though he had been expecting me to do it—produced a full-on first aid kit. He went to work bandaging my finger while another helper cleaned up my prep station. I began cursing myself for making such a stupid mistake.

And in no time—and with no time left to argue that we should reschedule—he had my finger wrapped up in a tremendous amount of thick, bright blue gauze. I took a second to think what a terrific medic he'd make, before I noticed that my bandaged middle finger was just smaller than a baseball bat. It was bright blue and jutting straight out from my hand.

So for the entire show I had my big blue finger peeking up very rudely at all the guests. The people in the audience were laughing their heads off. They found it very funny. I managed to keep a pretty good sense of humor about it. What else are you going to do?

Those quick, simple embarrassments are one thing—everyone burns toast on television once—but there are others that stay with you for a long time.

One of my worst, most personally distressing disasters happened during a promotion I did in Scotland. I had been hired to do a dinner for the CEOs of something like the top two hundred Scottish companies.

I've done these kinds of promotions all over the world. They are ripe with the chance for something to go wrong: you are not getting your ingredients from the purveyors you know and trust; you are cooking with a skeleton staff because you can't just close down your restaurant every time someone wants you to fly to a corner of the world and cook a meal; you are cooking in a totally foreign kitchen.

But it is like a musician playing gigs—you have to do it, you have to go out on the road and play what you play for people in places away from your restaurant. And because I am a deeply rooted masochist—I must be for the contortions I put myself through—I always serve a very elaborate menu, something that I feel will not just represent what we do at Le Manoir aux Quat'Saisons, but what we do there on a great night.

I remember when I did a dinner in America many, many years ago and I was very exacting and very demanding about the quality of the quails I wanted from the restaurant where I'd be cooking. And I scared them so much that their purveyor threw up his hands, practically raised me my own little flock, and delivered it to me as such. As a result I had to eviscerate, defeather, and butcher quails for two hundred guests—on top of everything else that had to get done that night. I curse myself when something like that happens, but I never expect anything less than the best, so what can I do?

Luckily, there was no quail problem to be had in Scotland, where I was preparing this dinner for the Scottish captains of industry. The ingredients they obtained for me were top notch, and since we were so close to London, it wasn't hard to spirit away a couple of extra cooks and make sure the event was a success.

When we arrived and surveyed what the hotel had procured for us, I remember being absolutely amazed by the oysters. They had a wonderful meatiness to them; they were some of the plumpest, most outstanding oysters I had seen in a long time. I was overjoyed, because the course I really intended to bowl the guests over with that night was a new creation of mine.

We prepared the meal with little trouble. First, the oyster course: I sterilized the dishes and pans I'd be working with, marinated cucumber ribbons in dill and lime for the garnish, and made a batch of beautiful pink horseradish sauce for the plate and then the seaweed-cucumber gelée that the oysters would sit on.

Everything went flawlessly. My new dish looked stunning, completely stunning—it was very fresh, very clean. The guests were happy. I was happy. Plates came back to the kitchen licked clean, the hosts told me I was brilliant. We even got the kitchen shut down at a reasonable hour. I retired to my room at around one a.m., pleased to get in a full night's sleep before traveling back to the restaurant the next day. I was floating on a silver cloud. No matter where you are in your career as a chef, that kind of unanimous approval from your guests is truly satisfying.

I'd been asleep for about an hour when I got a call from the front desk. A couple of the hotel's guests had gotten sick, it seemed, and they wanted to know what we had served at the banquet. Maybe they had been allergic to something. Maybe they had all been sitting at the same table. Maybe they all had had too much to drink. It was a thorn in my side, but I didn't give it too much thought: I was half asleep and you can't please all the people all the time, right?

My head was on my pillow for maybe five minutes when the phone rang again. This time it wasn't the front desk. It was a hospital. They had a couple guests from the dinner I had cooked and wanted to know . . .

This was not good. I answered all of their questions and then hung up. I was so upset that there was no chance I was going to sleep again any time soon.

Not that it was an option, anyway: the phone rang every ten minutes, then every five minutes, and then every time I wasn't on it. Phone calls from private residences, other hotel rooms, hospitals. The hotel's telephone system was overwhelmed by calls from guests complaining of food poisoning.

I started to replay every scene of the day, searching for a mistake. But everything we had done was right. I was certain of it. My oysters were sparkling fresh. All the equipment I had used was sterilized—there was no way it could be my fault.

At three in the morning a reporter from the local newspaper called me looking for a quote. In this business, you're as good as you were yesterday. And my morning was shaping up to be terrible. The headline the next day, on the front page of the Scottish *Times*, read:

RAYMOND BLANC POISONS 200 GUESTS

Oh my god, I thought to myself, I am finished.

When the hygiene people came along the next morning to interview me, I made my case, "Look," I told them, "I did nothing wrong. It cannot be me—it could not be neglect on the kitchen's part that sickened all these guests. There must be something else, it must be in the oysters . . ." And of course they told me, no, they are fresh, the oysters are fresh. It couldn't be the oysters. They had the receipt from the fishmonger stating the oysters were received the day before I arrived.

I was positively lambasted in the press for another day before I got back in touch with the health department, and I begged them to analyze those oysters. After enough of my pestering, they acquiesced.

And what did they find? The oyster beds where these beautiful oysters came from were flooded with some unusual seasonal pollution. And it was that contamination that had made all of the guests very ill, not any mistakes the kitchen had made.

Though we got the front page for allegedly poisoning two hundred people, the retraction—the truth about what had happened that evening—warranted only two lines on the back page.

Sure, I was vindicated. I had done nothing wrong. But it was still one of my greatest disasters, regardless of who was at fault, and it played itself out on the front page of a national newspaper. And both of these episodes underscore another universal truth of the kitchen, learned again and again: people love to see a great chef getting it wrong.

Found in Translation
HESTON BLUMENTHAL

One of the most celebrated culinary figures in England today, self-taught chef Heston Blumenthal opened The Fat Duck in 1995 in Bray, Berkshire. The Michelin Guide *awarded the restaurant its first star in 1999, which was retained in 2000 and 2001. It was awarded a second star in 2002, and a third star in 2004. Blumenthal was the first winner of the Chef of the Year award in the 2001* Good Food Guide. *His first book,* Family Food, *was published in 2001, the same year he hosted the program* Kitchen Chemistry *on the Discovery Channel.*

I T WAS A stroke of luck, a business deal gone right. As unromantic as it sounds, I owe my interest in food and my career as a chef to a particularly profitable deal my father struck for the leasing company he owned. With the money he made, he took our family on an unexpectedly influential vacation to the south of France.

I was in my teens, and it was my first trip abroad. I was a good, if not particularly focused, kid. I practiced karate with enthusiasm and was entertaining the idea of becoming an architect. Cooking was far from an interest of mine. Food was a fact of life and, my mother's cooking aside, largely a grim one at that.

I grew up in London in the seventies, before the gastronomic revolution of the past decades, in a city where the "basket meal" was the basic form of sustenance for the majority of the people who lived there. A basket meal, for the uninitiated, is a combination of fried things—fish and chips, scampi and chips, chicken and chips, sausage and chips—served in a cheap plastic basket lined with red and white waxed paper that kept the grease from running everywhere.

It had become so popular that adults would no longer go out socially for dinner. They asked, "Do you fancy a basket meal?" And then they'd waddle down to the pub and polish off a pair with a few pints.

This was a time when olive oil was only available at the apothecary, when getting an avocado—or any dish, however misguided, featuring avocado—was the very height of gastronomy.

This was also the time when my dad hit it big, or big enough to take us on vacation, and we headed down to the south of France. He had read about a Michelin three-star restaurant called L'Oustou de Baumaniere in a travel magazine and was fixated on taking the family there.

L'Oustou de Baumaniere was nestled in the cradle of a bauxite valley in Les Baux de Provence, just south of Montpellier, one of our stops on the way to the Mediterranean coast. When we pulled up to the restaurant, I was shocked. I had never seen anything like it before. We were seated outdoors at one of a dozen perfectly appointed tables—linen, silver, china, crystal, everything immaculate—in the garden outside the restaurant. The scent of lavender, which grew wild in the nearby hills and in pots around the terrace, wafted past our table whenever a breeze blew.

Up until that point the height of my gastronomic exploits were family trips out for Chinese food, basket meals, and the weekly trip to my parents' friends' house where my sister and I would pass out on the couch after dinner at the kids' table. My parents would scoop us up around two in the morning and deposit us in the back seat for the drive home.

L'Oustou de Baumaniere was a stunning change from all of that. The regimented beauty of the restaurant managed a peaceable harmony with its setting: the whirring of crickets in the distance, the gurgle of a nearby fountain, the quiet crunch of gravel underneath the waiters' feet. The waiters were themselves very smartly dressed in leather aprons and, in my memory, they all had handlebar mustaches. Playing against type, they were friendly and patient with us.

The wine list looked like something out of a Cecil B. DeMille film; the cheese trolley, laden with wheels and wedges of cheese, each with a little flag stuck into it, was the size of a chariot. I had never seen a cheese trolley before. But I had never seen so much of what I saw that night for the first time— waiters artfully pouring sauces into soufflés and carving legs of lamb at the tables. I remember my parents' aperitifs, champagne cocktails—champagne poured over a little bit of armagnac, orange juice, and a cube of unrefined sugar dipped in angostura bitters—served in balloon glasses that were so big they looked like something you'd put a bunch of flowers in.

It was hard not to be seduced by it all. The meal could have been so-so and I think we still would have had a fantastic time: the surroundings were that enchanting.

The meal, however, was anything but average. I had a few fillets of delicately cooked red mullet to start. It was sauced with a light vinaigrette and paired with tomatoes, basil, and green beans that the waiter told us were grown on the property. My next course was leg meat and kidneys from a baby lamb baked in puff pastry (which I had never eaten before) and a little gratin of potatoes and aubergines. Dessert was preceded by a slew of petit fours and followed by a train of *mignardises*. Each course was more impressive than the one that came before it.

There was something about the experience, something so fantastic yet so tangible, that I knew that this was what I wanted to do. I didn't want to stand there in a top hat and trousers, but I wanted to be part of creating an experience like the one I had just had. That night is when I got the cooking bug. And whether I liked it or not, I couldn't get rid of it. It was there for good.

A couple of days later, still on vacation, I bought my first cookbook. It was by the Troisgros brothers, Pierre and Michel, from the series of books published by Robert Lafont. (Robert Lafont printed about twenty of these books, by chefs like Michel Guérard and Roger Verge, and I eventually owned all of them.)

I couldn't speak a lick of French, so I translated the cookbook word for word, working out of the dictionary. I translated every single word, from the front cover to the last page, copying it down into a notebook. That's how I started learning about cooking—and how I began learning French. By the time we got back from vacation, I could walk into a bank and confidently ask for twelve-month-old oak-aged sherry vinegar. If I wanted to ask about converting pounds to francs, however, I'd be up the river.

For the next few years, I focused on working, saving, and reading. While my mates spent their money down at the pub, I squirreled mine away for another trip to France. When I was eighteen, I headed back.

My first stop was at Alain Chapel's restaurant—I had fallen hard for the food I'd made using his cookbook, and I wanted to taste the real stuff. From there it was anywhere: I visited chicken farms, foie gras farms, dairy farms; I met vegetable growers, a man who spent his life catching frogs, an armagnac producer—anyone who would give me a little of their time.

After that trip, I sent letters to the thirty best restaurants in London, seeing if any would let me work as a part-time apprentice. Few responded and most that did gently mocked what I think they saw as my hobbyist's interest in their craft.

Only Raymond Blanc invited me into his kitchen at Le Manoir aux Quat'Saisons. It was there that I got a real look at what professional cooking was all about: you were part of a team, and you needed to know a great number of elemental preparations and be able to duplicate what you did with great precision. The kitchen staff worked at a different speed than I did, they spoke a different language than I did, they seemed to be a breed apart from me, making me realize that I wasn't yet ready for a professional kitchen; I needed more time to study.

I met my wife when I was twenty, and she became as interested in my eating tours through France as I was. We didn't have the right clothes to be dining in these restaurants, and the proportion of our income we spent on them was completely out of kilter with the rest our lives, but we did it anyway.

Back home in London, I cooked furiously and studiously. But I wasn't throwing dinner parties. I was researching. I'd plate one dish at a time, study it, figure out how to do it better and faster and with greater precision, and then I'd plate it again.

Even if I was making something simple, like vanilla ice cream, I would gather all the recipes for vanilla ice cream from all the great chefs, and then I would rack my memory: What was the best vanilla ice cream I had ever tasted? In my mind I had a taste memory, an exceptional flavor memory that was fixed and very clear. I can remember most mouthfuls of food that I've tasted over the last twenty years. And I would try to take my taste memories and the methods from the great chefs and use them to make the best vanilla ice cream in the world. (I feel bad now about all the times my drive kept me up until all hours, and I'd wake my wife up at three thirty in the morning, wide-eyed and buzzing with excitement, asking her to taste this and tell me what she thought of it.)

After years of traveling and eating and reading and translating, I realized that I wasn't getting any younger. My daytime work—as a repo man, for the most part—wasn't fulfilling at all. It was time to bite the bullet and open a restaurant. After a few fits and starts, I finally found a 450-year-old pub for a price I could manage. My friends helped me renovate it. I put together a menu of affordably priced classic bistro dishes, and The Fat Duck was born. It was time to put everything I'd learned cooking in my cottage kitchen and eating my way through France to the test.

Blanc Cassis
DANIEL BOULUD

A native of Lyon, France, Daniel Boulud, is one of the most acclaimed chefs in New York City. His empire includes the four-star Daniel, as well as Café Boulud and DB Bistro Moderne. Trained under some of the legendary chefs of France, Boulud made his name as the executive chef of Le Cirque in New York City, before opening his own restaurants. He is the author of several cookbooks, and the designer of the Daniel Boulud line of cookware.

IT IS IMPOSSIBLE to overstate Paul Bocuse's importance or his influence. Not only did he elevate French cuisine, he elevated the status of chefs everywhere. There was no more famous chef in the world for a long, long time, and there are very few, if any, who have had the wide-ranging influence he has had over the course of his eighty years on the planet. He is a living legend now, as he was thirty-seven years ago, when I was a fourteen-year-old apprentice at Nandron in Lyon, France.

At that time, however, I knew nothing of Paul Bocuse, other

than having a passing familiarity with his name because I grew up on a farm outside of Lyon and his was the most celebrated restaurant in town. But it only took a few months of working in the business for me to learn who he was.

He was like the godfather in Lyon. When Paul Bocuse walked through market in the center of town each day, everybody walked behind him. (The market is where I first laid eyes on him; my chef took me there every morning to lug whatever he bought back to the restaurant.) When he joined the other chefs at the café after the market, where they'd eat tripe, drink wine or coffee, and share stories and recipes, he was always at the head of the table. Everybody sat around him.

I was alternately afraid of him—How could I not be afraid of a man regarded as infallible by everyone I worked with?—and intrigued, because I wanted to be a great chef like him some-day. But I was never so presumptuous as to speak with him at the market or in the café.

It was Gerard Nandron, my boss, the chef at Nandron, the two-star Michelin restaurant where I was an apprentice, who introduced me to Bocuse.

Nandron used to do a brisk business in private parties—dinners for rich families at their homes and big events at the prefecture of Lyon or the town hall. One afternoon we were driving along the Somme River, going up north of Lyon to cook a private dinner at someone's home. The lighted sign for the l'Auberge du Pont de Collonges, Paul Bocuse's restaurant that everyone referred to by his name, was visible on the other side of the river, and as we passed, Nandron asked, "Have you ever visited Paul Bocuse?"

"No, chef," I told him, "I've never been to the restaurant. But I see him at the market with you all the time."

"Okay, so on the way back, we'll stop there." Of course, I

didn't think we actually would. Were we going to sit down to a meal at the most widely revered restaurant in France in our soiled kitchen clothes after a night of work? But I was buoyed by the idea of the slim chance that it might happen.

We went to our event, we cooked, the guests gushed about Nandron's cooking, and afterward, as promised, Nandron took me to Paul Bocuse's restaurant.

He pulled his car around back of the l'Auberge and we entered through the back door. Bocuse was there, presiding over his kitchen, intense as always, but he cracked a smile when he saw my chef had come to visit. Nandron walked through the kitchen to shake hands and chat with him, while I stayed back by the door.

Bocuse noticed me standing there nervously and, with a twinkle in his eye, commanded one of his waiters to bring "a little something to drink for the apprentice." The waiter brought me a huge blanc cassis—a wineglass brimming with white wine and cassis liquor.

As a kid in France, you learn how to drink at a young age. Not much, but you can drink. I wanted to be polite, and I didn't want to look like a chicken, so I nonchalantly polished off the whole thing in a matter of minutes. It was a killer.

I kept it together at Bocuse, but on the car ride back to the restaurant, it was clear to my chef that I was smashed. I mean totally smashed. Nandron couldn't stop laughing about it and my colleagues thought it was pretty funny. After I'd unloaded the car—a far more difficult and time-consuming task than I remembered it being when I unloaded the same equipment full of food at the house we had cooked at—Nandron put me in his backseat and drove me home so I could sleep it off.

So that's how I met Paul Bocuse: he was the first guy to get me drunk. After that initial meeting—and once I had recovered from my first hangover—I was eager to work under him, to win his approval. I had heard rumors of how tough he was, but my first experience with him showed me his lighter side and I thought I might have an in.

But our subsequent meeting was not to be as cordial as our first.

My boss, Nandron, had started sending me to fill in at other restaurants—when a cook would burn himself, say, or had to take a leave of absence. I enjoyed meeting the challenge of cooking in a foreign kitchen where I had no knowledge of the repertory, of the way the kitchen worked, of where anything was kept. I liked jumping out of the pan and into the fire. When I was about fifteen and a half—about a year after Bocuse gave me my first blanc cassis—Bocuse was looking for a two-week replacement for one of his apprentices. Nandron gave me the nod.

When the day arrived, I showed up to work with my shirt unbuttoned, my Ray-Bans hanging around my neck, and my hair a little long. I strode into the restaurant with a youthful swagger, proud that Paul Bocuse, the greatest chef on the planet, "needed" me to help him in his kitchen.

Bocuse looked me over from my feathered top of shaggy hair to the untied laces dragging behind my shoes and barked, "We don't need anybody working in sunglasses here! Go and get a haircut if you want to work in my kitchen!"

Immediately, I slunk right back out of the kitchen. I went into town and got my hair cut and came back an hour later, asking for his permission to work. He nodded his approval. It was his kitchen. You just cooked in it. He never let you forget that.

My two weeks in his kitchen didn't go perfectly, and perfection was what I aspired to. Luckily, a few months later, I had a chance to redeem myself. Another short stint filling in for another absent cook came up. This time, I told myself, I would perform flawlessly. I made sure to get a haircut the day before I was to start. It wasn't my sloppy appearance that sabotaged my second stint with Bocuse, but it was sloppiness that did me in.

The kitchen staff was allotted what we called a "privilege" of drinks every day: a certain number of bottles of sparkling lemonade and a set quantity of beer. On one of the first nights that I was there, Bocuse went to inspect the walk-in refrigerator—something a chef typically does—and he came across a few open bottles of lemonade and beer on a shelf that was not designated for cooks to store their drinks. (I swear they were not mine.)

Sloppiness is anathema to any good chef and it was doubly so to Bocuse. He snapped. He grabbed a case of lemonade, opened the door, and threw it out onto the kitchen floor. The lemonade was quickly followed by a case of beer. Then he started to throw *everything* out of the walk-in. Carrots, celery, hulking heads of cabbage—whatever he could get his hands on went flying through the air and crashing across the floor. In a panic, we had to scurry to clean up this disaster before the first guests arrived. Bocuse was the only person who was going to make a mess in his kitchen. He never let you forget that.

Toward the end of my time as an apprentice, I was considering where I wanted to try and get my first real cook's job. I had more or less ruled out Bocuse—mostly because his raging temper was a frightening sight and I didn't want to put myself in a position where I could be on the business end of one of his rages.

As luck would have it, though, I did.

Nandron arranged for me to serve one last stint as a substitute in Bocuse's kitchen. But the night before, like an idiot, I went out drinking with the guys. I had wanted to ease my nerves a little, but I ended up taking it *too* easy—we drank until dawn and I slept through most of the following day. When I didn't show up for work, Bocuse was rightly furious. He called my boss and shouted, "Send me another one!"

He was done with me. And Nandron was pretty angry himself, because I had made him look bad. I ended up having to get my parents to come in and apologize to him, which meant *they* were furious, too.

That, I thought, was the end of me and Paul Bocuse.

As it turned out, though, not working for him—and not having it go terribly well when I *did* work for him—might have been the best thing for our relationship.

I went to cook at Georges Blanc's La Mère Blanc, where I'd see Bocuse every once in a while as a dinner guest. After that I worked for Roger Verge, who was Bocuse's best friend, so he was there all the time. I left Verge to work Michel Guérard's Les Prés d'Eugénie, another spot where Bocuse would frequently drop in, and when I moved to America, first to Washington, D.C., and then to New York, we would always be at all the same events.

Over the years Bocuse forgot about the sunglasses and me not showing up and getting me drunk for the first time—I'm certain each of those events loomed much larger in my mind than they did in his—and he started to take a liking to me, a kid from Lyon he kept running into in kitchens and events all over the world. He'd stop by my station and make small talk about what was going on back in Lyon. He was not treating me like a kid anymore, but like a grown-up. It was a real thrill to be taken seriously.

I finally got the long-desired stamp of approval from him, years and years after I had left Lyon, when I was the chef of the

Plaza Athenée hotel in New York. Bocuse turned sixty in 1986, and restaurants all over the world were hosting meals fêting him and celebrating all he has done for our profession. I had the pleasure of cooking a meal in his honor in New York.

I made a menu that had classical and modern elements, including a couple of riffs on dishes I had helped to make at Bocuse—it was an unqualified success. Afterward, Bocuse and Verge came to see me in the kitchen and poured me a congratulatory glass of champagne.

And then they dropped a bomb on me: they had been talking, and they were going to recommend that Sirio Maccioni hire me to take over the kitchen at Le Cirque, the most famous restaurant in New York, and one of the most famous restaurants in the world.

And that recommendation, from those two men, hit me harder than the blanc cassis Bocuse had poured for me fifteen years earlier.

Ready for My Close-Up
ANTHONY BOURDAIN

Anthony Bourdain has been a chef or a cook for nearly three decades, and in 2000 he chronicled that experience in Kitchen Confidential, *which has been translated into twenty-four languages, leading Mr. Bourdain to the conclusion that "chefs are the same everywhere." He is the executive chef at Brasserie Les Halles in New York City.*

T HE MORNING-NEWS ANCHOR is choking. Her co-host, the guy with the perfect hair, is covering his mouth, trying not to cough. The camera people, director, and even the weather-wuss are dabbing their eyes, tearing up from the acrid cloud of brandy and black-pepper-fueled smoke that's billowed through the studio. Yet the anchor perseveres. She soldiers on, a tight rictus of early morning cheer stretched across her face as she leans forward with her fork and spears a hunk of steak au poivre from the daisy-patterned plate. The fork goes in her face—to suitably orgasmic accompanying sounds—and then she hits a whole peppercorn, cracking it between her teeth. The smile evaporates.

"Oh my *God!*" she screams, waving a palm furiously in front of her mouth. "That's so spicy! Oh, my *God*!! My mouth is *burning!*"

It has not been a successful cooking segment for me. Eight cities into a long book tour, I'd thought I'd been smart: I'd changed up my menu selection. I'd already done Mussels, Normandy Style for one television station across town, and Frisée Salad with Lardoons for another. Both were sensible choices in that they were fast, uncomplicated, and easy to put together in a three-minute cooking segment—while exchanging banter with a hyperactive host and promoting the virtues of my cookbook. But for this gig, I'd found another dish. You don't want people turning on yet another local news show and seeing you doing the same damn dish in the same market. Steak au poivre had seemed like such an obvious solution. I'd made it a million times. It too was fast, easy to prepare—and had the added virtue of significant razzle-dazzle as the "deglaze pan" part of the recipe involved a brief column of flame when the brandy hit hot fat.

I'd gracefully encrusted my filet mignon with crushed black peppercorns, attractively seared both sides of the steak in butter and oil in the preheated pan. I'd removed the cooked steak and artfully nestled it atop a cloud of premashed potatoes. Two gaufrette potato chips and a festive sprig of rosemary awaited completion of the sauce. They would tower like an angel's outstretched wings over my steak—a monument of enticingly edible verticality. And though steak au poivre was not, admittedly, a common breakfast item, experience had taught me that free steak was popular in television studios. I fully expected the staff to fall on my steak like starved remoras as soon as we went to commercial.

The only thing I hadn't considered was ventilation.

Used to the airplane-engine sized exhaust fans of the professional restaurant kitchen, the massive range hoods that I'd come to take for granted, I hadn't anticipated what would happen when I poured the brandy into the hot pan, the searing, blinding, caustic wave of airborne pepper oil that would be released into the air—the near-impenetrable fog of white smoke that would roll out over the set, obscuring the happy bouquets of yellow flowers, the smiley-face coffee cups, and faux kitchen geegaws. I hadn't foreseen that worried producers and stagehands would have to bolt for the control panels in a panicky rush to disable the fire suppression system, before the smoke detectors tripped and the sprinklers ruined all those professionally applied layers of makeup, all that expensively poofed and tinted hair. Thankfully, total disaster was averted. The sprinkler system did not go off and drench the beleaguered news team midbroadcast. Choking and red-eyed, they forged on to read their breaking stories about jackknifed trailers, a cat trapped in a tree, and the turnip that looked like the guy from *American Idol*.

But I doubted they'd be asking me back anytime soon. And their clothes and hair would stink like beef fat and burnt peppercorns for the rest of the day.

The steak au poivre was only the latest (in this case, misguided) attempt at finding a stock selection of dishes that could be demonstrated on camera. It's a surprisingly tricky thing. Not just any old dish will do. When cooking on television, there need to be some visuals, some technique. You can't just slap a few ingredients together and say "voilà!" Presumably you want to be able to demonstrate a process, a little technique—to show off the skills that make you a motherfuck-ing professional. You want to accomplish this without looking like an asshole or an incompetent, avoiding the clumsy acci-dent, the unforeseen mishap: the soufflé that might not rise, the salmon filet that doesn't skin, the sauce that breaks. And you want to be able to do it in under three minutes, yet eat up enough air time so as to be able to adequately describe your lat-est project—and ultimately move some units. Stabbing yourself or the host with a boning knife is to be avoided. Splattering face or genitals with molten duck fat or caramelized sugar is not good. Softshell crabs and escargots, for instance, make bad costars, as they are prone to exploding at unpredictable mo-ments, showering those within proximity with boiling hot guts. A cooking segment that ends with maxillofacial mutilation and screams of agony is not a successful cooking segment. I had learned these painful lessons—among others—over time.

You know, for instance, before you leave your home city, that the equipment on location will be unreliable. When the pro-ducers say, "We have a full kitchen and all the tools you'll need," they usually mean, "We have a smelly, underpowered dollhouse electric stove and some donated crap-quality cook-ware that's still encrusted with the remnants of the camera as-sistant's reheated chili." When they say, "We can get all the ingredients you'll need," they mean, "If they don't have it at the local Stop & Shop—you're fucked. What is arugula any-way?" When they say that your segment host is "a really ad-venturous eater" it means they like mayonnaise on their curly fries.

I learned this last lesson when I found myself feeding steak tartare to a regional "gourmet" host on yet another morning news-and-banter show. You know the one: unnaturally happy blond cohosts in fright makeup, pausing between anecdotes of their weekend and sips of coffee to read news stories. Often there's a "chef" on these programs—some hapless burnout from a nearby country club kitchen—typically with a cheery moniker like "The Sexually Repressed Greengrocer" or "The Prozac-Gobbling Gourmet" who makes the occasional appearance to signal the advent of rhubarb season, or to show people how to make their bundt cake uglier. They are introduced to visiting chefs as "*Our* chef . . ." who is (of course) "happy to help you with anything you need." They usually hover in the distance, glowering at you from their dim cubicles, exuding failure, smashed hopes, with only the prospect of a return to a lonely apartment populated by one too many cats in their future. The crews love them, though. They give them bundt cake.

I thought the steak tartare was a shrewd idea. I wouldn't have to rely on the studio for any cooking equipment. I'd bring my own plates, my own locally (and easily) acquired ingredients. I had a metal ring and a knife and a spatula in my kit. I figured to chop the steak by hand—impressing with my fast, furious, and precise knifework. I'd quickly fold in the mustard, capers, chopped cornichons, and shallots, swirl in the egg yolk, and neatly shape the result in the metal ring. A few pre-toasted croutons would make it easy for my host to take an on-camera taste. "Mmm! Now that's tartare!" Retire to the hotel to the sound of deafening kudos . . .

Didn't happen. Apparently, the practice of eating raw meat had not penetrated this far into America's interior. News of mad cow disease *had* reached the state, however, because the host looked on in terror as I forced the uncooked egg and beef concoction into the metal ring, the idea dawning on her that yes . . . yes . . . she would be required to eat this thing absolutely raw. The word *Ewww!* actually escaped from her lips as she tenuously reached for a meat-smeared crouton. Like a nun giving a

blow job, she took the tiniest nibble, fighting the urge to gag—
her head swimming with images of spongiform bacteria rid-
dling her brain, turning it into swiss cheese. When the segment
was over and she'd spit the tiny taste out into a trash bin, she
fixed me with a look of such pure loathing that it haunted my
dreams. (A vengeful and enraged morning-show host invading
your dreamscape is a terrifying image, believe me.)

I thought I'd learned.

I'd learned to bring my own ingredients. I'd learned to bring
my own equipment. I'd learned to check and double-check every
detail. I'd learned to keep it simple—and fast—and to plan for
the possibility that things would have to be sped up or slowed
down, keeping fully prepared "swap-out" versions of whatever
dish was ready and at hand. "And in fifteen minutes—when
your salmon is done—it should look . . . like . . . this."

My first experience of cooking on camera had, of course,
brought many of these lessons embarrassingly home. It was ages
ago, in the early years of food television, and the—oh, let's call
it . . . the Cooking Channel—was in its infancy. In those days,
their studios were not the well-laid-out, well-equipped facilities
they are today. No donated Calphalon or Sub-Zeros. The
Cooking Channel operated out of a midtown office building,
high over Sixth Avenue. There were just a few bare-bones studios and a central prep "kitchen"—an office space littered with
the decaying remnants of the few shows they produced between
paid infomercials. One, as I recall, was a cooking competition
in which well-known chefs would be paired with nonprofes-
sionals to prepare a meal in thirty minutes. The winner was decided by a hooting studio audience of clueless fucktards who
never even got to taste the results. I vividly recall watching the
great master chef Jean-Louis Palladin lose one of these Battles
Not So Royale to a vastly less-talented audience favorite.

Another show paired a failed local talk show host with the wife of an ex-mayor, I believe. What either of them had to do with food, I have no idea. They would feature remote reports shot elsewhere: "A Lumberjack Meal Like No Other" prepared and filmed at a bed and breakfast in, say, Ontario. The results were then FedExed to the studio and reassembled in the septic kitchen, then presented to the studio hosts who would take a few desultory, on-camera bites. (The leftovers were then relegated to the "prep kitchen" where they were first picked over by crew and office help before being left for the prodigious insect population.)

I arrived at the studios full of hope, all atwitter, with a painstakingly assembled collection of ingredients and my knives. I did my best to clear a work space among the rotting detritus of the prep kitchen. An unwashed and shell-shocked looking "chef" hosed off a stained cutting board pulled from a piled-high sinkful of dirty pots and pans, and I managed to push aside enough sinister-looking, plastic-wrapped parcels in the jam-packed, petri-dish-like refrigerators to store my fish.

The plan was to grill a piece of salmon, quickly roast some yellow peppers, skin and puree them with a little vinaigrette, puree some roasted beets as well, and build a colorful and delicious presentation around a salad of mâche and belgian endive. The process was simple, the result pretty (at least back at my restaurant). The pink salmon fillet, crisscrossed with black and brown grill marks, would contrast beautifully with a moist, glistening, freshly dressed, dark-green-flecked-with-white pile of salad. Both would sit atop a vibrant yellow field of roasted pepper vinaigrette, drizzled with a restrained Jackson Pollock pattern of bright reddish purple roasted beet sauce.

But it wasn't to be so easy. First, for reasons I was never able to understand, I was instructed to assemble a finished and fully prepared "beauty plate"—the "when it's done it'll look like this" version of the dish, for the close-up shot that would introduce the scene and end it. This, I dutifully did—only to watch my baby sit unattended under the lights, the dressed salad wilting into sludge, the sauce separating, the fish attracting a cloud of copulating fruit flies. Also, as I quickly learned, the fire department frowned on the use of open flame or gas ranges on the upper floors of office buildings. The Cooking Channel, therefore, did not allow "cooking" per se. There would be no grill and no broiler. I would have to prepare my salmon in an ancient and much abused grill pan, a filthy, reeking, cast-iron beast that had never been seasoned or maintained. When I found it under a landfill of dirty pots and once-edible sediment in a stagnant pot sink, it was already beginning to take on a patina of rust. My heat source—on camera—was a food-spattered hot plate, wheeled onto a barebones set that made public access sets look like the finale of a James Bond film. You would have been embarrassed to shoot porn there. When my beauty plate had finally festered into adequate unrecognizability, I was summoned with my mise en place to take my place and begin cooking.

I tore the fucking salmon. Lifting the fish fillet out of the pan, the damn thing stuck to the cooking surface, leaving behind a sizable hunk. I did my best to cover the incident with a stealthy movement of the hand, depositing the remaining fillet atop the salad and field of sauce with as much panache as I could muster under the circumstances. The hosts jabbered enthusiastically enough. (But then I'd seen them happily eating from the diabolical Buffet of the Damned scattered around the prep areas in various stages of decomposition.) I slunk home encouraged only by the fact that no one at that time really watched the Cooking Channel. You found it now and again, as you channel surfed between Robin Byrd and the Weather Channel, and moved on. Yet on arriving home, the phone immediately rang.

It was my old friend Bigfoot, a restaurateur and until recently my boss and mentor.

"Asshole! You tore that salmon!"

Skull Man
JIMMY BRADLEY

Jimmy Bradley worked in kitchens in Philadelphia and Rhode Island before becoming executive chef of Savoir Fare, a progressive Martha's Vineyard bistro where he began his trademark style of straightforward, boldly flavored seasonal cooking. In New York City, he has opened a string of restaurants that started out as neighborhood joints and wound up as destinations for diners from across the country: the Red Cat, the Harrison, and the Mermaid Inn. His first book, The Red Cat Cookbook, *written with Andrew Friedman, debuts in November 2006.*

I N 1985 I graduated from high school and headed off to the University of Rhode Island, moving into an apartment in Narragansett, the little town right next to Kingston, with my older sister who was already going to school up there. It was my freshman year, so I didn't have a major yet. While I did enjoy the history and political science classes in the liberal arts program, my focus was on girls, and I was starting to like Scotch.

My sister was working as a waitress at a restaurant called the Boathouse in Narragansett. (Names have been changed to protect the innocent.) Seeing as I needed some scratch and that I had been a pretty good busboy back in Philly where we grew up, she put in a good word for me at the restaurant.

I had done all kinds of odd jobs in the business in Philly: stocking deli counters, making sandwiches, slicing pickles at the Jewish deli, you name it. (Except for dishwashing, oddly enough. I never was a dishwasher.) The general manager at the Boathouse, Lionel, agreed to take me on as a busboy. Lionel was an explosive Irish man with fiery red hair. I called him the Wig—actually, I started out calling him Wiggenheimer, but he wasn't going for that, so I settled on calling him the Wig. He had these episodes where he'd wig out, where you didn't know where you stood with him, but he was generally an okay guy.

I did well as a busboy, and after the season picked up a little bit I got promoted to waiter. I was a quick study, and, soon, whenever they had VIPs they gave me the table.

Don't get me wrong when I say VIPs: this was a classic coastal New England upscale restaurant, which means it was just one step above a fry shack. It was more than broiled scrod and Ritz cracker crumb topping on everything, but it was hardly refined. Veal marsala was three slices of veal with a pat of butter, three times around the pan with a bottle of cheap marsala and a fistful of raw mushrooms. Composed seafood platters were the Boathouse's stock in trade: baked, broiled, steamed, or fried. You couldn't set up your station without coleslaw, lemon wedges, and a bunch of butter—everything came with them. It wasn't gingham, but it was close.

The Boathouse was a nice enough place though, situated out on a long point, with water lapping up on three sides and giant picture windows facing out to sea. It did a gangbuster business throughout the season.

At one point during the year, my father, who lived there in Narragansett, went on holiday for a couple weeks. I decided to throw a party at his house. There were kegs and strangers, long rows of parked cars, people passing out on the lawn—it got pretty off the wall. I don't remember the exact details of *why* it happened, but a couple of us shaved our heads bald that night.

This was long before being bald was fashionable. We looked like carnies or maybe, in a best-case scenario, street thugs. It was not a comfortable sight to behold. I was so well shorn I could stick a plunger to my head and it wouldn't come off. (I'm not exaggerating—I actually did it that night. I had to dunk my head in a bathtub full of water and pry the plunger off with a butter knife.) That's how bald I was.

A couple of days after the party, I went back into work. The Wig took one look at me and said, "You're fired."

Prior to this, he had told me how much he liked working with me, and I knew for a fact that my sales were the second highest of any waiter working there. "You can't fire me," I replied. "I'm a good employee. You said so yourself."

So we got into this kind of exchange, the Wig and I. In the middle of it, he suddenly held his hand out. I didn't know if it was a handshake he was proffering or what, but I reached out and he took my hand in his and walked me toward the kitchen like I was six years old.

He burst through the kitchen doors and yelled for the chef, John. "Hey, Chef," he said, "you know this kid?"

Chef said, "Yeah, the kid. He's been doing good."

"Right," said the Wig. "He works for you now." And he stormed out of the kitchen.

The chef looked me over and told me to go stand in the corner. Which is what I did for a day or two. But the season had been building—one Saturday we did a hundred covers, the next Saturday two hundred, and that Saturday four hundred—so it couldn't have hurt to have some extra hands on deck. After a couple of days the chef finally gave me something to do back in my corner, in the larder, in the cold: make the coleslaw. Making coleslaw for this place was nuts. I took a brand new fifty-five-gallon Brute trashcan and slid it under the vegetable grater and shredded a case of carrots, a case of red cabbage, and two cases of white cabbage. Then it was time to get in there and mix it. I was eighteen; the thing was half as a big as I was. Seeing cooking on that scale—making four hundred portions of something at once—was really eye opening for me.

After a while, I graduated to opening shellfish. I still had to work in the corner, and I still wasn't really part of the kitchen crew, but it was a step up from cabbage detail. The main work was prying open clams, oysters, and scallops and busting open conches. I'd also cook up a case or two of lobsters, pick all the meat out of them, and portion it out for the cooks. I was taking care of all the grunt work that needs to be done to run a seafood restaurant.

The Boathouse served baked clams two ways and baked oysters two ways, so I'd go in and shuck three, four, five hundred of each. Luckily, my dad had taught me to shuck shellfish growing up, so within a day or two of working the shellfish duty, my chops were polished. I was probably the second best shucker in the kitchen. That was the first point, I think, at which the chef noticed me. He would come by my station and see that I was already done and say, "How the fuck do you know this? You're that stupid busboy," or, "You're done? What do you mean you're done? I'm not ready for you to be done."

But he was clearly happy with the fact that I was completing the work quickly.

Now even though this was a fried seafood place, it served a little pasta—there are a lot of Italians in Rhode Island and they like their pasta. There was linguine with clams, pasta fra diavolo with half a lobster on top, that kind of stuff. One day the chef decided that we were going to make ravioli. It would be my next task: making the ravioli. So he set me up in the corner with the filling and the dough that he'd made and he showed me how he wanted the raviolis put together. Then he split and I got to work. An hour later, when I'd finished, I ducked out back to smoke a cigarette. The chef, however, who had only just returned, saw me out there and immediately assumed I'd cut corners because I'd done the ravioli so fast. He dragged me back to my station to look over the ravioli, ready to bawl me out—and saw that mine looked better than his. Not just better, much better.

"Where the fuck does this come from?" he said, kind of amused that I'd done something right again. "The oysters, the clams, I get that: you live in Rhode Island. But what do you know from ravioli?" I told him about growing up in an Italian family with an even larger extended family in Philly. On Sundays we went to church, we made dinner, and we ate. That was all you did on a Sunday. I didn't think there was any kind of pasta I hadn't made.

Anyway, the chef always made the dough and the filling and had me form the ravioli, until one day, while no one was watching, I threw out his pasta dough and made my own. And everybody—the cooks, the waiters, the customers, the dishwashers—everybody reacted with, "How come these are better?" I didn't tell anyone, of course. I wasn't trying to show off; I just wanted to try it, to see how it would come out. The chef didn't know, so he kept making the dough and I kept throwing it out and remaking it.

Soon I started to change the filling a bit, mixing a little shrimp in with the cheese. There's this standard rule that you're not supposed to mix cheese with shellfish, but when you don't know anything, which I didn't, you're free to do whatever you want. I was going on flavors from memory, not traditional culinary technique; I hadn't gotten to that point. It seemed like a no-brainer to me: shrimp and Parmesan cheese just taste good together. Nobody knew what the story was with the pasta except for me, but on my days off people would say it wasn't as good as it usually was.

Then one day one of the cooks didn't show. He'd gone to a Grateful Dead concert the night before and no one ever heard from him again. The chef came over to me, stuck in my usual corner, and said, "You're going to work the combination fry station tonight. We'll see if you sink or swim." This was a Saturday night, and maybe the third most beautiful day of the year. The restaurant was going to be unbelievably busy. And it was the first time I'd been asked to cook anything in the kitchen other than a lobster—which is not that hard.

One thing you should know is that working a fry station is a dirty job. Usually in the kitchen you only soil one hand: when you're working the grill, you've got one hand that you touch the protein with and an instrument like a fork or tongs in the other—you never have two dirty hands. But the fry station is a mess, and so was I that night.

We got slammed. I did sixty-five fried seafood combination platters—french fries, clams, shrimp, and oysters, all fried, all the seafood hand battered, all with different cooking times—on top of all the regular orders of fried clam strips and single-seafood orders and french fries that went with half of everything we served.

I think if you can do that station well, you can figure out almost anything else in the kitchen. You have to have your timing down, because your food goes up at the same time as everyone else's. But you might have six things on one plate—lemon, coleslaw, chicory and melon wedge (the standard garnish), plus four kinds of fried things and two sauces (and that's when there aren't any substitutions)—whereas the guy next to you is making filet with a béarnaise sauce, which is prepared in advance, and a pile of asparagus that someone else just hands to him. Fry is a bitch of a station.

But at the end of the night I was still standing. There was a dull buzz in my ears, and the clickety-clack of the printer that spat out the orders all night was still rattling around in my skull. I was reeling a little from the shell shock of everybody constantly yelling at me. But I had made it. I never lost track of where I was, I never fell behind, I never failed to complete a repetitive task in the time allowed. And I know now that it's the ability to master those repetitive tasks that makes a good cook—not a good chef—but a good cook. I was pretty pleased with myself, despite the fact that I was a filthy, stinky, barely upright french fry of a human being. I smelled like the inside of a McDonald's ventilator hood.

The chef came over to me and said, "Let's go downstairs." I thought he was going to yell at me about something. But he didn't. He passed me a beer and he offered me the job. "If there's a holy trinity, I guess you passed it. There were so many opportunities to stick that knife through your hand when you were shucking, but you didn't. You did the thing with the ravioli and I still don't know what's going on there—I'm kinda pissed about that and I'm kinda not. And then you walked on as a looper tonight and you didn't get beat. I gotta give you the chance."

That was it. I was in. I thought if this—cooking—was going to come like this, I had to welcome it with open arms. And much to the dismay of all concerned parties, I dropped out of school and started the journey of the journeyman cook.

And the Winner Is . . .
ANDREW CARMELLINI

After graduating from the Culinary Institute of America, Andrew Carmellini trained in the best kitchens in New York, including San Domenico and Lespinasse, and under Valentino Mercatile, the highly regarded chef of the Michelin two-star San Domenico in Emilia-Romagna. In 1998, after two years as sous chef at Le Cirque, Andrew took on the chef's position at the new Café Boulud. In his six years there, Andrew earned a three-star review from the New York Times, *won the James Beard Foundation's Rising Star Chef of the Year award, and was named to* Food & Wine *magazine's roster of best new chefs. The month before Carmellini left Café Boulud to open his own restaurant, A Voce, he won the James Beard Foundation's award for Best Chef: New York City.*

FAT CHEFS IN tall hats standing around giving each other medals: that's what cooking competitions were in this country for a long time. Shows like *Iron Chef* have conferred more legitimacy on kitchen showdowns over the last decade, but I've always been a little leery of them. Too frequently, they seem like self-congratulatory exercises in self-promotion and rarely, if at all, centered around the food itself.

Still, you can only distance yourself from some things for so long in this business, and I guess I was at that inevitable point in the early nineties, when I was working as the sous chef under Daniel Boulud at Le Cirque. One afternoon, I got a call from a well-known Italian restaurateur who asked me if I'd like to participate in a world olive oil competition. He said there would be a qualifying heat in New York and the winner would go on to cook against chefs from around the world in Italy. The challenge was to come up with a recipe "highlighting the distinct taste of a regional olive oil."

It was an interesting proposition to me: I had trained in Italy and was (and still am) committed to using artisanal products in my cooking, so I thought I should open my mind up a little bit and give this competition a try. I was running a risotto with rosemary and five different types of tomatoes as a special at Le Cirque that I felt gracefully highlighted the fruit and acid of the olive oil we cooked it with. The olive oil was from Liguria, grown in my friend Marco Binaldi's orchard—it's great stuff, very fruity, and I knew it would shine in my dish.

When I showed up for the showdown in New York there were a couple of well-known chefs from the city, a few guys from out of town, and little to no organization to speak of. At some point we were ushered into a dirty subterranean kitchen in an ugly midtown hotel and were told we had one hour to prepare our dishes for the judges.

The event felt strangely unofficial: there was no audience, no distinguished panel of judges, no dinner, and no reception. Just five portions for five judges, none of whom I can even remember at this point. We got busy in the kitchen, cooked our dishes in silence, and sent them out to be judged. I was standing around talking with the other chefs I knew when, only minutes after we had finished cooking, one of the judges came in and announced, "Andrew Carmellini is the winner," and that I would be traveling to Italy to "represent America" in the world competition. It was surprising, as it was only my first cooking competition, but also kind of anticlimactic since it had happened so fast.

But when it hit me that I was heading to Italy in a few months and in the middle of the summer—always a good time to be there—it was hard to feel anything but enthusiastic. I went home with a grin, thinking, Italy, summer, tomatoes, risotto: What can go wrong?

Maybe a week before I left I got my itinerary and a little information about the competition. It was being put on in a little town outside Milan in the lake region of northern Italy, hosted by a consortium of olive oil producers that I had never heard of before. Federations—*consorzios*—of olive oil producers throughout Italy organize trips all the time where they invite chefs and journalists to learn about tasting olive oil, how it's produced, and about the producers themselves, so that didn't put me off. I thought I might even learn about or meet some great new olive oil producers whose products I'd never encountered before.

After I arrived in the town, however, I learned that it wasn't a *consorzio* of tiny producers like my friend Marco Binaldi. It was a lobbying group of huge conglomerates from countries like Tunisia and Turkey and Morocco—and not the quality producers over there but the guys who ship their cheap olive oil in tankers across the Mediterranean. That raised the first red flag.

I started to get progressively more worried as I watched the many presentations that had been arranged for attendees throughout the week. Not a single one of them focused on artisanal production or the regional nuances of olive oils from around Italy. They were almost strictly about world market stuff. During one, the presenter actually stated that the chief intention of the conference was to convince Asian chefs—and, more broadly, home cooks from Korea to Kuala Lumpur—to start cooking with olive oil. "What happened to 'highlighting the distinct taste of a regional olive oil'?" I muttered to myself.

The cooking competition was the big draw, the media focus of the whole conference, and where, I still faintly hoped, the experience might redeem itself. On the day of the main event, I met the chefs I'd be cooking shoulder to shoulder against. There were chefs from Brazil, Germany, Japan, Korea, China, Thailand—around twenty countries in all.

Whatever dim optimism I had miraculously managed to retain up to this point vanished the moment that I saw the kitchen we would be using. You know those beautiful, spacious stainless-steel-and-glass kitchens featured on television cooking shows today? This was *not* one of them. Dim, dirty, and cramped, the cheap hotel kitchen (yet another one) was a far cry from what I had been expecting; it was about as appealing as cooking in a gas station. In the corner, the dishwasher stood next to his machine and sullenly chain-smoked cigarettes, which he would continue to do without stopping (except for when he was making himself espressos). To make matters worse, all the Italian TV stations were there, which meant we would be on TV sweating and cooking and struggling to look half-presentable in this terrible little kitchen.

About an hour before we were to start cooking, they showed me where my mise en place and stove were. As I checked over the ingredients they had supplied me with for my risotto, I realized that the tomatoes were terrible—the cherry tomatoes were still half-green and the beefsteak tomatoes were profoundly tasteless. Here we were, in the middle of summer in Italy, and these tomatoes were as bad as anything you'd find in an American supermarket in the middle of winter.

I had no choice: my dish was about the quality of the ingredients I was cooking with and the olive oil I was cooking them in. I ran out of the kitchen, hopped in my rental car, and started driving, desperate to find tomatoes that tasted like something. I ended up at supermarket down the road where the tomatoes were better than what I'd been supplied with at the world olive oil competition.

By the time I got back to the kitchen, people were already cooking. I hurried over to my station and hastily unpacked my find. As I prepped the risotto, I glanced around to get a sense of what the competition was like. The guy next to me, from Germany, was smoking lobsters and making sweetbread strudels that had, all kidding aside, about seven sauces on the plate. And I could tell from five feet away that his strudels were burnt on the outside and raw on the inside. The Korean chef on the other side of me was making a version of vitello tonnato, poached veal with a tuna-mayonnaise sauce. What either of these dishes had to do with "highlighting the distinct taste of a regional olive oil"—or olive oil at all—I still don't know to this day.

After this initial observation, I started to relax. After all, I was doing great: keeping it simple, letting the olive oil taste like olive oil. What does smoked lobster have to do with olive oil? Nothing. I was confident that I had the competition in the bag. Who's going to beat me, the guy with the burnt strudel? There was no way.

Then it was time for the tasting. We all put our dishes up and waited for the judges . . . and waited . . . and waited some more.

You *might* think that someone behind the event would have given some consideration to the time between when our dishes were finished and when the judges were going to taste them. And, hey, you *might* also think that since we were in Italy, someone behind the event would have considered the fact that cooked risotto waits for no one. But as the minutes kept ticking by, and the dishes cooled and thickened and irreversibly hardened, it became clear that none of these things were being considered. I'm certain that by the time the judges got around to trying my once perfectly creamy risotto, it was close to the texture of spackle. I was disappointed and disgusted with the whole spectacle.

We were told that the winners would be announced at the gala dinner the next night. I tried to take comfort in knowing that at least if I was going to lose, it wouldn't be in front of anyone I knew personally, just the conference attendees and anyone who tuned into Italian television that night.

Of course, when I arrived for the dinner the following night, who was I seated with? Fourteen American journalists and a chef from New York, all of us clustered at a big table with a little American flag on it. I knew everyone.

After some now-familiar speeches about the virtues of cheap olive oil, they started announcing the winners. Korea, Taiwan, and Japan took the first three spots. The Korean guy who had made a practically olive-oil-free bastardization of vitello tonnato had beaten me. God, was that embarrassing. At that point I just wanted to leave.

But I had to wait for six more chefs to collect their awards before I was called up to take my tenth-place certificate. After the famous Italian restaurateur who had gotten me involved in this mess handed me the piece of paper, he leaned over and whispered in my ear, "You couldn't have possibly expected to win, Andrew. You knew this whole thing was put together so they could sell olive oil to China, right?"

I didn't even go back to the table. I dropped the certificate in a garbage can, got in my car, and drove overnight—sleeping briefly in the backseat after I crossed the French-Italian border—all the way to Alain Ducasse in Paris.

The competition was ten years ago now, and I have never cooked in another one since.

The Noodle Whisperer
DAVID CHANG

David Chang opened his noodle shop, Momofuku, in New York City's East Village, in 2004. Chang's personal take on Japanese and Korean cooking won the affordable and tiny restaurant national media attention. In 2006 Chang was nominated for the James Beard Foundation's Best New Chef award and was named one of Food & Wine's *Best New Chefs. His next project, Momofuku Ssäm Bar, will open in the fall of 2006.*

I AM CRAZY ABOUT noodles. I have been since I was a kid.

My noodle obsession started to take hold of me in my early twenties, when I was working as a cook under chef Marco Canora at Craft, Tom Colicchio's three-star, green market-driven New York City restaurant. Most of my colleagues were making their bones at Craft with dreams of later in life running their own similar, fine-dining venue somewhere. But I knew I wanted to take a different path: get the hell out of the fancy restaurant world and open a ramen shop.

While I was at Craft I daydreamed about traveling to Japan to really study the ramen culture there, eat as much ramen as I could, and, if I was lucky, get a job in a ramen shop. But I didn't know how I was going to make it happen.

I had taught English in Wakayama, two hours southeast of Osaka, right after college, though my real ambition was to get a job making ramen. I gave up after two months of consistent rejections. Subsequent attempts, after I had gone to the French Culinary Institute, worked at Mercer Kitchen, and was employed at Craft, were equally fruitless: I had sent letters that a friend translated into Japanese to a number of ramen houses in Tokyo and I hadn't heard back from any of them.

Toward the end of my second year at Craft, an acquaintance of my father's—he might even have been a relative, I can't keep track because my dad has eight brothers and sisters, so I've got uncles and aunts all over the place—caught wind of my situation and passed along word that he could set me up with a kitchen job in a ramen shop in Tokyo if I was interested. There'd be free lodging for me, too, and some visa voodoo that would make it legal for me to work there.

I didn't ask any questions. I didn't care what the place looked like. I was so singularly focused on working in a ramen shop that I was ready to buy a ticket as soon as I heard the offer. Without a moment's hesitation, I gave three months notice at Craft and called a travel agent.

The arrangement I had agreed to turned out to be more than a little unusual. The man who had expedited my being there was a successful businessman who had left the corporate world behind to follow a more spiritual path. (I think the fact that I majored in religion in college must have been one of the selling points that got me the job.)

He had purchased a nondescript, vacant seven-story office building in the Kudan-shita district of Tokyo and installed a Korean born-again Christian church on the top floor. The five floors below it were a mix of low-rent office space and a men's halfway house, a hostel of sorts. Rooms on one side of the building looked out onto the red and yellow façade of a Mc-Donald's across the street; on the other side they looked out onto the Budakkan, where I'd catch a concert every once in a while. The first floor housed two restaurants, a *ramenya*—in Japan, a *ramenya,* or ramen shop, serves ramen and almost nothing else—and, an *izakaya,* a Japanese pub.

The core constituency of the church on seven and the occupants of the hostel rooms were homeless or borderline-homeless, overeducated former salaried men in their fifties and sixties. My Japanese was terrible when I arrived (and, truth be told, is not so hot now, either), so while the old men's hostel was a strange place for a kid in his twenties to be living, it wasn't the worst place I could have ended up, since most of the guys spoke English. And it was free.

The plan was for me to work at the *ramenya* during the week and help out at the *izakaya* on weekends. But, even though working in a ramen shop was my life's goal at that point, it was apparent only days after I arrived that there was going to be trouble. The problem was the guy who ran the place. He was an old man, tiny, wrinkled like a shumai, with a short, gray buzz cut; he lived in the room directly below mine in the hostel. And he was absolutely fucking crazy.

He had clearly worked at some really good restaurants during his career: his knife skills were outstanding. But he'd also spent some amount of time living on the street before our mutual patron had installed him at the restaurant—the rumor was that he had had his own sushi shop in the Ginza district before he started drinking all the time and eventually lost it—and I think the sum of his experiences had gotten to him. Most days, he just strolled around the building, whether it was in the hallways of the hostel or the kitchen at the *ramenya,* dressed in only his sagging tighty-whities, chain-smoking cigarettes. He had a prohibition against paper *and* cloth towels in the kitchen, so he kept a few folded sheets of greasy newspaper tucked into the apron he wore over his underwear. It was a sight to behold. (Though not if you were thinking about eating the soup.)

My breaking point came early. On one of the first days I was there, a delivery of pork came in. I went to put it in the refrigerator, but the chef stopped me. He pointed to a counter. I didn't understand what he meant. He continued pointing, now gesturing emphatically for me to put it down. So I did. Satisfied, he walked away—and proceeded to leave it out all day. Hour after hour, the seeping, warm pork sat in that dank little kitchen that stunk of cigarette smoke. It freaked me out. I'd gone from working in a top-notch, superclean kitchen to the least sanitary kitchen in the world.

I knew I had to move on.

There were a couple of tense weeks where I still helped out at the *izakaya* before I was put in touch with another relative's friend's friend (sometimes having more relatives than you can count is a good thing), Dr. Hosoda, a well-to-do doctor. Dr. Hosoda's nephew, Akio, many years my senior, operated a soba shop in Tokyo. And though he and his wife had never employed another soul in their restaurant, and he'd never taken on an understudy, he agreed, for whatever mysterious reason, to allow me to come and work for him.

I had come to Tokyo to study ramen—which I was doing plenty of on my own time, eating all the meals I could manage in *ramenyas* around the city—but, hey, soba are noodles, too, I thought. Sometimes things don't go as planned.

Soba-ya Fuyu-Rin was in Mei-dae-mae, a residential neighborhood in Tokyo, and it was housed on the first floor of Akio's home. He lived upstairs, rolled his soba upstairs, and cooked and served customers on the first floor. It was just him and his wife, and the restaurant never did more than ten or fifteen covers a day.

Akio was a strange guy. He didn't talk much. In fact, I'm not sure what his last name is, even today. I just called him Akio, and that sufficed. But his restaurant was the perfect place for a kid who wanted to learn as much as possible. It was the diametric opposite of the filthy ramen shop where I'd started out: superclean, super-high-end, and Akio cooked everything *à la minute.*

The ingredients he worked with were top-notch. He wouldn't just have scallions, he'd have scallions that looked like leeks and were purple at the root end. One of the details I had teased out of him during our usually silent time together was that he used to work at Tsukiji, Tokyo's legendary and labyrinthine fish market, which explained the unbelievable prawns and sea urchins he'd manage to get his hands on. I've still never seen the purple sea urchin roe that Akio served anywhere else. The sake he cooked with is better than the sake most people drink in this country, the soy was artisanally brewed, and the mirin was real mirin, not the corn-syrupy stuff we get over here.

Akio taught me that it wasn't enough to make your own dashi (the seaweed and dried fish broth that is the most basic and essential of Japanese preparations). He taught me that if you were serious, you had to shave fresh *katsua-bashi* from a whole block of dried bonito flesh every day and have just the right kind of dried *konbu*, a variety of seaweed, on hand.

He would grind his own coarse *sobakoh*, or buckwheat flour, for the soba noodles every morning and taught me to use a second kind of buckwheat flour, the whitest, lightest variety, ground from the center of the buckwheat kernel, for dusting the noodle dough and the cut noodles.

The plates and platters and bowls he served food on were all handmade one-of-a-kind pieces that a friend of his crafted especially for the restaurant. The guy was some sort of national living treasure, and all his dishes—there weren't that many of them—were beautiful. Delicate. Perfect.

In the mornings, when Akio would make the noodles for the restaurant, he would set me up with my own allotment of sobakoh and water and let me try and duplicate what he was doing. (Though he *never* let me make noodles that he would serve to paying customers).

Since he wasn't in the habit of explaining what he was doing—nor, really, in the habit of talking very much—he would send me to his friends every couple weeks to study soba making.

There was a stretch where he had Yuki, Dr. Hosoda's wife, take me to spend time with his friend in a farmhouse nestled up against the mountains, a two-hour subway train ride west of Tokyo. I lived there for a few weekends, learning about mixing soba from the guy, who was both a soba maker and a knife sharpener.

Then, one weekend, Akio came with me. The knife sharpener

showed me how to mix the flour and the dough, and then indicated that I was to give it a go, just like he did every weekend. I did as I was told. The knife sharpener and Akio silently stood there, against a backdrop of cloud-covered mountains, watching me, like something out of *Kill Bill*. They had me do the same thing, this kneading and mixing motion, over and over. Practice, practice, practice, they told me. They nodded with mild satisfaction at my progress.

At that point, I'd done enough kneading and mixing—not that I had made noodles that anyone had eaten yet—and it was time for me to learn how to cut soba.

That was less like *Kill Bill* and more like *The Karate Kid*, with me in the Ralph Maccio role. Before I was allowed to slice real noodles—even from dough that I had made, and that wasn't going to be served to customers—Akio made me practice on newspaper. I spent what seemed like a week's worth of mornings slicing newspaper into ribbons with this big battle-ax soba knife, like an inefficient but determined human document shredder. I wanted to protest, and ask Akio to let me just cut some goddamn noodles, but I knew better. Eventually, my paper shredding was satisfactory and Akio let me start cutting my own noodles. (Noodles that were still unfit for anyone to eat).

Seeing as that my training was progressing, I went out and bought my own soba knife at about that time. Chefs everywhere, no matter if it's Tokyo or New York, hate lending out their knives. I hoped that Akio would be relieved that I wasn't going to need his anymore and maybe even heartened by the fact that I'd gone out and dropped whatever the yen equivalent of $220 was on a soba-cutting knife.

When I unsheathed the knife the next day, however, it turned out to be anything but cool. He looked over at me, then quickly came and took it out of my hand. He held the knife limply, like a spoiled fish he wanted to rid himself of, and gave me a look that said, "How can you bring this piece of shit into my temple of soba?" and told me to put it away for good. We'd be going to Kappabashi the next morning, he said.

Kappabashi is to kitchen equipment what Tsukiji is to fish: an impossibly giant city of stores in Tokyo, one after another, selling nothing but knives, pots, and plates. It feels about the size of Manhattan when you're shopping there. It is a cook's dream.

A cook's dream, that is, unless you're a twenty-something cook living off his credit cards and being taken there by a grumpy soba master who feels he needs to teach you what a *real* soba knife is.

Did he ever. He showed me how nice Japanese knives have handles you can remove, that they are made with these particular sorts of steel and are forged by guys whose families have been making blades since the era when there was a brisk business to be done in samurai swords.

I listened attentively, but at the time, I wasn't interested in buying heirlooms. I bought the knife that I did because it was razor sharp and the guy who sold it to me assured me it kept a great edge.

Then Akio handed me this gorgeous knife he'd been sermonizing about and told me to buy it. In my head, I thought, "Why do I need this? What do I need with a detachable sharkskin-covered handle? How am I going to pay for this?"

But I didn't know how long I was going to stay there, under Akio's tutelage. So I bit my tongue and bought it. If buying the knife was the price I'd have to pay to stay, then it would be worth it.

*   *   *

The knife cost $2,200. It took me years to pay it off. And, funny enough, it turned out that my time with Akio was almost at its end.

My purchase of the cheap—by Akio's standards—knife was certainly one of the contributing factors to the end of my stay. (And I later realized my buying the serious knife was simply redressing my inadvertent insult to him, not a step toward absolution.)

I also had chipped one of his priceless, irreplaceable bowls when I was washing dishes one night, and though he didn't say much about it, his silence seemed angrier that night.

But the turning point came when one of the few friends I had met in language school came to the restaurant for lunch one day. He spoke Japanese pretty well—or better than I did—so I don't know exactly what he said to Akio, but it was along the lines of, "Yeah, David wants to open up a ramen shop back in America."

My friend knew I was enthusiastic about noodles, but he did not adequately appreciate the fact that in Japan ramen and soba are different worlds, different disciplines, practically like different religions. So Akio didn't like hearing that one very much. He sat me down that night, probably for the only man-to-man talk we ever had, and told me, "It's either soba or not. Soba or nothing."

He'd thought I'd wanted to become a soba guy. I told him as delicately as I could that I wasn't then and there committing my life to soba. I said I was really interested in ramen, too, and he said, "No, no, no. You're either soba or you're not."

Apparently I wasn't. About a week later, he took me out to a yakitori place. We had a couple of beers. Ceremonious and gracious to the end, he gave me a rolling pin as a gift. (The difference between the soba-rolling dowel I owned and this beautifully simple piece of wood he had just handed me was the same as the difference between the first knife I'd bought and the one he made me buy.) Then he said, "You can try to replicate, but I've taught you everything I know. All you need to do is practice and you can do it."

But the subtext was as obvious to me as it was hard for him to disguise: for someone like Akio, who had worked by himself for decades and knows, in his bones, everything about soba, explaining things to some kid who's not utterly serious about it was just too much work. I was a pain in his ass and he didn't want me around anymore. It was the end of my *stage* at Sobaya Fuyu-Rin.

I lucked into a third great situation in two different restaurants at the Park Hyatt Hotel with a little help from Marco Canora before I came back to New York. And I visited Akio once before I left because his food was so good. It was just so fucking good. It was dead simple. It was honest. And though I've had other soba—lots of other soba—it's next to impossible for it to be as good as Akio's. He could coax water, buckwheat flour, and wheat flour into such a remarkable substance. There was no way to write a recipe or for me to possibly replicate what he was doing.

The plan had always been to go to Japan, train, learn, eat, and then come back to New York and open a ramen shop. I was going to call it Momofuku, because I loved the sound of the word.

I had eaten more ramen than I thought possible (I kept a journal chronicling meals at the almost three hundred different ramen places I ate in and, I'll ruefully note now, very little else about my time there). I had learned how to make soba from a master.

But Japan fucked me up. It made me realize there was no way I could open a proper ramen restaurant. Even if I could have gotten a job at real ramen place in Tokyo, I would have been thirty before I touched a stove. You spend a year taking orders. Then you wash dishes for three years. Guys who have their own ramen shops started in the business when they were fifteen. Not that I could get my foot in the door anywhere, anyway.

And it was preposterous for me to think about opening a soba place. Akio hadn't even let me boil noodles for his customers. The noodle cutting lessons were lessons about respecting and understanding a tradition, not lessons in mastering it. It would have been disrespectful of the time I spent with him to sell my version of soba.

So I went to work for Andrew Carmellini at Café Boulud when I got back to New York, and the time I spent there taught me something else I wasn't: a fine-dining chef. The guys I had the pleasure of working alongside of in the kitchen at Café Boulud could cook circles around me.

But I knew that Akio was doing what he did on his own terms. He was basically making enough money to get by. It made him happy. He and his wife served the best food they could, Akio cooked with the best ingredients he could get his hands on. What he was doing wasn't contrived in the slightest. So I figured I would set out to do what I could do as honestly as possible, with the best ingredients, and try to make the best food I could at an honest price. I'd open Momofuku, serve what I was going to serve—a mix of Korean dishes, Japanese-style dishes, and whatever else seemed like it would make sense for me to cook, using good American ingredients—and hope that it worked.

I couldn't be soba, as Akio had put it, and I couldn't be ramen. I couldn't be the next Marco Canora. But I was crazy about noodles.

The Swim Club
TOM COLICCHIO

Tom Colicchio, originally from Elizabeth, New Jersey, is the chef/co-owner of New York's celebrated Gramercy Tavern, ranked by New Yorkers as their favorite restaurant in the 2005 Zagat Survey, as well as chef-owner of Craft, the 2002 James Beard Foundation's Best New Restaurant in America. In 2002 Colicchio opened Craftbar, a casual adjunct to Craft, and CraftSteak in Las Vegas's MGM Grand Hotel. In 2003 he followed up with 'wichcraft, next door to Craftbar in New York's Flatiron district, bringing Craft's ethic of simplicity and great ingredients to the ever-popular sandwich. His first book, Think Like a Chef, *won the James Beard Foundation's Best General Cookbook in 2001, and was followed in 2003 by* Craft of Cooking: Notes and Recipes from a Restaurant Kitchen.

SOME FAMILIES GO to fancy resorts in the summer; others to beaches or yachts. My family had the swim club in Clark, New Jersey. The club was no more than a few locker rooms grouped loosely around a giant pool, a picnic area, and a fleet of towel-draped chairs, but as far as I was concerned, it was the center of the universe from June until the end of August. Our mothers would play cards and smoke cigarettes, while our fathers worked the grills. My brothers and I would stay in the water until our skin had shriveled and our lips were blue. We smelled of chlorine and sun and Hawaiian Tropic and it was heaven.

It was at the swim club that I discovered salt. It was a late afternoon, just cooling into evening with the light growing soft. My father had brought along a few club steaks to grill later for the family, but I was too hungry to wait, so I tossed one on the grill for myself, pulling it off when it seemed done. I started to wolf down the meat when I realized something— with a jolt of surprise—that had never occurred to me before . . . It needed salt.

Up until now my food had been cooked (and seasoned) for me, so this was an altogether new thought. I added a little salt and took another bite. I remember being literally blown away by the difference it made. The steak was so good I grilled another one then and there and then a third, salting each one and eating it on the spot. I started to play with the idea, adding a little more salt each time and tasting the difference that made— the point at which the steak went from being flavorful to overly salty. I was completely focused, cooking and salting and eating as I went. Suddenly there was an angry chorus of grown-up voices around me. The steaks for the whole family were gone.

What I discovered that day is that salt does far more than add saltiness to a dish. It interacts with the flavors of the ingredients and your taste buds, "waking up" everything along the way. Salt coaxes dull flavors toward vibrant, makes acids brighter, and sweet flavors sweeter and more complex. I like to walk my new cooks through this by having them taste a finished dish while adding salt just one or two grains at a time so they can learn the power of salt for themselves.

A few summers later, back at the swim club, I had just discovered girls and realized a couple of bucks in my pocket could advance my cause. I lobbied Don and Lucy, owners of the club's snack bar, for a job scooping ice cream. That job would change my life. Almost overnight Don and I switched roles and I was the one cooking burgers and grilled cheese sandwiches, double deep-frying hand-cut fries, and dreaming up specials for the club's patrons. Life was uncomplicated: Don would pick me up in the morning in Elizabeth and we'd make the half-hour drive to Clark together, getting in the right mindset for work (with a little help from Don's personal stash). The words *health violation* never seemed to come up, and I cooked shirtless and barefoot, my long hair trailing down my scrawny back. I got my first taste of celebrity in this job—I was The Kid Who Cooked, and everyone at the club knew me. It's not that I learned to cook on the job—by this time I had been experimenting in the kitchen for a couple of years. But at the snack bar I suddenly grasped the simple science of it—cooking makes people happy. And even more important, I learned something crucial about myself—I was good at this. It felt right.

Soon Don and I were catering Fourth of July and Labor Day picnics, to the delight of the swim club members, who lined up for roast chicken, coleslaw, and baked ziti. Don paid me $275 a week under the table, which catapulted me into an economic stratosphere far beyond that of any fourteen-year-old I knew. With that money I bought my first stereo. I also happened upon a copy of Jacques Pepin's *La Technique,* and bought it. That book became my own personal culinary school; its introduction suggested that the reader "treat this book as an apprenticeship," so I did. I spent my days baking in the sun (pun intended) and my nights practicing my knife skills. With the money from the swim club I bought chickens and twine and followed the photographs until I could truss a chicken for myself. I bought bones and made stock and learned to clarify consommé with a raft of egg whites. The snack bar taught me I could make people happy. *La Technique* would teach me how to do it right.

Teacher's Pet
GARY DANKO

In 1995 Gary Danko earned a rare San Francisco Chronicle four-star rating while chef of the Dining Room at the Ritz-Carlton, San Francisco, and the James Beard Foundation's Best Chef: California award. Within months of opening his eponymous restaurant in 1999, Danko received the highest accolades possible from both San Francisco daily newspapers and the first of three Mobil Travel Guide *five-star ratings. In May of 2000 Gary Danko won the James Beard Foundation's Best New Restaurant award, and in August of that year* San Francisco Magazine *named Danko Chef of the Year. In January of 2002 the restaurant was selected as a Relais & Châteaux property, one of only eighteen such dining venues on the continent. Later the same year, Gary was nominated as Outstanding Chef of the Year by the James Beard Foundation.*

B ACK WHEN I went to cooking school, professional cooking was a very macho thing. This was the early seventies, an era when most people ended up in vo-tech schools if they weren't good in math or science and didn't have the ambition to become a doctor or a lawyer. Thus they would train to become a cook, beautician, or plumber. One of my instructors in cooking school, for example, taught that the measure of a great chef was how fast he could bone a chicken. (He further reinforced his stature by doing his best to bag every one of the very few women going to the school.) I had been working in restaurant kitchens since I was old enough to be trusted with a knife, so, while I appreciated my time at culinary school, I was revolted by the idea that cooking was this chauvinistic act and that speed and quantity were everything.

I escaped that whole scene by sequestering myself in the school's library, where I worked my way through as many of their food books as possible. I'd comb through the shelves, find something that looked interesting, and devour it. One night, I came across a book with white lettering running down its thick blue spine: *The Making of a Cook*. I snatched it off the shelf and sat on the floor where I had spread out all my stuff.

It had me from the first sentence, declaring itself, "not another French cookbook." It wasn't: its author, Madeleine Kamman, took a very different approach than most other cookbook authors of her time. Her tone was personal and inquisitive. It hit a chord with me—despite the amount of time I spent with my head buried in cookbooks, Madeleine's was the first that really jumped off the page and spoke to me directly.

In school we were learning to cook in large batches—150 portions of beef bourguignonne or fifty pounds of puff pastry. It's tough to wrangle that quantity of ingredients into something resembling food, I'll admit. But Madeleine's book offered more than just formulas: it explained the process. In *her* puff pastry recipe, instead of saying, "don't knead the dough before you add the butter," Madeleine wrote:

> *Do not knead or handle it any more,* whether it is smooth or not. What is essential at this point is that the *détrempe* contain as little gluten as possible. You may have heard of kneading a *détrempe* for 20 minutes before enclosing the butter in it. This method is perfectly correct, for the more you knead a dough beyond 10 minutes, the more the gluten strands lose their rigidity. At 20 minutes, they have completely slackened and the *détrempe* will assimilate the butter easily. Choose: either no kneading at all or 20 *full minutes* of kneading, but *never* in between.

She would teach how to make a half pound of puff pastry, but if you truly understood what happened with a half pound, it was easier to make fifty. She knew and was writing about the art and science of cooking back when almost no one else did, back when my teachers at school were more interested in wearing big white hats.

Their authority emanated from those toques; Madeleine's authority came from her clear, assertive writing and comprehensive knowledge. When a teacher at school wanted to make a point he yelled; when Madeleine wanted to make a point, all she needed to do was use italics.

Her approach and tone got me hooked on *The Making of a Cook*. In the coming months, I'd follow up a day in the kitchen at school with a nighttime reading from her book, to deepen my understanding of whatever we'd covered that day.

I decided I wanted to study with her but being that she lived in France at the time, I didn't know if it would be possible.

After graduation, I moved to San Francisco and took a chef's position at a bookstore and bistro called Vanity Fair, a great place to cook and to keep up on new cookbooks. Madeleine had come out with *Dinner Against the Clock* shortly before I started at Vanity Fair, which was a major departure from her first book. But even in writing about quick cooking, she didn't compromise her tone: the book was far from a simple compendium of "express" recipes; it was a theoretical, practical approach to fast cooking. "This volume does not pretend to be the definitive book on quick cookery," she wrote in the introduction, "for there is actually no quick cookery, there are only methods of cookery that allow one to prepare certain foods in a relatively short time."

Then in 1976 she published *When French Women Cook,* her gastronomic memoirs. The book was both an engrossing account of the way women really cooked in France and a collection of moving stories about the women who influenced how Madeleine cooked and who she became. It was a classic as soon as it was printed. After I read it, I knew, somehow, that as much as I had learned about cooking and as capable as I was in the kitchen, being tutored personally by Madeleine Kamman would make me the cook that I wanted to be. I became transfixed with the idea.

Around that time I learned that Madeleine was making regular trips from France to New York to teach classes at Peter Kump's cooking school. I missed the East Coast a little—I had grown up in Massena, New York—so I figured I'd move back east, find a chef's position somewhere, take a few of

Madeleine's classes, and maybe persuade her to take me under her wing.

I scored the chef's position at a country inn called Tucker Hill in Vermont and, watching Peter Kump's class schedules like a hawk, made sure that I had a seat in the very first class Madeline taught in New York after my return to the East Coast.

When I walked into that classroom, I was beside myself with excitement. I had been waiting for this day for years. Finally, I was going to meet Madeleine.

I had brought along a stack of my menus, because at Tucker Hill I was writing a very unique menu. I had started to include farm-specific language about the products I used, and I tried to be direct about the techniques; also I didn't muddy the name of any dish with extraneous French terms (unless they didn't translate). Dishes were called things like Grilled Maine Halibut with Orange Segments and Saffron Beurre Blanc. Not many chefs were doing those kinds of menus back in 1981. But I didn't bring them to Madeleine to impress her; I brought them because I wanted her to see that I was serious about cooking, and perhaps so she could divine the influence her books had had on me.

The class was two weeks long, held five days a week, and it was mainly lectures and demonstrations. She went through classic French cooking and then modern French cooking, covering technique and theory, and demonstrating recipes. It probably looked like almost any cooking class but there was something in the way that Madeleine taught, something in her passion and wonder about cooking, that made the lessons really sink in.

At the end of the two weeks I asked to work with her, and while she was very polite about it, my earnest pitch went nowhere. We exchanged information, she went back to France, and I went back to Vermont. Maybe she thought I was just flattering her.

Over the following months, whenever I'd get wind that Madeleine was teaching again in New York, I'd try to get a seat in the class, but the enrollment was almost immediately filled, and I would always get shut out. A few times I called her and said, "Madeleine, I really want to study with you," and she would say, "Oh, my class is full, Gary. I'm so sorry, I'm booked up." I'd tell her to keep me in mind if something changed. We went back and forth like that.

Over time I became friendly with Madeleine's publicist, Lyla Spencer, who worked out of St. Louis and would keep me in the loop about any Madeleine-related goings on in the States. About two years after that cooking class in New York, I heard that a French woman was coming from France to open a cooking school at a country inn in New Hampshire. I thought it might be Madeleine.

I called Lyla, told her what I had heard, and she verified it: "Yes, that's Madeleine Kamman, and she's moving back to America." Instantly, I jumped on the lead. I got a hold of the people who were helping her organize the school to see if I could get in as a student. They said they were sorry but they were full. I was out of luck.

I kept in touch with Lyla, waiting to find out when the next session would start so I could be sure to get a spot. When Lyla gave me the nod, I made the call and left a message looking to enroll. A few days later, I got a call back: sorry, we're full. Again.

I mustered up enough courage to call Madeleine herself and see if she could make an extra spot available for me. But every time I got her on the phone, the response was something like, "Gary, please—I am in the middle of my son's graduation—would you please have the courtesy to allow me to celebrate properly and to call back . . ." And she never would.

Then, just before that second session of her classes at the school in New Hampshire was about to start, I received a call from Lyla. "One of Madeleine's students is pregnant and she has been confined to bed for the rest of the pregnancy, so that means there's a spot open . . ."

I called Madeleine—who was in the middle of something important again—and I confronted her with my findings. She told me she was full and that she would call me back. At this point, I couldn't believe it. I was really frustrated—and it was time for some resolution. I really wanted to study with Madeleine, to learn from her firsthand, but if she was going to keep rebuffing me, I had to move on.

I had a pet theory going that she might not have wanted me in her class because I was a man. Gender was an issue in her cookbooks: in the dedication to *When French Women Cook*, she wrote that the book was "in its own way a feminist manifesto." If I was being shut out because I was a man, I wanted to know. So I paced around the kitchen all day long, getting up the nerve to phone Madeleine again, and find out why she wasn't giving me a spot that I knew was open. (My friend Avery, who stopped by the restaurant that afternoon, still teases me about how worked up I was.) Finally I made the call up and said that I had heard there was a vacancy in the class. She denied it, "Gary, I'm full, full, full."

She wasn't. I knew she wasn't. And even though it meant challenging and possibly insulting one of my role models, I demanded an answer: "Madeleine, what is the problem here? Is it because I'm a man?"

Now, Madeleine is a very proper French woman. She had always been terribly polite to me, even when she was blowing me off. But I guess I struck a nerve with that question, because she just hit the ceiling. She told me I was full of shit and, in true Madeleine fashion, belted out, "The reason I will not work with you is because you are a culinary school graduate and those people give me grief. Do you understand that, Gary?"

I tried to reassure her, "Madeleine, I am a very different breed. I am not a typical chef. I've worked in small restaurants all my life, and the reason I want to come and work with you is to refine my skills and use you as a finishing school. I would really value your critique of my food."

She paused a moment, said she'd think about it, and hung up the phone. I thought I had permanently ended my nonexistent relationship with her. At least you got an answer out of her, I consoled myself, though I was distraught at the thought that I wasn't going to ever get a chance to study with her.

But the next morning she called and, in her simultaneously sing-song and stern tone, she said, "Gary, I have a seat in the class for you. Please send me five hundred dollars, and I will see you November first." I was overjoyed. I put in my notice at Tucker Hill.

The day before I left for New Hampshire, I filled my Volvo's trunk with every great product that I'd used in Vermont, from home-churned butter to bread baked in wood-burning ovens by local Vermonters, to lamb, duck, guinea hen, geese, blue cheese, goat cheese, and more.

I arrived in New Hampshire, backed my car up to the front of Madeleine's cooking school, an old pizzeria that she was just beginning to convert into a school and restaurant, and started unloading the car. I thought of the food as kind of a housewarming gift. What chef doesn't love the gift of great handcrafted products? She must have thought I was a really odd duck at that point—Who brings ingredients to cooking school with them?—but behind the funny look she was giving me, I could tell that she was happy to have all these beautiful artisanal products on hand.

Classes started the next morning. From the get-go, Madeleine was incredibly hard on me: she directed every pointed or technical question at me, acted disappointed when I didn't know an answer and unimpressed when I did. She had mentioned to her assistant that no chef was going to be giving her grief in her school. I didn't care. I was there to learn. If Madeleine's firmness toward me in front of the class was part of the cost of my attendance, I was okay with it.

On the third day, while making a dish of beef with mustard, cassis, and lavender, I had been peppered with endless questions from her about why I had chosen each of the elements for the recipe. When I told her that it was because those ingredients were all things that grow in and around Dijon, I saw a little flicker of acceptance in her eyes. I knew she would like the theory behind the practice because I had learned it from her books.

And over the next couple of days, she began to accept that I was a serious, disciplined, and dedicated cook, and slowly started changing her tune from "Oh, let me humor this arrogant-ass kid" to putting her arm around me and saying, "Okay, Gary, now I want you to take the foie gras and make something . . ."

I was in.

Waiting for, working, and cajoling my way into a spot in Madeleine's school was one of the most protracted and intense pursuits of my life. Once she finally accepted that I wasn't a chauvinist meathead and that I really did care about cooking, we started to get along very well. Well enough that we worked together regularly over the next decade. Well enough that we've stayed close friends ever since.

But having a relationship with her was—and is—never easy. She is exacting and she is critical—the exact reasons I felt I needed to go to her for finishing school, though it was Madeleine who taught me that your schooling is never finished. She was always challenging me—the challenge sometimes could be painful, it sometimes could be liberating, it could be many things. But there is a saying of Frank Lloyd Wright's that sums up exactly what I think of Madeleine: "A teacher is a man who sets men free. He is the most eager learner in the class." It fits Madeleine Kamman to a tee, and I'm grateful that at least a little of it has rubbed off on me.

Madeleine is the one who sent me to the California wine country. I wouldn't be where I am—a California chef with a wine-country connection—without her. I became her de facto right hand whenever she organized trips, classes, demonstrations, anything. I used to help her with all her events, because she only cooked on a small scale, and I could put out a meal for five hundred people if that's what the occasion called for. It was a deeply satisfying moment when, after years of working with her, Madeleine said, "There's only one person that can really reproduce my food the way it is supposed to be, and it's Gary Danko."

Cooking the Books
TAMASIN DAY-LEWIS

Tamasin Day-Lewis was a documentary filmmaker for fifteen years before she wrote her first cookbook, West of Ireland Summers. *She has since written eight others, including* The Art of the Tart, Tarts with Tops On, *and most recently,* Tamasin's Kitchen Classics. *She has filmed three TV series in her kitchen in Somerset, England, and is currently writing a book about this year's foodie travels to be published in the autumn of 2007. She wrote the* Saturday Daily Telegraph's *food page for six years, and is a regular contributor to* Vogue, Vanity Fair, *and* Country Homes & Interiors.

I WAS NEVER TAUGHT how to cook. That is, I was never thrown into the Dante-esque flames of a professional kitchen to be eaten alive by a brutal chef intent on his own self aggrandizement and the flaying of the young, inexperienced flesh of his apprentices until they could raise soufflés like he could raise hell and bone chickens by merely showing them the scalpel and giving them the eye. Nor did I go the cooking-directors-lunches-in-the-city route, as did a certain class of girl whose background and academic achievements meant that cookery school was for her what university was for the rest of us and who ended up feeding stuffed pink-shirted ex-public-school bankers. In fact cookery school was really just somewhere she passed her time until she met her future husband, which was meant to happen when she "did the season" and "came out," after which the city was deemed the most fertile hunting ground other than the shires for securing a future Master of the Universe. There she could seduce the prospectives over the balance sheet and the beef Wellington, all between the hours of twelve and two p.m., after which they would retire with port and cigars and she would slink back to the kitchen, drink the dregs of the Chateau Margaux, wrap up the extra veal *escalopes* she'd bought on the bank's budget, and decide what to wear that night at the dinner party she was throwing with the leftovers.

I know all this because, despite being wholly untrained for it, for a few ghastly weeks after I'd left university I filled in for these girls in between my interviews for jobs in television. I had hoodwinked one of those agencies that provides "the right sort of gel" for "the right sort of family or business," a charmingly trusting place called Lucie Morton, into believing in my culinary credentials, despite my lack of diplomas and references and experience. They took me on as a director's lunch cook or general dogsbody—one lady wanted me to do her darning, another needed a serving wench for her dinner party, yet another huge firm of insurance agents hired me as a tea girl and were most taken aback at my accent and my Cambridge degree, and, on finding out that brewing up wasn't my only skill, immediately offered me a traineeship. I could have been a shipping insurer!

Anyway, I was let loose on an unsuspecting clientele whose eating habits I was rather nervous about, as I had never cooked for anyone other than friends and family before, and it became clear almost immediately that it wasn't just my culinary skills that were found wanting. These seemingly dizzy, Sloanie girls didn't think too highly of their well-upholstered clients or else were determined that I didn't usurp their positions, because they left me details of the particular dishes their "boys" liked best, which bore no resemblance to the truth. "They all adore pears stuffed with Stilton" read one message, so I dutifully stuffed dozens of pears and surrounded them with watercress and walnuts. Every one of them was returned uneaten, so this had to be some kind of a joke, though I never did discover whether they were playing it on me or the banker boys.

They suggested I cook turbot and sole Veronique, *escalopes de veau*, chateaubriand and steak Diane, *vacherins* and soufflés; they enjoyed spending the bankers' food budget in the most expensive shops in town, but I had spent the past three years as an impecunious student at Cambridge learning how to cook page by page from Jane Grigson and Elizabeth David, and only cooking the dishes whose ingredients I could afford, none of which fell into the directors' lunches category. I had never bashed out a veal *escalope*, let alone made a collared soufflé rise high as a turret above its neck. I had never shucked an oyster or made a mirepoix, whisked up a béarnaise sauce or flambéed crêpes suzette. What techniques I had were entirely self-taught, or, in the case of a few favorite home-cooked dishes like belly of pork and beans and chicken cacciatore, picked up from watching my godmother, novelist Elizabeth Jane Howard, cook—usually for an army of novelists, poets, painters, and the intelligentsia who hung out with her and her then husband, the novelist Kingsley Amis, who she was trying to feed frugally or at least economically, since she ran a semi-permanent soup kitchen for all their friends and every dispossessed writer or adolescent like me trying to finish a book or escape their parents. And as Kingsley's monthly booze bill was big enough that it would probably have fed several large families, Jane kept the kitchen under a pretty tight rein, budgetarily speaking. What I learned from her was somewhat vitiated by the city boys and their expense account spending, but at least I could learn to cook these new dishes and extend my repertoire. Of one thing I was quite sure, this was no place for *me* to find a husband.

Jane's food was hearty, earthy, one-pot fare, not the sort that financial-world sophisticates expected for lunch, so I invested immediately in the *Constance Spry Cookery Book*, which the eponymous writer, who founded both the Cordon Bleu School and Winkfield Place near Windsor, had published a couple of decades earlier to help her pupils. Her book was still pretty much a blueprint in the seventies despite having come out in 1956. English food, particularly English country house food, had retained its roots and much of its French influence. Our great houses had often employed famous French chefs, and the English influence had been confined to our roasting skills and our superior raw ingredients: great beef, lamb, pork, and game; wonderful soft fruits and orchards; superb cold-water and river fish; some great unpasteurized farmhouse cheeses; and good butter and cream.

However, the mystery of *choux* pastry and *gougères*; of how to make crème pâtissière as good as any French pastry shop; the strange, secret world of the galantine and of setting every mousse and soufflé within an inch of its life with aspic; the chasseur; *truite meunière*; lobster thermidor; cold, pressed tongue; cold collations; sauces remoulade, tartar, verte and gribiche, hollandaise, supreme, and aurora; puff pastry, forcemeats; farces and stuffings—these had all so far eluded me. So I went to bed devouring the pages hungrily, memorizing techniques to secretly try out the next day—for God forbid anyone should see me with my crib sheet in the heat of the professional kitchen.

My other mentor was my cousin David's first wife, Serena Bass, now a well-known caterer in New York. On weekends I was her kitchen slave in London or Dorset where I was seconded to peeling and mashing potatoes. It was from her that I learned that no amount of butter can be too much for mashed potato, not even in equal proportions, and how to make beef carbonnade, which was very different from the watery school stew I was familiar with, since she used chuck steak not lumps of gristle and her meat was braised spoon tender in one and a half pints of Guinness. It was Serena I observed make the smoothest and most velveteen béchamel sauces, the best lemon mousses and lemon meringue pies and fruit tarts and apple pies with perfect, buttery crusts. I peeled and I chopped; I watched and washed up; I asked questions, whisked, creamed, and folded. No book is a substitute for watching an expert and learning exactly what the terms you thought you understood really mean: *bring to scald point, whisk to soft or firm peaks, deglaze, reduce, caramelize, blanch, bake, brûlée.*

From Jane and Serena I learned that most valuable of lessons: it is actually no more difficult nor time consuming to cook for a dozen, or two dozen, than it is for four. The preparation and shopping is everything. And the ease with which you rope in willing and competent helpers—even if it is just to wash the earth off the carrots and peel the spuds—will sharpen your delegating skills while saving you time and entertaining you in the kitchen. Cooking is by nature a communal activity, not a solitary one.

So, I say I am entirely self-taught, since I took my own route through the cookery books of my teens and twenties, watched a couple of good cooks cook, clipped out recipes in the newspaper and began by following them to the letter, and stored up other people's wisdom and lore like a magpie stores stolen jewels. Otherwise I was led by my nose, and my determination to master the art, or the craft, of good cooking. What I have learned and continue to learn has come through greed and taste alone: good taste and a good palate being the only requisite skills or attributes you need. Teaching by example, though, and by the generosity of spirit of the cooks and chefs I have asked questions of, have been my mainstays. The best cooks are always generous with their detail and their instruction—none of that "it's a secret recipe; I couldn't possibly give it to you." They would rather someone enthusiastic and interested learn how to get it right and then adapt it if talented and creative enough to do so.

However, I would say I have been lucky to experience two formative moments, both of which taught me by splendid example and fueled my already burgeoning curiosity and love of food and cooking more than any cookery course or school domestic-science lesson ever could have.

When I was nineteen, a much older but not much wiser boyfriend took me out to dinner with a rich American friend of his. I'm not sure whether I was also being offered up like the head of John the Baptist, but I expect that, as a nineteen-year-old model who was about to study English at King's College Cambridge and with what would have been interpreted by that sort of American as an impeccable English background, I did somehow fit the stereotype pretty well. The American friend was three decades older than me so I remained almost innocent of any ulterior motive; after all, he was old enough to be my father.

He had booked us into La Tante Claire, the most famous restaurant in England at the time other than the Hole in the Wall in Bath and the Roux brothers' two emporia, Le Gavroche and the Waterside Inn. Pierre Koffman, the French chef at La Tante Claire, was legendary, and his establishment had two Michelin stars. I knew nothing of any of this and had never before been brought to a restaurant like this one. The frequenting of such places, few as they were, was somewhat frowned upon by the upper echelons of society, I imagine because restaurant culture was nonexistent and there was still a postwar rationing mentality among my parents generation that eschewed conspicuous consumption.

The moment the fine linen was napped across my knee, the menu perused, the champagne poured, and the bread served with sweet, unsalted French butter, I felt as excited as one does after a spectacularly fine overture or the first act of a brilliant play. But it wasn't until the dessert that I was really blown away. I had ordered the *feuilléte aux poires*, not really knowing what to expect. A coffin of the most stratospherically light puff pastry into which was set a perfectly poached half pear covered with a thin veil of caramel arrived. The pear was perched on a soft bed of *crème légère*, and beneath the crisp leaves of pastry that shattered like glass to the bite, was a satin sabayon flavored with Poire Williams. This dish has had an extraordinary influence on my life, showing me, as it did, a level of cooking that went beyond anything I had suspected possible, yet remaining trenchantly rooted in the real world of achievable, honest cooking. It wasn't about setting goals I could never achieve, it was about trusting to cook from the heart, learning how to achieve taste, the taste of the thing itself, with little or no interference from too many other ingredients; it was about texture, about surprising the palate, the eye, the nose. It was about entering a world that I had seen as somewhat frivolous before, realizing that it could be serious, that perfecting the craft of cooking could be a lifetime's very happy work, even in the domestic kitchen of an enthusiastic amateur.

Then there was my hero George Perry-Smith. George had been the chef-proprietor of the Hole in the Wall in Bath in the 1950s and 1960s and had single-handedly transformed British food in the latter half of the twentieth century. George, who called himself a cook, not a chef, had zero interest in the celebrity status that modern-day chefs so often seek, indeed was mortified when he overheard a customer, on arriving at the Hole, ask "Should we bend down on our knees and kiss the threshold?"

"We were there to cook, not to become famous, just to cook," was George's Philosophy. He was self-taught and had studied French at Cambridge before entering the portals of the professional kitchen, where he cooked mostly using Elizabeth David's books on French, Italian, and Mediterranean food, which had inspired a generation. I was too young to remember George's first place, the Hole, as it became affectionately known, but when George and his then-partner-later-wife, Heather Crosbie, opened a restaurant with rooms in the absurdly beautiful village of Helford in Cornwall, I quite by chance booked into it for my two-day honeymoon, little knowing how it would influence me for the rest of my cooking life.

The perilously steep field behind Riverside was covered in vegetables that were dug daily for the restaurant: thumbnail-sized broad beans and pebbles of Cornish new potatoes, bushels of fresh herbs, asparagus, squash, and sweet, young peas. Fish was brought in straight from the boats, the meat was local, the breads homemade, including a particularly good walnut loaf that George served with cheese. If you took room 3 above the kitchen, you would awake not just to the sound and the smell of the sea, but to the scent of the croissants being baked with the rolls for breakfast on the terrace, which were served with homemade jams and bowls of sliced oranges and tiny local strawberries. The Sunday night cold table was like a medieval banquet, with its homemade patés, terrines, rillettes, potted meats, and fish and salads. And every dish, from the tarragon chicken that was brought whole to the table with second helpings offered, to the salmon baked in pastry with currants and ginger and a sauce messine, George's signature dish, was transformed the following day into something equally delicious. Here were the classics like sole Dugléré and entrecôte à la bordelaise; *brandade* of smoked mackerel; la bourride, fish soup served with aioli and a rouille; a ragout of shellfish, chocolate St. Emilion; walnut treacle tart; and Tia Maria ice cream accompanied by hazelnut meringues, the latter served to my children for tea after their wild-salmon-and-mushroom croquettes.

I asked for recipes from George and his staff, returning twice a year for several years and never once being disappointed by the food, the ingredients, or the manner in which they were served. Sitting at George's table was a joyous privilege, and everything was done properly with the finest ingredients from start to finish, without ever being too rich, too much, too pretentious or ever striving to be anything other than what it was. George's food was about what and how George liked to cook and to eat with no compromises or nods in the direction of fashion or what he imagined people thought he ought to do. He was influenced by what he chose to be influenced by and sought always to refine the dishes and the style of cooking that were, essentially, his own. It takes years and it takes exceptional talent and judgment to get to the level George got to, but giving people the sort of happiness that he did can, in fact, be done by cooking something simple for the people you love and serving it to them with the minimum of fuss and decoration. It is all about a kind of honesty and integrity and respect for the ingredients, but in a lighthearted way. It is, after all, only putting a good supper on the table. I have learned most of what I have learned from sitting at George's table and from always thinking, I wonder how George would have done that, or, What would he have thought of that?

After several years, I finally plucked up the courage to invite George and Heather to dinner. I can't pretend it wasn't stressful. I knew I mustn't show off but that everything should appear simply, effortlessly perfect.

I poached wings of skate and made a sauce by reducing white wine with finely chopped shallots, adding anchovies, butter, chervil, and dill and finishing it with a little lemon juice and cream. There were minted new potatoes and braised fennel, but I can't remember what I made for pudding. Quietly, George turned to me and asked "So when are you going to open your restaurant?"

I had a lifetime more to learn but felt that at least I was on my way. I couldn't have asked for more.

The Crack-Up
JONATHAN EISMANN

Jonathan Eismann is the chef-owner of South Beach, Florida's, perennially hot Pacific Time restaurant, which has been at the center of the Lincoln Road scene since the restaurant was launched in 1993. A graduate of the Culinary Institute of America, Eismann began working professionally with Pan Asian flavors in New York City in the 1980s as chef of the Acute Café on West Broadway, and then at such restaurants as Batons, Fandango, Mondial, and China Grill. In 1994 he became one of the first chefs to receive the Robert Mondavi Award for Culinary Excellence.

YOU LEARN ALL kinds of things in culinary school. The difference between an allumette and a batonnet is a life-or-death matter. There's coursework that covers how to break down big animals into ready-to-eat cuts. You turn out sauce Espagnole by the bucketful. And then you get turned out into the real world, where you learn how much there is left for you to learn.

Back in the eighties, especially in the kitchens of the white hot Manhattan restaurants where I spent most of the decade, there was a particular professional dynamic that my instructors at the CIA never really touched on: how to manage a kitchen that was half out of its mind on drugs.

It's hard to explain how widespread cocaine use was in the New York restaurant biz in the eighties. These days it's different—there are no drug issues to speak of in my restaurant today, and it's not because of my policing the staff: kids just come into the business with a different mindset. But even the owners I worked for back then were cokeheads, some of them doing Pablo Escobar-style mountains of the stuff, and not too discreetly either.

My most scarring memory from that era came when I was working as the sous chef of a restaurant in lower Manhattan. It was a high-profile place, with a very large and very drug-dependent staff that, through all of its dysfunction, provided high-quality food and a dynamic dining experience. The dining room was wall-to-wall celebrities—it was one of the most celebrity-ridden restaurants I've ever worked in—and it was also a late-night model haunt.

Though I was young and only the sous chef (a second-in-command position), everyone counted on me to get things done in the drug-fueled anarchy of the place. My chef, who was a really talented guy, had a drug issue of his own—he was very lax about drugs and drinking in the kitchen—and so my job was to make sure that dinner ended up on the tables.

I'd get into the kitchen at eleven in the morning, two hours before everyone else was supposed to arrive. Of course, *no one* was ever on time. Figuring out who would straggle in when every day was one of the first tests of my new skill set. The guys with the really bad drug problems—your heroin and coke guys—would usually show up in the neighborhood of on time, since they didn't sleep much. That is, unless they were on a bender, in which case you didn't know when—that day? that week?—you'd see them next. The heavy drinkers would roll in a little later.

And that was one of the trickiest things about managing the staff: we had guys doing coke, pot, pot and coke, coke and booze, heroin, pills. Everyone had his or her own self-medicating regime. Staying on top of who was on what was of critical importance during service because there was a kind of pharmacological Darwinism at play in the kitchen. Who could survive service?

With the potheads, there was no problem: they could make it through the whole night. They'd get stoned before staff meal, be really focused, and work hard and then want to go outside, smoke a joint, and do it all over again. You could count on the potheads, you just knew at some point in the evening (usually around ten o'clock) they were going to disappear for a few minutes to smoke a joint. That was easy enough to take.

Then there were the cokeheads. They'd start out okay, but soon enough they'd be out of control and spastic. They'd get distracted, thinking about how they wanted just a little more coke, and would end up cutting or burning themselves or carelessly leaving hot pans out and knives unsheathed and unattended to. Some tried to quell that mid-evening jones with a few bloody Marys but that never worked out well, because then I had to contend with a twittering drunk who couldn't walk or see.

Anyone who did heroin would inevitably become completely useless during the peak hours of service—they'd either look like they were having some sort of seizure or pass out against the wall. But on the other hand, they didn't typically do it every night—or at the same time every night—so once in a while you got almost a full night's work out of them.

The restaurant had a kitchen that was open to the dining room, but I don't think any of the diners ever noticed that there was a cook taking a standing nap in the corner, or that if we had ten cooks on the line at seven thirty, we might only have nine an hour later, and by ten o'clock we were lucky if we had six men left standing.

I worked the pasta/hot apps station, and everything to my right side—the wok and pantry stations—was generally okay. The two guys on those stations and I were consistently sober enough to work a full shift. To my left was where the drug addict contingency worked the five busiest stations in the kitchen: pizza, grill, double sauté, duck/lobster (a special station we had that did nothing but put out the restaurant's two most popular dishes), and plating.

Among this band of wannabe Johnny Rottens we had one cook, who I'll call Augusto Ramirez for the purposes of this story, who is still to this day the fastest line cook I have ever worked with in my life. He could somehow get his hands moving faster than *anyone,* and with unbelievable precision—from removing something from a pan or grill, getting it to a cutting board, putting it in the correct position, getting the edge of his knife on it, sticking his tongs or fork in it, slicing it perfectly, plating it properly, garnishing it—and then repeating the process over and over again. It was amazing to watch this kid work.

So when things started to fall apart in the kitchen, as they did every night, I'd grab him and say, "I know you're working the grill, but—*insert the name of whatever jackass was nodding off in a corner or doing bumps of coke downstairs in the employee's bathroom*—and I need you on that station." He could seamlessly shift into gear, managing the work of two men, and always bail you out.

Of course, the incredible part about this is that Augusto had one of the biggest coke problems in the kitchen. But all the coke seemed to do was to make his hands move faster—which wasn't a bad thing, especially when you were relying on him.

At some point Augusto, like plenty of people in the late eighties, migrated from coke into crack. So in between periods of being the line cook king of New York City, he'd go on a two-day crack binge, then show up the next morning, cry his way back into his job, and promise he'd change his ways. But when Augusto was there, regardless of whatever was coursing through his veins, he could be counted on. He was my secret weapon: when everybody else fell apart, Augusto was the way to manage the mess.

There was one night in particular that I thought it was a godsend to have him on the line. His associate on the grill station came unglued unusually early in the evening, so I figured that we were looking at a night spent at the edge of the weeds. Then the chef abruptly knocked off as the first orders came trickling in, and I knew we were in real trouble.

This was at a place where were doing four hundred covers a night, easy, and serving food that had earned two stars from the *New York Times* on Villeroy & Boch china with Christofle sterling on the table. It was a legitimate restaurant, and it was amazing to me how small a portion of the staff treated it as such.

That night, the other cooks just started falling apart one after another, like a bunch of drugged-out dominos: the coke knocking over the Stoli knocking over the mix of Vicodin and Valium. Half my line was unmanned by eight thirty. That was particularly bad news, since we were well known as a late-night place. While the dining room was full at eight thirty, at ten o'clock there'd be a swarm at the bar and every banquette would be filled with models looking for a post-cocktailing, preclubbing snack. It was going to be a brutal night.

I immediately eighty-sixed a whole section of the menu and closed down the pizza station, because I was down to a ragtag team. Luckily, Augusto was part of it. Between the two of us we covered pasta/hot apps, grill, sauté, duck/lobster, plating, and expediting.

Around nine, I realized that we were starting to fall behind. We weren't shorting tables of dishes, and customers weren't sending the food back, but we were getting backed up. The kitchen normally picked up between twenty and thirty plates at a time, but, given the vicious mess of weeds were in, I saw that we were going to have to do three pickups of forty or fifty plates each. That's a lot of work.

We set to it and got the first batch up and out. It looked good, it was properly cooked and it was on time.

I yelled, "That was great," to my guys and told them we're doing fifty this time. Same thing again, just a few more plates. So we've got plates, scorching hot out of the oven perched everywhere, and we're trying to get this food done and looking pretty and out so we can do it one more time and be caught up before the late-night crush started. That's when I noticed that Augusto had disappeared. I let it go for about thirty seconds before I shouted, "Where the fuck is Augusto?" One of my sober compatriots said he thought he saw him go downstairs.

I dashed for the stairs, slid down the railing, and frantically looked around for Augusto, to tell him to abort whatever mission he'd sent himself on and return to the line at once. I was jetting past the employee restroom, which had a little window in the top of the door, when I caught something out of the corner of my eye.

It was a vision the likes of which I had never before beheld: I can honestly say that if I'd seen an elephant crammed into our staff restroom I wouldn't have been more taken aback.

I stopped dead in my tracks, rubbed my eyes, and, disbelieving, looked again. But there was no denying it. There was Augusto, standing on the toilet, his eyes clenched shut, his houndstooth checked pants in a puddle around his ankles, his tighty whiteys stretched taut across his pale thighs, with a lit crack pipe in one hand and his dick in the other, masturbating full speed ahead.

I was speechless. I was paralyzed. I could never have expected to find Augusto, who'd been killing for me all night, half-naked and getting high when there were a couple of hundred customers upstairs and ninety plates that needed to be finished in the kitchen.

When I could move again—it took a few seconds—I pounded on the door and yelled, "Augusto, put that shit away! Get back upstairs!" While normally I would have just left, writing him off as another loss, we were in the middle of a pickup, and I was in survival mode. I couldn't handle losing another cook.

Miraculously, he reappeared upstairs two minutes later, hopping back into action as if nothing had happened. He started working even faster and more furiously than he had earlier in the evening. We got the food out and we never spoke of what had transpired downstairs. Not that night, not ever.

As the insanity dissipated and the orders started to trickle in more slowly, I took a second to catch my breath and, for whatever reason, my eyes settled on the EMPLOYEES MUST WASH HANDS sign over one of the sinks in the kitchen. I earnestly and sincerely hoped that it was a sign that everyone paid attention to. Especially Augusto, especially that night.

Everything I Need to Know About Cooking I Learned in an Ashram

SUSAN FENIGER

Inspired by a love for bold flavors from all over the world, Susan Feniger first garnered national attention in the early eighties at the tiny restaurant City Café in Los Angeles, where there was barely enough room in the kitchen for both her and co-chef, Mary Sue Milliken. Today the two own the popular Border Grill restaurants in Santa Monica and Las Vegas at Mandalay Bay, and Ciudad restaurant in downtown L.A. They have authored five cookbooks and appeared in 396 episodes of their television programs Too Hot Tamales *and* Tamales World Tour *for the Food Network.*

PROFESSIONAL KITCHENS WERE a different world twenty-five years ago, when I was starting out in the business. I was one of the first women to work in the kitchen at Le Perroquet, a fine-dining French restaurant in Chicago where, even though I was a recent graduate of the Culinary Institute of America, dead serious about becoming a chef, and hired to be a line cook, I was assigned almost exclusively to daytime shifts working with the prep cooks. Did it have something to do with my being a woman? Probably. The chef wasn't used to having women his kitchen, much less women with formal culinary training, so he started me at the bottom.

The guys in the back of the house were predominantly Hispanic—from El Salvador, Guatemala, and different parts of Mexico. During the day we'd slave over huge cauldrons of stocks, and reduce, re-reduce, and reduce yet again, creating these very dense, very classical sauces for the elaborate and sophisticated haute cuisine the restaurant prided itself on.

When it was time to drum up "shift meals" for ourselves, my fellow cooks would spring into action, run a sheet pan full of onions, tomatoes, chiles, and garlic under the broiler until they were charred and blistered, whiz the vegetables through a blender, and a few minutes later pour an incredible salsa over some grilled meat or tortillas covered with melted cheese. Every meal our crew ate—breakfast and lunch most days—was crowned with a spectacular and simple sauce. The salsas these guys made tasted truly inspired.

I was ten times more excited about a good salsa verde than I ever had been about a beurre blanc or a truffle butter or a red-wine reduction. The first time I admitted that to myself came as a surprise and was also the beginning of an awakening awareness about—and affinity for—how cooks, especially home cooks, around the world approached cooking.

During my time at Le Perroquet, I learned more valuable cooking lessons from the Latin American guys on the day shift than I did from the guys who didn't want me around during dinner service.

I left Le Perroquet to work for Wolfgang Puck at Ma Maison (where I struck up a friendship with Wolf that has lasted decades and fell in love with Los Angeles) and then went on to spend a year in a Michelin three-star restaurant in the south of France, where I knew the cooking—less Parisian, more Provençal—would suit me better.

It did. I found that I'd much rather eat my lamb with fresh thyme, chopped shallots, lemon, and olive oil than with a reduced red-wine demi-glace sauce. I also got to delve into the way French people—not French chefs—cooked at home. I learned all about salt cod *brandade*, confit of duck, pot-au-feu, and cassoulet.

When I returned to the states, I convinced Mary Sue Milliken, whom I had met on the day shift in the kitchen at Le Perroquet, to move out to Los Angeles and open a restaurant with me. We opened a tiny place called City Café, where there was barely enough room for the two of us in the kitchen from which we served casual, home-style French cooking. From time to time we would sneak dishes you might find around the Mediterranean onto the menu: a great moussaka, an excellent baba ghanoush, a few other little ethnic treats. Our customers, we were delighted to see, responded well to the new dishes.

After City Café had been open for a year or two—by then it was 1982 or 1983—I finally found a block of time where I could take a real vacation and get away from the restaurant for a few weeks. A friend of mine was running the kitchen at an ashram in a town called Ahmadnagar in the western state of Maharashtra in India. If I really wanted to get away from L.A., I reasoned, what could be farther than a Hindu hideaway out in the Indian countryside? I booked my flight.

Ahmadnagar is very far inland, as I learned on my first trip there: I flew into Bombay, then from Bombay to Poona, and from there traveled another three hours on a bus before finally arriving. But once I disembarked from the bus at last—a touch stiff and slightly overwhelmed from all the travel—I had a great feeling about the place.

The sun was beating down hard and the air was crisp and hot. There was a giant metal-frame tent covered with huge swaths of wildly patterned fabric whipping in the wind, big enough to house the thousands of guests who would be coming for a wedding a few days hence. Women were loosely wrapped in fabric, hand-died in intensely vivid colors—mustard and blue and orange—and they were festooned with dozens of bangles, rings, and piercings. It was a welcome change from the white uniforms and brown sauces of minimalist France.

After I had settled in and caught up on my sleep, my friend Alan showed me around the kitchens. There were two: one indoor and one outdoor. They were where I'd spend almost all my time while I was there, either with my friend or working alongside one of the dozens of other cooks he worked with.

I remember squatting on the floor of the outdoor kitchen on one of my first days there, pitching in with the work: grinding whole spices in a stone mortar and pestle, peeling sticky tamarind pulp out of its crumbly pods, pounding cilantro to a paste for a chutney. There was a fire burning in an alcove-like fireplace where two women were cooking pappadums, naans, and other breads. They were sitting on either side of the hearth, the fire in between them. They'd pat the dough to the appropriate thinness with their hands and then cook it over the fire. One had a baby lying just an arm's length from her, and I watched her keep an eye on the fire, an eye on the breads she was cooking, and an eye on her infant all at the same time.

A few days later, I got to help with catering the wedding. We made tons—almost literally—of all different types of appetizers. Most were vegetable fritters, dipped in a chickpea-flour batter and fried in big pits of boiling oil. Every dish had its own dipping sauce with coconut or cilantro or tamarind; chiles were deployed with abandon. There was nothing dainty about any of it—no delicate trays of tiny toasts pristinely topped with fish eggs, being passed between prim and proper people in black and white. Hundreds of laughing revelers, decked out in celebratory colors, were sharing giant platters of deep-fried red cabbage wedges.

At one point during the party, I stopped to look around, trying to absorb the scene, and just fell in love with it. I liked the rough, rustic presentations and the bold, fresh, and direct flavors of the food. I liked how the meal was made up of many dishes with many condiments—not just one piece of meat with a potato.

It was such a far cry from the way that I was used to eating. And it spawned the style that I cook in now. My partner Mary Sue Milliken and I don't just serve a starch and a protein— when we're serving a skirt steak, we serve it with corn relish, with a cucumber-watercress yogurt salad, with black beans, with a flour tortilla. A lot of that style, I think, comes from India, because that was how food was presented there. You never just ate a thing, just a lonely piece of chicken. There was always more to the plate.

Once I was back from that trip there were curries and raitas and chutneys and all kinds of Indian accents on our menu at City Café. It was an overnight change—pushed through by a woman who had never made a curry before she left on that vacation—and I've never looked back. The trip moved me into a whole different direction in terms of the kinds of food I wanted to cook and eat and serve.

Looking back, I'm sure it could have been Thai or Mexican food that transformed me—it didn't have to be Indian. I think I was just ready to be done with "fine French cooking" no matter what. The techniques I learned from the French school of cooking are still valuable, and I still have a place in my heart for French home cooking, but for me the time of butter and cream and red-wine reductions had passed. I was ready for cumin and fennel and turmeric and chiles and epazote and cilantro. I was ready to leave behind the Old World and explore the new.

French Lessons
SUZANNE GOIN

Suzanne Goin graduated with honors from Brown University and trained in restaurants around the world, including Chez Panisse, Al Forno, L'Arpège, and Le Mazarin, before returning home to Los Angeles. She spent two years helping Nancy Silverton and Mark Peel run their celebrated restaurant Campanile before opening Lucques in West Hollywood with her business partner, Caroline Styne, in the fall of 1998. The restaurant was an instant success, awarded three stars by the Los Angeles Times *and hailed by the national press as one of the city's best tables. Suzanne was named one of* Food & Wine *magazine's best new chefs the following year. A.O.C., the pair's second restaurant, opened in 2002 to similar fanfare, earning another three stars from the L.A.* Times *and more national attention. Suzanne was nominated for the James Beard Foundation's Best Chef: California award for the first time in 2003 and has been nominated again in 2006. Her first book,* Sunday Suppers at Lucques, *was nominated for the International Association of Culinary Professionals' Julia Child Award and won the James Beard Foundation's award for Cooking from a Professional Point of View.*

I WAS RAISED TO be a Francophile. Most of it came from my dad, an unrepentant lover of all things French.

He enrolled my sister and me in French classes at an early age. When there was a special occasion of any kind to be celebrated, there was no question as to what kind of restaurant we'd go out to, just whether it would be L'Orangerie or L'Ermitage. Every summer, my family would stay for two or three weeks at a rented house in France. During those stays, my sister and I would make friends with the neighborhood kids during the daylight hours and the family would make regular nighttime excursions to distant Michelin-starred restaurants that my father would have been talking about since before we'd left Los Angeles.

I had a trove of idyllic memories from those trips to back up the idealized version of France that my father had so firmly imprinted on my imagination. So as a kid, I could never understand why Americans always made generalizations about French people being snobby or mean or derisive. As far as I was concerned, everything in France was perfect.

And, as I made my way up through the ranks of the kitchen world, I didn't encounter much that was contrary to my way of thinking. Though it's no longer the case—not by a long shot— the best restaurants in any city in the United States were French when I was growing up. (And thanks to my dad, I knew that very well: he planned vacations around visiting them.) They were the model; the pinnacle.

When I was twenty-six, I was cooking at Chez Panisse, Alice Waters's exceptional restaurant in Berkeley, California. Chez Panisse has been the standard-bearer for seasonal cooking in America for more than three decades now. Alice is the godmother of California cuisine and some would say (myself among them) of New American cooking today.

After cooking at Chez Panisse for two years, I made the

decision to head to France to *stage*—the French word for a limited-time, low-pay or no-pay externship in a fancy restaurant—at a two-starred Michelin restaurant that will, for the purposes of this story, remain nameless. I was enormously excited about the opportunity to cook in France. I thought of it as where everything came from, as the source.

My *stage* began in the winter. The restaurant was out in the country, so it was pretty slow, businesswise, during the colder months. I figured that would work in my favor: start off slow, learn the recipes, the ethos of the kitchen, the way a Michelin two-star restaurant runs, and then stay through the spring, when I'd really get a chance to put it all in play.

After a couple of days of walking around with my head in the clouds—I was in France! I was a *stagiaire*! I was going to learn so much!—reality started to bring me back down to earth.

In fact, I started to understand the shape of my situation within minutes of my first day on the job at this idyllic little hotel restaurant. I was familiarizing myself with my station when I opened one of the reach-ins (in chefspeak, there are reach-ins and lowboys, which are the small refrigerators peppered around a kitchen, and walk-ins, the big refrigerators that you walk into) and was hit by a smell so foul, so intense, and so wretched that I immediately slammed the thing shut.

My mind immediately tried to process the smell and come up with a reason—if any—for it to exist in the kitchen. I figured it must be a garbage drawer or something that hadn't been cleaned properly. Or recently. Or maybe ever. I let out a little "Omigod what's that?" gasp, and a nearby cook nonchalantly told me, "That's the fish drawer," before going back to his prep work.

It turns out that the chef was regularly driving to Spain,

buying dirt-cheap fish—here I thought I'd be working at a place where if the chef was driving to Spain, he would be on a mission to buy the freshest, best seafood—and freezing it on these Styrofoam boards. (And it was all the more confounding since there was a river that ran right next to the restaurant, teeming with edible fish.) That was problem one.

Problem two was the very low-tech approximation of sous vide cooking that he was practicing. Sous vide is a legitimate cooking technique that's fairly widespread in high-end kitchens these days. It involves a complex process of vacuum-packing meats or fish in airtight plastic bags with sauces and flavorings and then cooking it in a water bath at a precise temperature—it's pretty high tech. What this chef was practicing was decidedly less so: we were putting portions of the already frozen-and-defrosted fish and the sauce in plastic bags and keeping them half-frozen—cold enough that it wouldn't immediately spoil but not so frozen that you couldn't use it for service.

His unique "technique" helped me to learn that high school French and kitchen French are different things. "*Coupe le sac! Coupe le sac!*" he'd yell. And I kept thinking that *sac* meant handbag—I was a teenager in Los Angeles the last time I had tried to regularly speak French—and what the hell is he talking about . . . until I realized he meant I was to cut open the bag and squirt the rancid fish onto the plate.

Though it didn't seem to bother anyone else, I had just left Chez Panisse, where the ingredients we cooked with were beyond pristine, so every day I would go to the chef and ask if the fish was okay to serve. Believe me, you didn't need a Michelin star to tell that it was past its prime. You needed a nose.

But he'd dismissively bark, "It's fine, just put more tapenade on it." And then the next day, when I'd ask again, he'd answer,

"Put more garlic in the tapenade." On the third day, he'd decide that we should make a fish terrine out of it. And when the fish terrine had sat around for a couple days in that dank fish drawer, then it was relegated to staff meal.

As you can imagine, with offers like two- and three-day-old fish terrine, staff meals were hardly something to look forward to. There was one casserole that, happily, we only had to encounter once a week. The chef was insane about not wasting anything, so he'd have the cooks save all the wonton wrapper trimmings from when we made ravioli. (Yes, you read right: the two-star Michelin restaurant I was giving six months of my life to didn't even make its own fresh pasta.) When the wonton wrapper trimmings reached critical mass, they'd be deep fried and made into a casserole with instant mashed potatoes. Instant mashed potato and wonton wrapper casserole and spoiled fish. That's what we were running on in the kitchen.

There *were* some bright spots during my time there, however. I remember the chef's wife was a really sweet lady—she would even sneak me a little money here and there because it was basically a no-pay gig. One time she asked me to prepare her a piece of fish—God knows why she wanted the fish—and I did. Why wouldn't I? It was nice to be able to do something for her.

Minutes after I had cooked the fish for his wife, the chef, always insufferable, stormed into the kitchen. With his wife in tow, he proceeded to dress me down, "Why are you giving my fat wife butter sauce? Why are you giving this to my fat wife?" And she was standing right there.

Every once in a while, the chef would start to extemporize about me in an indirect way, announcing, "Americans don't care at all about cooking or ingredients or food" or "The only food that Americans know about is hamburgers." I had already resolved to make it through my six-month commitment to this disaster in the countryside, regardless of the situation, in order to prove to myself that I could—and so I wouldn't feel like I had given up. But it was infuriating to listen to this guy and his ignorant, not to mention hypocritical, rants. All I wanted to shout was, "The food at the place that I just came from was five thousand times better than the slop you guys are serving!" But I didn't. I kept my head down and worked.

Not everyone was a committed masochist like me. Cooks were quitting left and right. Instead of hiring new people, of course, the cost-cutting chef figured he'd have the externs—me and two Japanese guys—take up the slack. Before long, that meant I was the new pastry cook. I am not a trained pastry cook and don't have much of a sweet tooth, so working the pastry station was a real challenge for me to take on, but I found some comfort in the fact that I wouldn't stink like rotten fish every night.

And the stink of that kitchen *did* stick to you. At the end of the day I would smell like the fish I was cooking, like duck fat from all the confit we made (at least that wouldn't rot), and like sweat from working from eight a.m. to one a.m. Not that it mattered much: my clothes were all musty, too. The lodging the restaurant had arranged for me was a dank, windowless room in the basement of a house owned by a lecherous retiree who lived down the road from the hotel.

Thanks to him, I didn't have a single satisfying shower in six months. I'd get home at one in the morning reeking of garlic, and have to sneak upstairs to the only shower in the house, down the hall from where the old man slept. I'd gather all my clothes and soap and lock the door and try to get it over with as soon as possible; since it was an old house with old plumbing, there was never any water pressure or hot water in the middle of the night, so it's not like it would have been a shower worth lingering over anyway.

Between the nighttime—when I prayed that my shower wouldn't wake my landlord from his snoring and provoke him into offering me, half-naked and freezing, a drink or tell me that I was in France and I didn't need my silly bathrobe—and the days of horrible food and regular abuse from the chef, my experience as a *stagiaire* was starting to wear me down emotionally. And it was doing a number on the pro-France attitude I'd arrived with. I knew, logically, that it couldn't be like this at every restaurant kitchen over there, but the longer my ordeal dragged on the less sure I became about that.

Toward the end of my stay, after I improperly tempered the chocolate for one of our desserts one time and had to scramble to remake it in the morning, I started losing sleep at night. I worried that I'd arrive at the restaurant to find that something I'd prepped the night before didn't set correctly, or, as happened on a few occasions, I'd be told that the chef needed puff pastry made by lunchtime for some special menu and that I'd have to scramble to put it together and then bite my nails all through lunch, hoping it would have enough "puff." In all the American kitchens I had worked in, you'd know you needed to make something as labor intensive as puff pastry at least a day in advance. Not in France, at least not here.

But I could see the light at the end of the tunnel. I was counting the days until I'd be free. Just eleven days, Suzanne, I'd tell myself on the walk to work. Then at staff meal later in the day, I'd cheer myself up thinking, Just ten and a half days left to go.

It was during one of my last days there when I finally gave the chef a real reason to go after me. We were serving a red wine sorbet with red-wine poached pears in this giant crystal wine glass. It was something like one of those fifty-dollar

Riedel Sommelier glasses—positively gigantic, decidedly impressive, and somewhat fragile. I called the waiter over to pick up the sorbet and he said, "No, the table's not ready yet. Put it in the freezer. I'll be right back."

I shouldn't have let him do that. I should have pulled the pears out, salvaged what was useable of the sorbet, and then replated the dessert when he was ready. But the chef was so psychotic about waste—which, hey, most chefs are, but there are honest mistakes and margins of error in this business you've got to be able to cope with—so I did what the waiter asked me to. I put it in the freezer.

When the waiter came back, he didn't ask me for the dessert, he just went for the freezer door and—it was one of those experiences I saw happen in slow motion—the glass tipped, wobbled, and then fell, crashing into a million little pieces on the floor. A spray of blood red ice shavings covered everything. Sticky chunks of pear and shattered crystal were everywhere. And the sound! It was like someone had fired a shotgun at a plate-glass window. The chef ran over to the pastry area and just lost it. It happened because Americans are so wasteful, we just throw everything away and only eat at McDonald's, we just spend money and we don't care about anything . . . He went on and on and on as I put together a replacement for the lost dessert and then tried to restore order to my station.

That was the last straw. I was frayed, I was broken, and I was struck with a weird sense of professional self-doubt that, until then, I'd never really known. I felt alienated from a country I had spent so much of my life identifying with. My *stage* was officially a total disaster, professionally and personally.

Most of the kitchen staff had turned over during the time I was there, so on my last night, I had a glass of wine with the girl who worked at the front desk of the hotel and that was it. The chef didn't even say good-bye.

After those grueling six months—what I like to think of now as my "character building" era—I was ready to leave France for a good long time, if not forever. But my friends back at Chez Panisse, whom I'd been calling with increasing frequency as I needed more and more emotional support (and who had repeatedly urged me to quit) insisted that I spend a few restorative days with the Peyraud family at Domaine Tempier in Provence. I figured, why not? Anything would be better than the little slice of hell where I had been living and working.

Now, when I look back on my arrival at Domaine Tempier, I can't help but picture myself as a wounded, pathetic creature, a bird with clipped wings or, at best, one that's flown into a lot of windows. It only took Catherine Peyraud, daughter-in-law of the famous family matriarch Lulu, seconds to assess my situation and about a day to undo the effects of my six months in the dungeon. We went to the market, bought armfuls of the most beautiful ingredients I had seen since I had arrived in France, returned to the house, and cooked them simply. We sprawled out on the couch, ate olives, and watched Wimbledon during the afternoon and drank Domaine Tempier's excellent rosé on the stone terrace when the sun went down.

For a week, that's all we did. And it was perfection. I was reminded of why I loved food and wine. I was reminded of why life was worth living. I remembered why and what I loved about France. It is no mistake that I named my first restaurant, Lucques, after an olive from southern France.

And the Peyrauds, after a week of my sob stories, set me up with a *stage* at Alain Passard's restaurant L'Arpège in Paris the very next week. Funnily enough, I was ready and raring to go. It turned out to be the experience that I'd come to France seeking—amazing ingredients, incredible food, a tough but professional and encouraging working environment. But I don't know that I could have fully appreciated my time at L'Arpège if I hadn't first spent those six miserable months slinging spoiled fish in the countryside. It might have been too easy.

"It's All Fun and Games Until . . ."
GABRIELLE HAMILTON

Gabrielle Hamilton is the chef-owner of Prune, which she opened in New York City's East Village in October 1999. Prune was named in Time Out New York's *"Top 100" in 2000, Gael Green's "Where to Eat in the New Millennium" in* New York *magazine, and also featured in the* Saveur 100 *in 2001. In 2006 Prune was named in* New York *magazine's "101 Best Restaurants" and in* Food & Wine's *"376 Hottest Restaurants in the World." Gabrielle has written for* The New Yorker, *the* New York Times, Saveur *magazine, and* Food & Wine *and had the eight-week "Chef's Column" in the* New York Times. *Her work has been anthologized in the Best Food Writing series for 2001, 2002, 2003, and 2004.*

THERE ARE PEOPLE—and as much as I'd like to distance myself from them, I once counted myself among them—who think that just because they have a stove and a good recipe for duck they can open a restaurant. Because it's "only cooking," any hardworking, dedicated person could do it. What seems effortless—you in the kitchen spooning reduced cider sauce over confited duck leg while your spouse hustles the front, overseeing the dining room with a warm touch and a glass of cabernet, just like the dinner parties you've been throwing in your apartment for ten years—is not. The difference between being a good cook and being a good chef is as big as the difference between playing online Texas Hold'Em in your pajamas and holding a chair in the World Series of Poker.

When I first opened my restaurant, I improvised everything. Other than having an ironclad work ethic and a certain compulsion for cleanliness, list making, and straightforward food, I did not know what I was doing. I ran out of items too early, too often. I drank wine during service. I sent incomplete orders out to tables, making the last diner sit empty-handed. I didn't really have the hang of the language of the line and would expedite tickets without phrasing them, calling out one giant, unpunctuated recitation of orders with no regard for their coursing, timing, or pickup. Worse, I would arrive in the morning and change the entire menu, without warning, for that evening. I did not rehearse or plot or spend months in the laboratory testing new items until I got them just so. I did not research an ingredient and its best technique so that I fully understood it from all sides. I did not prepare my kitchen staff, and most certainly failed to warn the floor staff, who had less idea about what they were serving than we had about what we were cooking.

I can assure you, several years later, that not everyone works this way. In fact, no one credible works this way and this is not at all how professional kitchens are run. I can also confirm that this amateurism can really piss some people off. Maybe it especially pisses off landlocked midwesterners who like to see something coming—like a tornado or the chocolate martini trend—from a long way off and who like to hunker down and get prepared for it, or possibly it's people born under water signs in particular, I can't say for sure but I am certain that my sous chef, A., was pissed.

She was from Nebraska, at any rate, possibly a Pisces, and she was—emphatically—not a spontaneous kind of girl. She preferred a life lived close to the ground, on all fours, ears cocked and cold wet nose quivering to sniff out dangers, predators, and treacheries such as the peril posed by your chef breezing in at ten a.m. with a deli coffee in hand, a bright, fangy smile, and an entire new menu to be ready by six p.m.

This concept was received with as much joy and "can-do" excitement as if I had proposed that she and I eat glass.

She, however, had actually run kitchens before and worked in real professional restaurants with pedigrees and French terms, and she had been to cooking school. She had not spent the past twenty years, as I had, in shitty tourist restaurants where everyone just added cheese, curly parsley, and an orange half-moon to the plate to make it look better, or working for shitty catering companies where some poor bride's wedding food sat in the back of a cargo van, leaking onto the floor mingling with diesel fumes and the voices of five gay cater waiters sitting on buckets of "demi-glace" singing show tunes, while we drove out to the Hamptons.

No, A. had been diligently building her résumé because she wanted to be in this industry. She was the real deal, and I was lucky to have her. She had method, strategy, precision. My impulse to change the menu on a whim, like a gambler at the blackjack table asking to be hit in spite of eighteen showing, was an assault to her demeanor, training, and professionalism. Walking into a room of chaos and reining it in, my former preferred way of "rocking, dude," to show how competent I was, how durable under whatever circumstance, how willing and able I was to hump it, huff it, tough it out, bang it out (and then retire as soon as possible to the greasy mats outside by the dumpsters to smoke filterless cigarettes with the guys, K-Rock blaring out the screen door), was the equivalent of poking the dog with a stick until, at last, she's baring her incisors. While there are people who thrive on this kind of challenge, A. was not one of them.

She spent the day with the hackles up on the back of her neck, her low shallow breathing like the treble throaty growling of a dog who smells danger out in the black wilderness just beyond the campfire. She was the woman who put all kinds of order into this mayhem I called a restaurant in the first months. She scripted every improvised piece of this show we put on each night. She chased the butcher down when his meat came in too fatty. She put a prep schedule together that made us never run out of any item at any time. She coached us all in the language of the line: Order only! Order and fire! Picking up! All day! She permitted me some wine during service but dragged her finger across her throat as a signal to the bartender when I tried for a lemondrop shot.

Warm, fried fava beans with a perfectly cooked artichoke heart, salted. I thought it sounded delicious. But when I arrived with my notes and my prep list for the day and my freshly written menu, eager to try out my new ideas, I was received rather icily by A. It was not the usual convivial day of prep that we had come to enjoy. The amiable chopping and chatting and stirring the broth and having a spoonful of each thing to taste for salt or heat or body or acid had a very cool breeze blowing through it.

We had to be separated, in fact. I prepped in the basement on a stainless-steel table, singing along with the radio set on the golden oldies station, while she grimly prepped upstairs on the line. A. needed silence the way a lost driver needs the radio turned off and everyone in the back seat to halt all chatter until they find their exit.

As the hours passed and the waitstaff started to arrive, an impending sense of disaster began to poison the room. Not only was A. pissed off, but I, ever mature, I became pissed back at her. What was her *problem?* I asked myself. Where was her *positive attitude?* I wondered. Glibly dismissing my part in bringing her mood down to subzero, failing to understand that if I had suggested a new menu a week in advance, begun to test it on Monday, and maybe run it by the following Friday I would have had a much more pleasant, even cheerful, experience. Instead, I just thought she was being a big downer. Now I know better and I follow the latter scenario; but at the beginning, I just threw all of us onto the fire thinking: I can cook, you can cook, so let's cook.

But I'm also the one who thought soaking the dried fava beans in warm water would soften them enough that when fried, they would still have a starchy satisfying interior with a crispy delicious fried exterior. Of course, I had never tried it out beforehand, but it just sounded logical to me. I remembered eating fried fava beans in Turkey when I was a backpacking teenager, and though I had no idea how to cook them, I relied on my intuition. Since the prep day had gotten away from us, I hadn't had a chance to test all of the dishes before service started, and as the fava beans seemed simple, I'd played triage with them. There had been so much to do all day and such unfamiliarity in doing it that we didn't even manage a family meal that night, which meant that each server had to approach her tables all night not only bluffing her game but doing so on an empty stomach. This fava bean and artichoke item, naturally, came in on the first ticket of the evening, submitted by a leery waitress keeping her distance from the uncharacteristically frosty kitchen where A. and I were silently and bitterly finishing the last setup of our stations.

My kitchen is the size of your bathroom. It has been described as one of the smallest kitchens in New York City. I am not exaggerating to be funny. It is tiny, and we generate an astonishing quantity of food out of this very small space. A large part of the way it works is that the two people working the line are very tuned into each other at all times and do "the kitchen ballet" in such concert and harmony that Balanchine would be proud. Your knees are always up against your work station, your towel is always in your hand, your cutting board is always wiped clean and free of debris, your tasting spoon is always in your *bain* of clean water. You never ever stand with one arm akimbo or one leg casually out, you never leave anything extraneous on the counter taking up valuable real estate, and most important, you don't move—ever—without announcing it: "I'm behind you, Behind you, hot! Opening oven door! Open oven! Coming around! Coming around, hot!"

To work in this space, you have to talk a lot. You must constantly communicate, so that no one gets hurt. Because it's all fun and games until somebody gets, you know, their eye poked out.

But A. and I were not really talking on this evening. We were quickly in the weeds, reading tickets and cooking food that we had never seen before nor picked up on the line. One great part about learning your station is when you can do it on autopilot: as soon as you hear "lamb" your left hand moves to open the drawer that the lamb is in or pulls down the pan that the lamb is cooked in. You can be doing six other things but when a menu is internalized, your body can execute the food without your mind consciously thinking about it. Your eye registers the plate of mackerel in front of you and your arm automatically reaches over for the smoked almond vinaigrette to finish the plate—with no conscious thought process.

A new menu fucks everything up. You don't know automatically what goes with what—you have to read the notes you've taped up on your reach-in door. The pickup is the protocol or flight plan for a finished dish. It tells the cook what steps to follow and in what order. It's the map we follow to get to the plate. Does the duck leg go in a sauté pan on the stove top or on a sizzle plate in the oven? Do I reduce my cider sauce to order or keep a *bain* of it warm in my station for an easy ladleful at the finish? This can be complicated at the beginning, with ten or fifteen new items, all with their own unique pickup. Especially if you are not the person who conceived the dish or the menu. I, at least, had been mulling this stuff over in my mind for a few weeks and so had a decent mental picture of the pickup as well as the finished look of each item. A. was flying totally by instruments, no sense memory to guide her. It was grueling. And made no less so by having had to prep all day with so much adrenaline and urgency. When you are starting from scratch, there's a lot more to do, and by the beginning of our first seating—of what would become a long night of service—we were already exhausted.

So we weren't talking, and the atmosphere was thick and bitter and I hated A. and she hated me and I started to fry my first batch of fava beans for our first order. Wet beans in deep fat— wet *anything* in deep fat—make a raucous boil. I had, surprisingly, anticipated that; I'd experienced water in hot oil before. But what I didn't foresee is that the skins of the beans would burst when submerged in the fat, sending hot globules of fryer fat streaking through the air like sizzling missiles. There were somewhere between fifteen and twenty-five beans per order and 75 percent of them burst in the fat. First came a raucous crackling roiling in the fryer—exactly the sound of great sudden applause. I took a grandstanding Olympic bow to get A. to laugh but she was having none of it—and just then whistling, hot fat bombs began flying through the air, stinging us in the neck, the cheeks, the hairline. To call this painful is obviously an understatement. It was stupidly painful and more than dangerous. One of those in the eye and it really would have been an end to the fun and games.

This is when A. started to throw things. A sauté pan flung into the dish station. An empty quart container hurled into the recycling bin. She would come around to plate without warning, and if my arm happened to be in the way of her hot sauté pan, then the resulting corporal's stripe of punishing burn on my forearm was my own concern. A simple "I'm thinking about changing the menu next week and here are my menu items" would have gotten me the customary courtesy of a "Coming around, hot!" but on this night, any bare skin I had —and any utensil, sizzle plate, pot or pan, whatever the implement of "I'll get you back for this, bitch"—was fair retributive game.

When you are in the planning stages of your new restaurant, fantasizing about how great it will be to open your own little place and cook delicious food in a warm atmosphere of great congeniality and fraternity, this kind of scene doesn't come up. I kept my head down and my tail between my legs and worked as fast and hard as I could to just keep the food coming and the new menu running. Of course, the artichoke heart with fried fava beans turned out to be the hit of the evening—one on every ticket!—giving me ample opportunity to learn my lesson, to really internalize my mistake. I vowed to apologize to A. in the morning, at length, and thank her for teaching me how to not change a menu.

But that, unfortunately, was not to be the simple end of it. Deep in the middle of the eight p.m. rush, while we were ducking fat bullets flying through the already thick air and squinting so as not to get one in the eyeball, A. looked up and out into the dining room and said, "Holy shit, is that Mario Batali at the bar?"

I froze and, with disbelief, followed her gaze. There in fact was Mario Batali eating at Prune for the first time. Suddenly I saw all my new menu items with different and appreciably less confident and permissive eyes, and felt deflated, embarrassed, and ashamed. It's one thing to go along glibly thinking up some food ideas, but is that what you want to present— untested!—to a serious eater, a person who is hugely knowledgable and discerning, someone who will definitely know the difference between good enough and excellent?

I didn't have any idea where Prune was going when we opened. I didn't know that chefs would eat here and cooks and serious food lovers who were savvy and well traveled. In the very beginning, I banked on the adequate palate of the average diner—and often took advantage of the fact that, for the most part, most people can't tell the difference. My husband, for example, thinks the turkey spinach pesto tortilla "wrap" that he eats for lunch at the hospital where he works is "delicious," but he also thinks the monkfish liver with warm buttered toast at Prune is "delicious" and so he really can't discern between delicious and delishusssss. I think most customers are like this. The problem is that a lot of cooks and chefs and restaurant folks eat at Prune and you don't want to show them your decent pair of eights. You want to kill them with your straight flush.

That night ended, mercifully, and neither of us lost an eye. Mario nodded to us encouragingly, paid, and left. We fed the staff a midnight meal. And A., after we had cleaned up, generously joined me in a well-earned lemondrop shot at the bar.

I have seen a lot of chefs refuse to be humbled by their staffs, refuse to learn from their mistakes, refuse even to consider that they are mistaken, but I do not count myself among them. I am grateful to have learned from A.—albeit the hard way—how not to introduce a new menu, and how to take good care of my cooks and the people working for me. I also am glad, in the end, that Mario was in the house that night, as it made it crystal clear to me that every night matters, that it's amateur to hope no one will notice.

It's the difference, I discovered, between being a good cook and being a professional chef. Which I learned by trying to fry wet fava beans.

Lunch with Victor
MARCELLA HAZAN

*Marcella Hazan, a native of Cesenatico in Emilia-Romagna, is
the acknowledged godmother of Italian cooking in America. She
has written six influential cookbooks, including* The Classic Italian Cookbook, Essentials of Classic Italian Cooking, Marcella
Cucina, *and, most recently,* Marcella Says. *She is at work on a
memoir of her long life and brilliant career, which will be published in the fall of 2007. Marcella and her husband, Victor, himself an authority on Italian food and wine, live in Longboat Key,
Florida. This piece is based on a conversation with Marcella.*

I WAS IN MY twenties when I met Victor, my husband now
of more than fifty years. He had come to Italy to visit his uncle and the rest of his family who still lived there. Though he
was born in Italy, like me, his parents left before World War II
and raised him in America. Victor's cousin, whom I had met
once at a party, introduced us, and we immediately hit it off.

We spent most of the summer together. While we were
courting—usually over meals at restaurants—Victor talked

about food. He talked about food and ingredients and eating nonstop. He would talk about what he wanted to eat for dinner while we were still eating lunch. At the time, I had nothing to do with food or cooking. I was on the road to becoming a science teacher. I had earned my first degree at the University of Ferrara, in geology, and was working hard on the second, in biology. I had been staying in boardinghouses at the university, where they would cook for the students—very simple meals; it was a special thing if you got a piece of meat at the commissary—and sometimes I would rent a room and get all of my meals out at restaurants and cafés. The arrangements never bothered me because I didn't care much about what I ate. I thought that Victor's passion for food was very strange.

But I fell for him all the same. We married and came to America, to New York. I didn't know anyone in America. I didn't speak English, either. And since I had never cooked and never taken care of a house before—I had never even learned how to make a bed—it was a hard transition for both of us. But I knew that one thing that was very important to Victor was food, to eat nicely.

The first place he took me to see in America was a supermarket. It was around the corner from our apartment. I had never been to a supermarket before. I remember saying to Victor, "Everything is dead here. Everything is in a coffin, wrapped in plastic." Even as someone who had never concerned herself with what made for good meals, the supermarket seemed a world away from the fresh produce markets and farm stands in Italy.

But there was a silver lining: I didn't have to haggle, I didn't have to struggle to make small talk in English to buy my groceries. Victor explained, "You can come, pick out what you want, and you don't have to understand what anyone is saying. Just look at the amount on the cash register and pay."

So now I had a way to get the raw materials I would need to cook our meals. But buying groceries was only the first obstacle for me to overcome. I had never seen a big refrigerator like the one that we had in our rented apartment. It took me almost a month to start using it because I was so scared of it. And I didn't like the idea of taking the vegetables from one coffin to another.

Those first few months were tricky, to say the least. No one had ever taught me how to cook, or shown me how to do anything in the kitchen. I was a total beginner. Before we moved from Italy, though, Victor had bought a cookbook for me. It was an Italian cookbook that was famous in Italy, *Talismano della Felicità* by Ada Buoni. I read it a little, and then started cooking soups and vegetables and other simple things.

Since I was too afraid to take the subway, I was limited to what I could buy at the store around the corner. I also never paid attention to what was written on the packages because I couldn't read English. One time I bought a can because it had a picture of these tiny little peas on it. Thinking about how good peas are with butter and salt, I brought it home and prepared the peas for lunch. But the finished dish was terrible. It was so salty that I had to throw it away. And Victor looked at the can and showed me that it said "salt added." That was an important early lesson: read the can.

One of things that helped me, especially in the beginning, was when Victor would compliment me, telling me that I had a natural instinct for cooking. This is probably why I have taken the road I have in life: when Victor would taste a dish I had just cooked, he would jump from his chair and run over and kiss me, telling me how incredible it was. He made me want to keep doing it, to keep improving. And I think it was very smart of Victor to encourage his young bride in this way.

A veal cutlet was one of the first things I learned to cook well, and it was the first dish that really drove Victor crazy. He still likes it today. It was fried. I fried everything back then because I knew how to do it well.

At the time, I was working as a researcher in a biology lab to help pay the bills. I have always liked doing research, and my cooking benefited from this tendency. Every day I would comb through the book for recipes and search the supermarket for ingredients to try and make the food taste like we remembered from Italy. Though I never thought about being professionally involved in food, I was starting to realize that spending two hours cooking and eating well and spending time with Victor made me very happy.

After six or seven years in New York, we went back to Italy. Because I had learned to cook—and that I liked to cook—I tried to learn as many new dishes as I could. And I was looking at them in a different way, analyzing them, taking notes, treating them like my research in the lab. It still had not occurred to me that I might one day write a cookbook; I was doing it out of enjoyment. But looking back now, I can see that my eye had developed; the way I thought about and cooked food was changing.

When we came back to America six years later, I decided that I didn't want to return to the laboratory, partly because the hours were difficult, and partly because I wanted to spend more time at home. When I told my parents, they were surprised. They said, "What?! You study so much and now you go in the kitchen?" But the truth was I was happier there.

Once I was a little less afraid of taking the subway, I began going over to the ethnic grocery stores on Ninth Avenue in Hell's Kitchen, where they carried ingredients that I couldn't easily find in the supermarket. One time, I came across a big basket of Jerusalem artichokes; I had learned to cook them very well while in Italy, and had never seen them in America before. I said to the counterman, "Ooh. Give me two pounds."

He looked at me with a strange expression on his face and asked, "Two pounds?"

"Yes," I clarified, "two pounds."

"What are you going to do with two pounds?" he asked.

At this point I didn't know what he was getting at, so I har-rumphed: "I'm going to cook it. I know how to cook it."

I brought home my two pounds of Jerusalem artichokes and started to peel them and found out they were ginger. What was I going to do with two pounds of ginger? I had plenty of those experiences.

Around this time, when I had all that ginger on my hands, I decided to take a Chinese cooking course. I had come to like Chinese cooking while living in New York and eating at Pearl's, an upscale uptown Chinese restaurant that Victor's father frequented. After the very first class, however, our teacher, Grace Chu (whom everyone called Madame Chu), took a sabbatical in China. She was gone.

The women in the class asked me what I was cooking at home. I told them that I cooked Italian food for my husband and they decided, then and there, that they would hire me to teach them about Italian cooking. They wrote their names and phone numbers down on a piece of paper and asked me to call them to let them know when the classes would start. I was very surprised by this. When I got home I handed Victor the scrap of paper and told him it was a list of crazy people.

But Victor said, "You like to cook, you like to teach"—and I did like to teach; I had done so briefly at a high school in Milan—"so why don't put the two things together?"

And I became a cooking instructor, completely by chance.

After a year of teaching six of my former classmates in my cramped New York apartment kitchen, I took a break. Victor asked me if I wanted to teach again next year. I said, "Yes, I'd like to teach, but not to those same people, because I don't know how to cook anything else!" They had been coming twice a week for a matter of months—we had covered just about everything I knew about Italian cooking.

The *New York Times* maintained a list of culinary schools, and prospective students could write in and get a copy of it, so I thought I'd get the list and write to these schools to see if they could use an extra instructor. But the newspaper had run out of these lists. I thought, Well, that's the end of this new career. And I didn't teach anymore for a while because no one knew about me.

Then, one day, Craig Claiborne, the restaurant critic and food writer of the *New York Times,* called me. I think he must have run out of story ideas. He must have had nothing to do when he came across my letter looking for a list of cooking schools. For whatever reason, he called me.

Now when you don't know very much of a language, the telephone is a monster. It can be very difficult to understand people, especially their names. (I've always been very bad about names.) I didn't recognize Claiborne's name, but I knew that it was the *New York Times,* and I understood that he wanted to come talk with me on his lunch hour. I said, "My husband and I have lunch at that time." Victor and I always had a real meal at lunch. We still do.

Claiborne asked about the next day, and I said we ate lunch every day. And I didn't know what to do next, so I said, "If you really want to come talk to me at that time, then why don't you come here for lunch?"

The next day, he came and ate lunch with us. From that

lunch he wrote a nice article, a very big article, too, two-thirds of a page. He asked me for the recipes of what he had eaten, and I wrote them down and they accompanied the piece. And that jump-started the school: I was teaching again.

Teaching taught me a lot about America: everyone loved deep fried squid rings at Italian restaurants, but when I brought out a bowl full of whole squid at a cooking class no one wanted to touch it. I tried to teach a class on kidneys, but my students didn't want to cook them and they didn't want to eat them.

I was a few months back into teaching when another person called. I didn't understand who it was or what he wanted me to do or what he was even talking about. So I said come over for lunch. Victor would be there and he would understand what the man wanted, I figured.

The caller turned out to be Peter Mollman, the publisher of *Harper's Magazine.* He had just spent three months in Italy and had read Craig Claiborne's article in the *Times* when he'd returned. He said he recognized the food that he had eaten on his trip in my recipes. He wanted to know if I had ever given any thought to writing a cookbook, an Italian cookbook for an American audience. The answer was easy: No. Would I like to write a cookbook? he asked. And I said: No. Why not? Because I didn't write in English. But Victor said that if I wanted to write a book that he would translate it. So I said, "Okay, but I don't know a single thing about writing a cookbook."

I knew so little that when I went to sign the contract, Mr. Mollman asked me how much time I thought I needed to write the book. "I don't know, two months?" I said.

He smiled and said, "Let's make it ten months. At least."

And we did it, Victor and I. He is very precise, so precise that I started to get mad at him when we were working together on the book. Every time he couldn't understand something, he would come running into the room and ask me what I meant. *Every time.* It didn't matter if I was in the middle of a new recipe, he would barge in with a dozen questions: When you steam this how much water should be in the pot? Should the pot be closed or open? Why do you put salt here? Why this? Why that? So I kept rewriting and rewriting the recipes, until a recipe that was thirty lines ended up sixty lines. But they worked better because of it.

And now, nearly forty years later, they still work. I went on to write more recipes for more cookbooks. The cookbooks have done very well. Victor and I have moved to Florida, where the gigantic local supermarket—which would have even been more frightening to me than the little supermarket I patronized in New York in the fifties—is now where I do my shopping. I still teach cooking classes, and I still run across the occasional student who's afraid of squid when they're not cut into rings and fried. Victor and I still have a home-cooked lunch together every afternoon. And though he still talks about food all the time, it doesn't bother me at all these days.

A Brief History of Fate
FERGUS HENDERSON

Fergus Henderson trained as an architect before becoming a chef, opening the French House Dining Room in 1992 and St. John in 1995, which has won numerous awards and accolades, including Best British and Best Overall London Restaurant at the 2001 Moët & Chandon Restaurant Awards. He is the author of Nose to Tail Eating, *winner of the 2000 Andre Simon Award.*

A SERIES OF CURIOUS events and the fickle finger of fate are responsible for me finding myself in the kitchen, rather than any actual moment of deliberate culinary education. But in many ways, the deck was always stacked against me.

I had a very gutsy youth. My mother was a great cook and my father a magnificent eater. Generously, he enjoyed many gastronomic adventures with us, and our home was always ripe with eating and wine. Coming downstairs in the morning in the early seventies, I would encounter the seductive musk of the previous night's dinner party, and that tingling feeling that there was something going on that I wanted to be part of would seize me. These vibrations were strong, and enduring; they lingered straight through childhood and right on into my studies.

Even though I trained as an architect, I was never away from great food. At lunchtime, while working in an architect's office, I'd watch the architects run out and buy their sandwiches and bags of chips, return to their desks, and eat their gastronomic booty offhandedly, washed down with a can of Coca Cola. Architecture, I thought, was a creative profession, yet I could see no stimulative effect on the creative juices by this brief and meager meal. So I took on the mantle of going out and having a true lunch for the rest of the office— unfortunately with such rigor that often I did not return in the afternoon. But at least someone was making a stand for the importance of lunch.

Once my studies had ended, along came the fickle finger of fate. Before being offered a job in an architect's office, I was offered a job in a kitchen. It was a strange time of transition all around. I was brought in to change the menu, and suddenly an architect whose architecture had been influenced by food was telling chefs what to do. The realization was exhilarating and imperfect. It seemed easier for the world of architecture to understand my culinary sensibilities than for chefs to understand my architectural training.

Still an architect, and yet increasingly distracted by kitchens, I left the kitchen job to cook in a ropy club in Notting Hill, where the bouncer, named Danar, kept telling me to cook goat neck soup, which he said would enable one to go all night. I hasten to add that Danar was not one of my mentors, even though he made many such useful culinary suggestions. He had a very peculiar hairstyle that looked like someone had pushed his beard through to the back of his shaved head. For a large lad, he let in more undesirables than desirables, although many sincere eaters slipped passed him—despite the inevitable problem of enthusiastic ordering without the appetite to match.

Within this strange club much cooking was done with Charles Campbell, who sat on a stool in the corner of the kitchen, smoking and drinking warm vodka. As I bounced around the stove he would tell me stories of Elizabeth David while he made terrines, which did not require him leaving either his stool or his vodka. A wise soul who I learned much from. We made sausages, boudin blanc, overly salty cucumber soup (which we punted out as Cucumber and Sea Salt Soup). It was here that I roasted my first suckling pig. We were cooking. Chefs came in late, after service for ham (left over from Ham in Hay) and eggs.

As you can imagine, in this environment I was a little chaotic, possibly lacking in the rigors of running a professional kitchen. Fortunately into my life came love and self-discipline at the same moment, in the form of my wife Margot, who knocked me into shape, doing away with the chaos and disorder and making a chef of me.

Architecture was long gone. All my buildings now ended in a feast.

The Disciple
PIERRE HERMÉ

Heir to four generations of Alsatian bakery and pastry-making tradition, Pierre Hermé has been called "the Picasso of pastry." He began his career at the age of fourteen as an apprentice to Gaston Lenôtre, and by twenty-four he was the pastry chef for Fauchon, where he first rose to international prominence. Hermé opened his first Pierre Hermé Pâtissier Paris boutique at the New Otani Hotel in Tokyo in 1998, and his first location in Paris in August 2001. He is the author of a number of cookbooks, including two he coauthored in English with Dorie Greenspan: Desserts by Pierre Hermé *and* Chocolate Desserts by Pierre Hermé.

A S AN ASPIRING pastry cook, one learns to master hundreds of preparations, from the simple—like how to temper chocolate—to the elaborate—such as constructing grandiose wedding cakes covered in dozens of handcrafted marzipan flowers.

Much of this learning happens under duress: there's a brief

tutorial from a gruff superior who then leaves you struggling to replicate what he's just demonstrated. You get it all down after a while—at least I did—but it's hard to remember exactly when you learned every basic building block of the pastry cook's repertoire. But I'll never forget when I learned how to make crêpes.

It happened when I was fourteen, a newly arrived apprentice at Gaston Lenôtre's boutique in Paris. I had been there for maybe a month when my chef asked for volunteers to help cater an event. Since the closest I had yet come to handling food that was eaten by anyone was arranging the restaurant's spectacularly crafted, jewel-like petit fours on plates for the dining room, I figured that if I signed on I would be washing dishes or performing some other menial task, something I could certainly handle, so I volunteered. I was timid then, and fearfully respectful of the professionalism of the men I was working with, but I didn't want to miss out on any opportunities to learn.

You can imagine how surprised I was on the night of the event when, as we were setting up, I was told by my chef that I would be in the ballroom, cooking for the guests. He pointed to a crêpe station in a corner of the room, with a large flat griddle, and explained that I would cook crêpes to order, fill them, and serve them to guests.

I was, I will reiterate, fourteen. A little boy. Grown-ups made me nervous. Luckily, however, I had seen crêpes being made before—my parents owned a patisserie and bakery in Colmar, Alsace, where I was raised—so I did my best to imitate the method from memory. The plan was to swipe the griddle with butter, then, with a ladle, quickly pour out a thin slick of batter into a perfectly round puddle, cook it for a second, flip, fill, and serve it.

My first few attempts were awkwardly shaped and overly

thick, more like pancakes than crêpes. These aborted efforts caused me no small amount of grief, with all the well-heeled clients looming nearby. My subsequent efforts were improvements, but they still weren't the crêpes you'd expect from Gaston Lenôtre.

I had only been making crêpes for a few minutes when I noticed that Lenôtre himself was walking through the dining room, making nice with the guests. Lenôtre was the biggest pastry chef in France and probably in the world in the 1970s; his very presence in the room sped up my heart rate. I had only seen him once before and was not anywhere near presumptuous enough to have spoken to him. You do not get to where he was without an extrasensory talent for pastry, and I was sure that he could see from across the room that I was struggling with the crêpes. I'd wager he could probably feel it in his bones the way a farmer can feel rain coming.

All of a sudden he was there, beside me, and he wordlessly and gently took the spatula and ladle from my hands. He started pouring out crêpes, each miraculously thin, each perfectly round. I was amazed at his facility: not that it existed, but that it was so fluid, unharried and effortless. My amazement almost overtook my fear: I was waiting for him to dismiss me and end my career right then and there under that gilded ceiling in front of all these fancy people. I would be finished at fourteen.

But Lenôtre did not fire me. He spent fifteen minutes by my side, making crêpes and directing my attention to the elements of their preparation. He showed me how to run the spatula around the edge of the crêpe, peek at its underside, and when it was just colored but the overall crêpe was still very creamy, to flip it. I was to cook the second side of the crêpe for less time, to ensure that it was not cooked through—so it would be tender, not tough. His instruction was almost silent, but each utterance—"more," "less," "now," "no"—spoke volumes. Then he handed me back my spatula and stepped aside to supervise my work.

I was beside myself with anxiety. I was worried about looking like a dunce who needed special attention from the teacher, there in front of all those people. I was worried about whether or not Lenôtre was going to be firing me that night. I was worried about how I would explain it to my parents.

With the end of my budding career in sight and the chance to humiliate myself in front of an audience close at hand, I chose to focus, almost singularly, on my crêpes. I blocked everything out except for Lenôtre's occasional direction and, miraculously, they got better. Were they as perfect as his? No. Not even close. But they were flaky and tender, round and thin. They were good crêpes. And as soon as I hit my stride, Lenôtre was gone. I didn't see him leave, I just felt that there were no longer eyes peering over my shoulder, watching every minute step of my work, from the flick of my wrist when I poured the batter onto the griddle, to the delicate jerk of the spatula needed to flip the crêpes.

For the rest of the evening, I was a crêpe-making machine. I watched every single one intently. I wanted each to be more perfect than the one I had made before it. If Lenôtre came by to check on me again, I wasn't going to give him any other reason than he already had to dismiss me.

As it happened, Lenôtre did not stop by to check on my work. I took that to be a bad sign: he must have written me off. When I reported back to my chef at the end of the night, I was prepared to hear that I'd be packing up for Colmar in the morning. I skulked into the kitchen and sullenly kept my distance. But my chef said nothing of my crêpe-making mishap, not that night and not the next morning either. I was burning up inside; I needed to know what was going to happen to me. And when I blurted out the story of what had happened, my chef laughed a little and told me that when Lenôtre was unhappy with me I would know it. Now get back to work and quit my worrying.

Which is just what I did. I stayed on with Lenôtre for years: by the time I was nineteen, he had entrusted me with his boutique on Avenue Victor Hugo, a huge honor and responsibility for me. And every once in a while, when I start a batch of crêpes, I have this slight tingling sensation that Lenôtre is there behind me, watching my every move. He isn't, of course, but I make the crêpes perfectly, just in case.

Lost at Sea
BARBARA LYNCH

Barbara Lynch is the executive chef and owner of three Boston restaurants, including B&G Oysters Ltd. and the Butcher Shop. Her flagship restaurant is the elegant No. 9 Park, which has routinely been named as one of Boston's—and the country's—finest restaurants since opening in 1998. Lynch first won national acclaim when she was named Food & Wine *magazine's Best New Chef 1996. In 2003 the James Beard Foundation named her Best Chef: Northeast. She is working on her first cookbook, which will be published by Houghton Mifflin in 2008.*

I WAS THE LAST of my mother's seven children. My father died just a month before I was born, and after my stepfather and mother separated when I was ten, she was left to raise me almost single-handedly.

We lived in south Boston, a resolutely working-class Irish neighborhood that was the only world I knew, until my mother started working as a waitress at the Saint Botolph Club, a tony private club with one location in London and another on Commonwealth Avenue in downtown Boston. When I was little and one of my siblings wasn't around to watch me, my mother would take me into work and I'd hang out behind the scenes with her co-workers—the other waitresses and the maids— during her shifts. I liked the place so much that by the time I was fourteen, I was helping with the housecleaning and making beds, and I started working the occasional waitressing shift in my late teens.

My favorite part about waiting tables at the Saint Botolph was watching the chef, Mario Bonello, cook. He was doing this very classical, very Escoffier-style stuff, like cooking sweetbreads under a bell and serving Dover sole that was filleted tableside, that just seemed so refined—not that I necessarily wanted to eat all of it, or knew that much about what was "refined" and what wasn't, but you didn't see stuff like that down in south Boston. I was intimidated by the elegance and sophistication of the menu, but mostly I just thought that it was amazing. And I was really impressed with the command he had over his kitchen—he'd inspect every plate that was going out to the main dining room while simultaneously orchestrating a dinner for a small group in the club's library and making canapés for a reception in the music room. He did it all without ever breaking a sweat or losing his temper. Watching Mario cook got me thinking that I might want to try my hand at the whole chef thing, even though I had never cooked professionally and, for that matter, hadn't cooked much at home, either.

I finally got up the courage to try it when I was twenty-two and one of my girlfriends proposed that we quit our jobs in Boston and move to Martha's Vineyard for the summer, where we would get some seasonal work and hang out until the fall rolled around. I knew I wouldn't miss my full-time job at the dry goods warehouse where I worked, and the part-time gig I had at Filene's Basement wasn't exactly my idea of a good time either. And because he'd known me since I was knee high, I was sure Mario would give me my waitressing shifts at the Saint Botolph Club when I got back, so I consented. It sounded like a plan.

I figured that my summer on Martha's Vineyard would be a good place to give cooking a try. If I found a kitchen job that interested me, I could always just lie my way into it by saying that I had cooked all around Boston. Who on the Vineyard would know any better?

We moved into a house with a bunch of girls we knew from the neighborhood who spent every summer working—and, most of the time, not working—on the Vineyard. On one of the first afternoons I was there, one of my housemates volunteered that she knew the owner of a place called Percy Hayward's from south Boston. She called him and asked if he was looking for help. Since we were all Southies and people from the neighborhood tend to stick together, it wasn't likely he would turn us away. My friends jumped at the waitressing jobs—waiting tables during tourist season is easy money on Martha's Vineyard—but I lobbied for the opening he had in the kitchen. The menu was no great shakes, chowders and burgers and fries, but the kitchen was spacious and new and well put together. It seemed like a lucky break.

That is, until I realized what the job actually entailed. By the end of my first week, I had learned that it meant back-to-back twelve-hour days reheating frozen patties on a griddle and warming up canned soup. There would not, apparently, be anything remotely related to "cooking" as I understood it. It didn't take long before I got fed up with the tedious menu, with the nonstop hours, and with the irritable owner who wouldn't listen to anything I said. Suggestions I had for adding items to the menu that required actual ingredients and real cooking—and were the sort of dead simple things even a rank amateur like myself could pull off—were contemptuously dismissed. While my friends all loved the place because they were making easy money waiting tables, I began to dread it. At night, I would go to sleep still smelling the grease from the grill, and hearing the hiss and bubble of the Frialator in my head like a song you want to forget, but can't, no matter how desperately you try. I didn't know if I still wanted to work in a kitchen at that point, but I knew what I didn't want to be doing, and this was it. After three weeks without a day off, I quit.

It felt great to get out of there, but it didn't feel great to be back at square one, without a job, and still without any real kitchen experience—I had opened cans and reheated leftovers before so the way I figured it, my experience at Haywards didn't really count.

A few days later, I responded to an ad in the *Martha's Vineyard Gazette* for a cooks position on a boat that did nightly dinner-and-dancing sails from Pier 66 to the waters just off Falmouth on Nantucket and back. It took me two weeks of petitioning the owner of the boat to take me on as a cook; he wanted me as a server, but I held my ground. It wasn't just tenacity, I'll admit, that scored me the job—I fudged a few facts on my résumé. I said I had cooked at the Saint Botolph Club, at the Union Oyster House (another well-known and well-regarded Boston restaurant), and a couple other places where I would like to have worked. It must have been believable because in the end he went for it. I was instructed to come in the week before he started his sailing season to meet the chef and get my bearings.

I was so nervous that I barely remember meeting the chef that first day. Then again, it's hard to remember someone you only saw once. Five days later, barely twenty-four hours before we were going to set sail with our first load of passengers (150 men and women who had prepaid good money for their dinners) I arrived at work to discover that the chef had quit. Except for a quick meet-and-greet, we hadn't spent any time together. This was supposed to be the day when I learned the ropes: how to cook for 150 people at once, and how to do it in a ship's tiny galley kitchen.

The owner of the boat turned to me and said, "Well you can probably handle it, right? You can cook?"

I grinned nervously. What could I say? As someone who had supposedly worked in all of these high-end Boston restaurants, I didn't have any choice.

"No problem," I replied.

"Great," he said, and walked away, seemingly confident. As for me, I was battling a panic attack. Me, alone in a kitchen, making dinner for 150 people? I had never even cooked for *half* that number. And I'd certainly never cooked on a boat before.

The one thing I felt grateful for was that the set menu was simple, just two choices: broiled beef tenderloin or steamed lobster. Of course, I had never cooked lobster or tenderloin before, let alone cleaned and butchered whole tenderloins, so maybe "grateful" isn't exactly the right word . . .

As soon as the owner was out of sight, I rushed from the ship to the local library and grabbed up as many cookbooks as I could find. They answered one question—how to steam the lobsters—but none of them addressed the tenderloin problem.

I was in a frenzy, racing around the house, trying to figure out a way to deflect this imminent disaster. Meanwhile my roommates were hanging out, drinking beers, and enjoying a lazy summer on the Vineyard. One of them padded barefoot into the kitchen, yawned, and casually asked me what my problem was. I told her I was going to be the chef and sole cook on the boat starting the next night. She laughed, not believing me, and went back to join the others—who also didn't believe me. I just shook my head. I didn't have time for them. I had to learn how to cook a hundred steaks, and fast.

Thankfully, I remembered that a friend of a friend worked at the Beef Tender—a 350-cover-a-night steak joint where you'd go for a rare steak and a baked potato and that was about it—and I called him up, explained my situation, and asked him what to do.

He put me on hold for a minute, cleared it with his boss, and told me I could come in and shadow one of the chefs. A few hours later, I was situated next to the chef, a veteran grill jockey (and a patient teacher), and together we cooked a couple of hundred orders of steak. I had never worked on the line before, as part of a team cooking for tons of people, and it was an eye-opening experience, to say the least. The speed involved, the efficiency, the teamwork—I was as impressed by these traits as I had been by the chic menu of the chef at Saint Botolphs. The chef taught me at least a dozen tricks, including how to judge the rareness of meat with my closed fist, pressing on the flesh between my thumb and index finger. Rare steak felt like a loose fist, well done was a tight one, and everything else was somewhere in-between.

I left the Beef Tender sometime after midnight, after a round of beers with the cooks, and less than five hours later I was chasing coffee with more coffee and butchering my way through the day's allotment of tenderloins on the boat. While preparing them, I kept hoping that I would somehow make it through this alive. As the day wore on, I tried to discreetly make out how everything in the kitchen worked. I deduced that the bungee cord on the salamander—the super-high-power broiler-type oven that you cook steaks in at a lot of restaurants—was there to keep the thing shut so that meat didn't go flying everywhere every time we hit a wave. There was the same bungee cord safety system on the steamer drawers where the lobsters—currently incarcerated in a tower of cramped plastic crates in the ship's tiny walk-in refrigerator—were to be cooked. I personally gave each of those cords a good tug to make sure they were strong—the last thing I needed was a floor covered in half-dead lobsters. The owner stopped by a few times to check on me, and I gave him an earnestly enthusiastic though probably not too convincing smile.

That afternoon, I realized one thing I had going for me: most of the waitstaff was new to the boat and everyone except the ship's captain and his family was seasonally employed. So even though I was a fresh face in the kitchen, this was the first sail of the season and no one had any idea how much of a rookie I was. Bartenders and servers passing by the kitchen during the day would stop in and introduce themselves, and we all nervously joked about how we were hoping for "smooth sailing" that first night. Little did they know how palpable the nervousness behind my joking was.

Finally, 150 paying customers boarded the boat, and we lifted anchor and set sail. There was no going back. Nighttime sails on the boat started off with cocktails up on the deck, so I wasn't immediately thrown into action. I made sure I had my kitchen as organized as I could—dozens of ramekins of drawn butter lined up, a hotel pan of husked and halved corn cobs, potatoes baked and covered with foil to keep them warm—I was as ready as I was going to get. I was nursing my umpteenth cup of coffee of the day when the headwaiter poked his head into kitchen and told me we were about to get to Cape Cod and turn back toward the Vineyard, and they were getting ready to invite the ship's guests to their tables and start taking orders. That meant it was time for me to get cooking. (Later in the summer, I'd know we were at that point in the sail because the band played the same set list every night, and when I heard the tambourines go crazy during "Coming to America," muffled as it was coming through the ship's deck, I knew it was time to get some steaks started in the salamander.)

I dumped a few cases of rowdy lobsters, pincers snapping, tails flapping, antennae waving, into a steamer drawer, slid it closed, and bid them goodnight. I froze for a second and tried to remember how much time it would take for them to cook. I came up blank, and decided on seven minutes: check on them in seven minutes, and if they're not bright red, give them seven minutes more. I knew what a cooked lobster looked like, so I'd just have to go on that. These days I can tell you it takes longer than seven minutes to cook a lobster. Back then I went on how they looked.

And I cooked steaks by feel, as the Beef Tender chef had taught me to. I loaded up the grill with tenderloins, slid it under the salamander, and turned it up to the hellfire setting. He had sagely counseled me to start off with a batch of well-done steaks for two reasons: they took the longest to cook, obviously, and I could use that first batch to gauge how hot my salamander was and how long it would take for me to properly cook the rest of the tenderloins to temperature. I did as I had been taught.

Soon enough the kitchen was swarming with waiters, picking up plate after plate of steak and lobster and demanding more. I only had to make the mistake once to learn to lean back when I unbungeed a steam drawer full of cooked lobsters if I wanted to avoid the plume of scorching shellfish-scented steam that would billow out with them. As with any semi-traumatic event, I don't remember a lot of the specifics from that point on. I know there was lots of heat, lots of the ship pitching back and forth (the bungee cords held, thank God) and what seemed like an endless stream of seared beef and steamed lobster leaving my tiny little one-woman kitchen.

And then, miraculously, it was over. Hours had passed, and I was sweaty and dirty and I had my hands in more fire and boiling water that night than I had in my entire life—but I had pulled it off.

I sped home around midnight, exhausted and pleased, my hands shaking, my mind racing. As soon as I walked in the door, I had a lit cigarette in one hand and a full bottle of something in the other and I stormed in on my roommates, who were hanging out in the kitchen and told them, "I'm a chef! I did it. I cooked dinner for 150 people tonight." They looked up from their beers and started jeering immediately, insisting I wasn't a chef and having a laugh about it.

But neither their ball busting nor the ache in my feet could dampen the incredible sense of accomplishment and gratification I felt. I had never really gotten that out of any work experience before. I knew that this was what I wanted to do. This was *it*.

That night, when I was drifting off to sleep—not that I had that long to sleep, since I needed to be back at the boat at eight a.m. to get ready for the next night's sail—I told myself I'd work through the season on the boat and then maybe, eventually, open up a little sub shop back in my neighborhood in Boston. I'd find something simple like that. It sounded like a plan.

A Flower in Venice
MARA MARTIN

Mara Martin may be the only chef in Italy to divide her time between a Michelin-starred kitchen in Venice and a pizza joint around the block. She opened Da Fiore on a narrow street in the San Polo district in 1978 with no professional culinary education and, in the last twenty-five years, has become one of Italy's most sought after seafood specialists. Her husband, Maurizio Martin, runs the front of the house, and together with her son, Damiano, she recently opened Il Refolo, an outlet for her latest passion: artisanal pizza.

I WAS NOT CUT out to be a seamstress. And factory work bored my husband, Maurizio. But in the mid-seventies, there weren't many options in Mirano, the gloomy town outside of Venice where we lived. So when Maurizio's aunt, who owned an old osteria in Treviso, asked if we could help her in the restaurant, we hopped on Maurizio's motorcycle and went. Back then, we were looking for a place to put down our roots, a place we could call our own. Mirano was all farmland when we were growing up there, but the farmland was rapidly giving way to sour industrial sprawl. Even if the osteria in Treviso wasn't the final destination, it was as good a chance as any to explore new options.

In Treviso, Maurizio's aunt gave me more-or-less free rein with her menu. But I'd never studied cooking and hadn't planned on doing it as a career. All I knew I had learned from my grandmother, who was legendary in Mirano for her cooking and entertaining and ended up becoming a caterer without planning on it, either. People would ask her to cook for their weddings and parties, and she'd say yes, which meant I was often called in from playing outside to help her peel potatoes and roll out pasta.

Her cooking was simple. Roasted meats and polenta, big bowls of mussels, lots of fresh vegetables and wild herbs. Even though Mirano is close to Venice, it has a completely different cuisine, one that revolves around the mainland farms, not the fish from the lagoon. My grandmother's cooking was more rustic and seasonal—I still remember her telling me to go outside into the garden and bring her whatever vegetables or fruit were ripe and smelled good.

So my grandmother's dishes were what we served. The menu was a hit with the restaurant's small clientele and, somewhat to our surprise, Maurizio and I liked working in a restaurant. Working for family, however, was difficult. After a while, I started dreaming about doing my own thing while I was rolling out pasta in the afternoons. But I had just become a mom, and it was hard to juggle all the responsibilities I had and seriously entertain the notion that I would be able to open my own restaurant.

Then one night my father came to dinner after a day's work in Venice (he was a mason, which was good work in a city where the buildings are always in some stage of crumbling), and he told me the most serendipitous bit of bad news: the owners of Da Fiore—the flower—were retiring.

It was too bad about Da Fiore, I thought, because it had always been the kind of casual osteria—in Venice we call it a *bacaro,* after Bacchus, the god of wine—where men like my father would stop by for a quick snack and an *ombra* of wine. It was located on a small canal where it got a nice breeze whooshing through the dining room. There weren't many places like it left, because there weren't many old timers and natives left to patronize them. Venice had turned into a tourist magnet. The people who had lived there were moving to the suburbs, commuting into the city by day to work in the souvenir shops or restaurants. At night, the city was weirdly vacant.

I got it in the back of my mind that we should take over Da Fiore. This was 1977 and the whole "Save Venice" movement was in the works. There were pockets of young people, about our age, moving back—artists and such—because the city was giving them tax breaks and other incentives to restore buildings and revive the community. So we took a leap of faith.

Da Fiore had been neglected for years—the paint was chipping, the floors were scuffed, but it had good "bones." We spent the whole winter giving the place a face-lift—painting, polishing the woodwork, collecting knickknacks to hang on the walls. As for the menu, we didn't intend to do anything too different from what the previous proprietors had done: just a simple *cichetti*—Venice's version of tapas—which I would pile onto platters and serve from the bar.

But there was a little problem. Growing up in the countryside outside of Venice, I didn't know anything about fish. And in Venice, fish is what is served in restaurants. So Maurizio and I would get up early and go to the Rialto fish market, where most of the restaurant and home cooks shopped. We'd follow chefs around and see how they interacted with the old fishmongers—what questions they asked, what they paid. And when they finished buying something, we'd walk up and order the same thing. (Nowadays, many chefs go over to the large Chioggia market, but we take our boat to the smaller one in Torcello, which is run by the fishermen.)

I was lucky to make the acquaintance of an old cook named Ermano who had worked on cruise ships and was an expert on fish from the lagoon. He'd come to Da Fiore in the morning, after we got back from the market, and show us how to clean the local specialties, like the ink-filled *seppia* (cuttlefish) and the *granseole* crabs. He taught me how to make *brodo di pesce*, the powerful base for soups, risottos, and sauces. I learned all the tricks and techniques, things most chefs don't even do anymore, like reserving the ink from the squid and cooking with it, rather than using the packaged junk, which has preservatives and, in my opinion, a tinny, off taste.

At first we cooked everything on the grill. Traditional stuff, easy enough. And every now and then, I'd run a special, just because I was getting bored with doing the same limited menu.

For my specials, I'd mix the dishes I had learned as a child— like a stinging nettle soup—with the seafood that I was learning about in Venice, like *canoce*. Or I'd take freshly made taglioni tossed with radicchio, as my grandmother would have done, and mix in some sweet scampi to offset the vegetable's bitterness. It all depended on the season—what was growing in the countryside and what was swimming in the lagoon.

I'd bring it out to a regular, like our friend Gildo, to see what he thought of it. Once he told me my clams were sandy. I went back to the kitchen and learned how to let them flush themselves clean in a bowl of water, and never had that problem again.

But more often, I got encouragement—from people who were telling me my dishes were a refreshing change from the same old–same old served at most of the other restaurants in Venice—and that inspired me to do more.

I didn't have any preconceived notions of what I should be cooking, and hadn't been taught the old canonical Venetian recipes, so I didn't know that it was unusual to be mixing fish and vegetables in pastas and risottos. Traditionally, dishes were either fish *or* vegetables. Basta!

Before I knew it, I was cooking three courses a night. There was a lot of experimentation—mixing old recipes I had inherited from my family with fish I was learning about at the market and with Ermano. I spent a lot of time reading about the history of Venetian cooking, to try to understand some of the recipes I was seeing in other restaurants, and why chefs made them that way. And I spent a lot of time learning to taste, to become attuned to flavors as they are experienced on the tongue, by the nose, and how they linger after the food is eaten.

We use a lot of spices in Venice that you don't see in other dishes in Italy—saffron, for example—so I tried flavoring fish with them. But where to incorporate them—in the sauce? In the pasta? In a marinade for the fish?

When I started researching how other cultures prepare the kind of fresh fish we have access to here in Venice, I realized they were serving it raw (just as many Venetians once did.) So I started experimenting with *crudi*, or raw fillets of fish, with flavorful marinades or simply finished with a slick of good oil.

Over the years, the reputation of our restaurant grew. We had a lot of famous people—politicians and film stars—trekking out to our little place in an old residential neighborhood in Venice. One day Marcella Hazan walked in. She was teaching a class about our city's cuisine to some American students and her husband Victor had told her our restaurant would be a good one to bring the students to for lunch. We struck up a long conversation, and afterward kept in touch, becoming good friends. I've learned a lot by cooking at her side since then. And I've learned a lot simply by asking questions of other cooks.

That is part of a good cook's personality: to be curious. And curiosity—coupled with a streak of perfectionism—is the road to developing your own style.

Of course, when I started out, I didn't know that was where I was headed. Not knowing much about fish when I started meant I really had to be curious about all aspects of each species, and how it reacted to different types of cooking methods. Not having experience with other professional kitchens meant mine was not designed to fit some traditional model within which I had to learn to cook. My kitchen design may not make sense to other cooks—there's no line, I finish dishes other cooks have started, and, for years there was a chair by my pasta station where my young son, now all grown up, would keep me company.

But it's my kitchen, and I feel at home in it.

Early Riser
MARY SUE MILLIKEN

For over two decades, Mary Sue Milliken and her business partner, Susan Feniger, have transformed street foods and comfort foods into critically acclaimed cuisine and become some of the country's foremost authorities on the Latin kitchen. Today, they own the popular Border Grill restaurants in Santa Monica and Las Vegas at Mandalay Bay, and Ciudad restaurant in downtown L.A. They have authored five cookbooks and appeared in 396 episodes of their television programs Too Hot Tamales *and* Tamales World Tour *for the Food Network.*

B ACK BEFORE I hooked up with Susan Feniger, my partner in crime at the old City Restaurant, Border Grill, and Ciudad, I corralled various cousins for my culinary adventures. In fact some of my earliest cooking triumphs were the result of lazy, restless summers at a resort in Michigan, where my grandparents lived and much of our extended family rented holiday cottages.

My mom and dad would come up some weekends, aunts and uncles would come up others, but most of the time we cousins were under our own supervision, running wild, free to get ourselves into (and out of) all kinds of trouble.

My cousin Carol and I often babysat her youngest brother, Jimmy, who had a fiery temper and a penchant for throwing tantrums. At the beginning of one summer, when he was still too young to speak, we gave him a pile of carrot sticks in an effort to get him to stop yelling. They seemed to do the trick—until one got stuck up his nose and the end broke off. We tried to get it out, but it was unreachable. Not even the village pediatrician could get it to budge, but he pronounced it harmless, and eventually we all forgot about it. Then, during an evening downpour after a big Labor Day weenie roast, as we all crowded onto the porch swing watching the thunder and lightning, something made Jimmy howl with laughter. And out popped that carrot looking as fresh as the day it got stuck. No one has yet to come up with an explanation for that perfectly preserved carrot that lived in my cousin's nose for nine weeks.

We were always looking for something to occupy ourselves, and one afternoon we resorted to flipping through copies of one of our mothers' magazines—maybe it was *Redbook*, or *Ladies' Home Journal*—and we were intrigued when we came across a recipe for something called "apricot coffee cake." I was in fourth grade at the time and my cousin was just a year older than me, so neither of us had cooked much more than Bisquick pancakes at that point in our lives. We had never drunk coffee, and I know that I had certainly never eaten coffee cake before. I felt lucky when I got my hands on a doughnut as a kid, or if my aunt splurged on a tube of Pillsbury Poppin' Fresh cinnamon rolls.

I'd never been drawn in by a recipe in one of my mom's magazines before, but this one seemed so preposterous that my cousin and I couldn't help but read it again and again. It sounded like instructions to a science experiment. There were lots of precise measurements—the dough, the waxed paper, softened butter—so we got out a ruler and tried to figure out what the thing would look like. Then there were strange instructions for enclosing the butter, chilling, rolling, folding again and again—each time with hours in between when you were supposed to wait and let the dough "rest," whatever that meant. Every step of the way, the recipe just got more complicated.

My curiosity was piqued, big time. When we finally looked up from the pages of the magazine the decision had been made. "We gotta do it," I said, and we were off. We jumped on our bicycles—somehow I always forgot to hurry to the bike rack, which meant that I ended up on the blue black, fat-tired clunker we had nicknamed The Bruise. We pedaled our way over to the local A & P supermarket, me arriving hotter, sweatier, and several minutes after Carol. And then we started shopping, going up and down the aisles calling out to each other. Butter, check. Flour, check. Sugar, check. Yeast, check. Dried apricots, check. Soon we had everything we needed to make the coffee cake—not that we knew exactly what that was.

Despite the fact that we had no idea what we were doing, we *did* have the sense to follow the directions—to the letter, word for word. Mixing and kneading, rising, chilling, softening, smearing, we approached every detail with diligence and precision, rereading each step of the recipe to make sure we'd get it right.

A yeasted, butter-rich Danish dough, which is what we were making, is a day-long task. But since we were baking on impulse, we got a late-afternoon start on the dough. That meant that the final rising stage when the yeast worked it's magic ended at the less than convenient time of four a.m. The two of us were deathly afraid that any deviation from the rigid rules of the recipe would result in disaster, however, so we set our alarm clock for the middle of the night and tried to get a couple of hours of sleep.

Of course, being preteen girls embroiled in an exciting adventure, we could barely keep our eyes shut. I was afraid the alarm wouldn't wake me and we'd already spent so much time and energy on this darn cake that I was determined to see it through successfully. This was no Betty Crocker mix we'd spent twenty minutes on; it was a significant investment of time and concentration. I guess that's why we were up long before the alarm went off and caught our older siblings sneaking tipsily up the secret pine stairway to the bedroom window after a forbidden teen beach party. This observation would come in handy a few years down the road—but on that night we just hurried past them, rubbing our eyes. We were on a mission to see what this wacky concoction was going to look like and how it would taste. At four a.m. on the button, we did the finger test and the dough held the print—telling us it was ready.

Then came the moment of truth: we popped our creation into the (preheated, *exactly*, of course) oven, sat in front of it in wooden chairs, and watched the foggy window like a TV set, waiting . . .

Much to our surprise, out came a beautiful, burnished cake. It was perfection, buttery layer upon buttery layer of delicate dough; it rose up big and tall and flaky. I remember being absolutely blown away that I had made this thing, this coffee cake. It was so complicated, but it came out right. And that was it: I was crazy about cooking from that moment on. My cousin and I baked for every bake sale and cakewalk after that. We cooked for the family—our older siblings couldn't get enough of our buttery cakes in the mornings when they were nursing hangovers. We cooked every chance we got.

One year, when I was about twelve, Carol and I treated her parents to a formal anniversary dinner. We made cornish game hens and wild rice, we got dressed up and recruited some boys and taught them how to be waiters and had them hold folded towels over their arms—it was very refined. For dessert we were serving the pièce de résistance: cherries jubilee. But at the moment before the boys were to carry it, aflame and glorious, to the dinner table, we hit a snag. We couldn't get the thing to light. Not to save our lives. We kept bringing the matches close to the alcohol on the plate but as soon as we'd get the match really close we'd jerk our heads back—we had read the warning in the recipe and we didn't want to singe our eyelashes. Unfortunately, every time the match got close it would drown in the alcohol and extinguish. (We didn't know then that you have to warm alcohol a little to get it volatile enough to catch fire, though that's the sort of thing you only need to learn once.)

We went through an entire box of kitchen matches trying to get that thing lit, while Gammie and Gampie, Uncle Al and Auntie Frill, waited patiently. By the time we gave up, we had a big pile of ash and sulphur and crêpes and cherries and kirsch. I'm certain the dessert had more sulfur flavor from the matches than the taste of cherries.

Setbacks like those less-than-jubilant cherry crêpes didn't deter me. It was one of dozens of lessons I've learned from failures, like why not to drive all night with your cousin's wedding cake in the back seat of your Maverick while you're flicking ashes from your Newports out the window; unless you want to end up with a gray-speckled cake and have to make new buttercream in a church basement with only a bowl and a whisk, after which the stress of the cake repair will cause you to sleep through the entire ceremony and drink too much at the reception. But that's another story.

Through it all, I remained obsessed. I took all the home ec classes I could—there weren't any cooking schools for kids back then. I worked in a doughnut shop and a pizza joint and took extra classes so I could get out of high school early. I left Michigan for Chicago where I enrolled in chef school at seventeen.

The first time we made Danish dough in pastry class, a light bulb went off in my head. I realized I had made it before, though it took me a second to figure out when. And then that wacky day and night that my cousin and I spent slaving over that coffee cake came rushing back to me: it was my first kitchen triumph!

Curveball
MASAHARU MORIMOTO

Masaharu Morimoto—known to many from his role on Iron
Chef *and* Iron Chef America—*trained and cooked in his hometown of Hiroshima before moving to the United States in the
1980s. In 1993, Barry Wine of the Quilted Giraffe, one of New
York's most famous restaurants at the time, hired Morimoto
to head the sushi bar and Japanese kitchen at the Sony Club, an
exclusive restaurant high atop Sony Corporation's Midtown
headquarters. Just a year later, he was selected to be part of the
opening team at Nobu, where he eventually became executive
chef. In 2001, he opened his first Morimoto restaurant in
Philadelphia's Old City neighborhood, and in January 2006 he
opened his second branch in New York City.*

T HE TWENTY-FIFTH was the day my father, who worked
at a printing press, collected his month's wages. Our family was poor and my parents were at each other's throats constantly, but payday was a happy day in the Morimoto
household. After my father cashed his check, he'd take the fam-

ily out for sushi. It was the only time during the month that we typically ate out. While we were at dinner, my parents were relaxed, even enjoyed themselves. They'd pick up their bickering right where they'd left off the next morning, but during dinner at the sushi restaurant, we were the spitting image of a happy family.

Is it any wonder, then, that I thought becoming a sushi chef was a noble and worthwhile pursuit? The chefs were clean and precise, and they made pleasant dinner conversation with my family from across the sushi bar as they turned out tiny morsels of food that almost magically pacified my parents. The sushi bar was the one place where the problems of real life seemed to wait patiently beyond the door.

The only other place where I felt as good was on the baseball diamond. In high school I played catcher and had a powerful enough swing that I batted cleanup. There was nothing quite like baseball for me. I could escape everything on the field, or at home, glued to the television watching Sadaharu Oh hit home runs for the Tokyo team, the Yomiuri Giants. (I was really a fan of my hometown team, the Hiroshima Carp, but the only time they were on television was when they were playing the Giants, so I ended up following them both.)

At the end of high school, it looked like I was destined to wield a bat, not a knife: the Carp had sent scouts to watch me play and a representative from the team had met with my father to talk about my future. I could not have been more excited about the possibility.

Then, one afternoon, I injured my shoulder at practice. It was a serious tear, and not likely to ever heal completely. The Carp didn't seem any less interested in me, but I knew the situation I'd be getting myself into. If I could recover quickly enough and perform well enough at tryouts, they might keep me around for a couple years. But nobody needs a catcher who can't reliably gun down someone trying to steal second, or a power hitter whose power is gone. I knew that among professional players, the best I could become would be average.

After a few days of soul searching—one does not take walking away from the offer to play professional baseball lightly—I decided I would pursue sushi instead. There was no reason why I couldn't excel at being a sushi chef, I thought, and there was a clear obstacle in my path to being the best baseball player I could be.

I began my apprenticeship at Ichiban Sushi at eighteen, a few weeks after I finished high school. I worked there six days a week and lived right upstairs. I woke up at the crack of dawn, ambled down and into the restaurant's van with my chef to go to the fish market. All day I worked in the restaurant. At the end of the night, I turned out the lights after I had finished cleaning the restaurant and climbed up the stairs to my tiny room to catch a few hours of sleep.

It was a tough and occasionally lonely six years working for chef Oyama. Early on in my training I would sneak out of the restaurant after all my work was done to go drinking with my friends. It was an attempt to make myself feel like I was living a more normal life.

To get out of the restaurant, however, took finessing. Ordinarily I was locked inside every night. To escape I had to shimmy my way through a long, narrow, horizontal window above the cabinets in the kitchen. By the time I made it outside, my clothes were smeared with a thin film of kitchen grease that had settled on the top of the cabinets. And to make sure my getaways went unnoticed, I would shift the van into neutral and push it hundred meters away from the restaurant before I hit the ignition—making sure that I was not only filthy and greasy, but also sweaty, by the time I got to see my friends.

I started out as the dishwasher at Ichiban Sushi and slowly started moving up the ranks. As I did, my focus shifted from sneaking out to see my friends to how I could become the best sushi chef possible. I didn't just want to make the rice *good enough*. I wanted the rice to have the perfect texture, the perfect temperature, and the perfect seasoning. It wasn't enough that I could cut the fish professionally—I wanted to cut the fish artfully. I managed to throw myself headlong into my craft and, by the time I was twenty-five, I opened my own restaurant in downtown Hiroshima.

Was I disappointed that I didn't become a professional baseball player after coming so close? No. Honestly, I couldn't have stood being one of guys on the team that no one pays any attention to, who bats in the low .200s and gets replaced by the first hotshot rookie the team can get its hands on. I wanted to be the best at what I did. And with sushi, I felt like I had a fighting chance.

And a fighting chance it was. Or maybe a battling chance, to use the parlance of *Iron Chef*, the television show that helped propel me to where I am today. In the early nineties I was the chef at Nobu, Nobuyuki Matsuhisa's restaurant in New York—as popular a restaurant then as it is today—when a friend of the producers of *Iron Chef* discovered me.

Since then I have opened my own restaurants, one in Philadelphia, and one most recently in New York. I get to cook for famous baseball players—Hideki Matsui and Derek Jeter, among others—very frequently. But for all that sushi has done for me, there was one moment that confirmed that I had made the right decision back when I was eighteen.

It was 2001 or 2002, just after I had opened Morimoto in Philadelphia and when *Iron Chef* was starting to catch on as a late night hit on the Food Network, when I got a call from someone in the front office of the Seattle Mariners. The Mariners are owned by Nintendo, and the city of Seattle has a large Japanese population, but I still never could have anticipated what they were calling me for. They were inviting me to throw out the first pitch at a Mariners game.

The night of the game was like a boy's fantasy come true: when I was warming up along the left-field stands, throngs of little kids thrust out baseballs and pens, looking for autographs. When my name was announced over the loudspeaker, the crowd cheered me onto the mound. Briefly, I imagined myself as a poor kid from Hiroshima who had broken through the American minor-league system and was embroiled in a tough game in the majors. And then I threw my pitch. It hissed through the air and landed with a satisfying *thwack* in the catcher's mitt. It wasn't a ninety-mile-an-hour fastball, but it was a good, solid strike.

After the pitch, I got to watch the game from a perfect seat—another luxury—right behind home plate. All game long fans, probably fifty people in all, came over for an autograph or to make conversation about *Iron Chef*.

Even if I hadn't hurt my shoulder and had gone on to play professional baseball in Japan, I am almost certain that it never would have taken me across the ocean to Safeco Field, where an audience of American fans would cheer my arrival on the mound. It was sushi that did that for me. And if I ever had a doubt that I had made the wrong decision back when I was eighteen, it was erased from my mind that night, when my pitch hit the catcher's mitt and the umpire stood up and shouted, "Play ball!"

Blame It on the Del Rio
SARA MOULTON

A lifetime food enthusiast, Sara Moulton graduated from the University of Michigan in 1974 and from the Culinary Institute of America in 1977. She worked in restaurants for several years, including a postgraduate stagiaire *with a master chef in Chartres, France. In the early 1980s Moulton cooked at La Tulipe in New York City, and cofounded the New York Women's Culinary Alliance. In 1983 she taught at Peter Kump's New York Cooking School, then took a job in the test kitchen at* Gourmet *magazine, which led to her becoming the magazine's executive chef, a position she holds to this day. In 1995 she became the food editor for* Good Morning America, *making regular on-air appearances. Moulton has hosted two Food Network shows,* Cooking Live *and* Sara's Secrets. *She is the author of two cookbooks, including* Sara's Secrets for Weeknight Meals, *published in 2005.*

D URING THE MIDSEVENTIES, when I was inching my way through the University of Michigan's hippie-dippy

Residential College, the Del Rio was one of the coolest bars in Ann Arbor. The barroom was an airy space with soaring ceilings and exposed brick walls. There was blues or reggae music playing on the house sound system whenever there wasn't a jazz band performing live; it was always packed. I spent all my time hanging out there when I wasn't (or maybe should have been) studying.

The Del Rio served food, too: a short-order menu of bar fare like burgers and Greek salads. And though I'd grown up cooking much more ambitious food than they served at the Del Rio, it was the place where, in some strange way, I came into my own as a cook. Indirectly, and certainly unintentionally, the Del Rio led me to the steps of the Culinary Institute of America, where I got a much more formal culinary education.

I applied for the cook's job at the Del Rio after I heard that they had lost somebody from the kitchen. It seemed like a good way to make a living. I hadn't yet decided that food was going to be the focus of my professional life.

But it had played a huge part in my upbringing. Growing up, I spent summers on my grandmother's farm in Massachusetts where she taught me how to cook classic New England dishes like Johnnycakes and fish chowder. I was a little blimp as a kid, so I was especially interested in helping her with pies and cookies, which I think few kids have the patience for, because of the precision they require. Maybe I should have known I was destined for the kitchen back then.

As a teenager I attended a tough all-girl private school, and all I did was study. My release was cooking with my mom on the weekends. She started traveling to Europe with a friend of hers around the time I was in seventh grade, and when she'd return, we'd cook these over-the-top dinners for my parents and their friends that re-created the food she'd discovered on her trips. When we weren't conjuring a Greek taverna or Italian trattoria in our dining room, we muddled our way through meals out of Craig Claiborne's *The New York Times Cookbook*. By the time I was in twelfth grade my mom and I were a well-oiled entertaining machine.

When I got to Ann Arbor for college in 1970, I started taking it much easier—enjoying a kind of delayed adolescence. I flirted with a few different majors—I might have become a doctor except that I couldn't bear constantly having to give people bad news—and ended up with a BA in literature, in the "history of ideas." As advertised, the hippie era was a pretty carefree time.

But I always paid the bills by cooking, for a while as a private cook for two professors, and for a brief stint at a place called the Halfway Inn (Do restaurants with names like the Halfway Inn exist anywhere besides college towns?) before going to the Del Rio.

It was an unusual place, even in a famously relaxed town like Ann Arbor. Run like a commune of sorts, the Del Rio had two principal owners, but the staff made joint decisions about hiring and firing and all sorts of things. The interview process was intimidating, to say the least: I went in and sat at the end of a long rectangular table. On the other end was everyone who worked at the restaurant—from bouncers to busboys—staring at me. Anyone could ask questions, but the point of the process was to find out if you'd fit in with the rest of the staff. I did. We were all very left wing, very political, into co-ops, good food, and the potent local pot.

The interview was very cordial right up until the end, when one of the bosses abruptly adopted a solemn tone. "Sara, you understand when you are working in the bar you cannot drink. There is no drinking on the job."

I tried to look as penitent as possible and said, "No no no no. No drinking. I get the message." I was fine with that—I wasn't a huge drinker.

On my first day I spent most of the time in the kitchen getting my bearings. I use the term *kitchen* loosely since it was more like a metal-walled walk-in closet. There was a flattop, two burners, and a screen door to the outdoors that was the kitchen's main source of ventilation (and that was also the door my future brother-in-law would knock on when he hit me up for freebies late at night). Right before service began, a waiter shouted that I needed to report to the bar for a "staff meeting." I hurried out of the tiny kitchen, eager to make a good impression.

And what was lined up from one end of the bar to the other? Shot glasses full of tequila. I was hesitant to join in—Were they testing me?—until I saw every other staff member, including the guy who had sternly warned me about drinking on the job, happily slug back their shot. It turned out that whole bit about not drinking was a put-on: *every* night at the Del Rio started with a round of shots.

The menu was simple bar food, with a few flourishes. One was the daily soup special that it was the cooks' responsibility to invent. We all worked from the same basic recipe: start with some butter and onions and garlic and cook them until they soften. Add whatever vegetable the soup was going be—say cauliflower or broccoli—then a jar of soup base (this was not gourmet cooking), and a few gallons of water to dilute it. Simmer, puree, and serve.

Simple enough, right? But I started to develop a reputation for my soups. I was following the basic recipe, but sometimes I'd get a little wild and add some wine or some fresh herbs at the end. I had certainly been aware of the importance of seasoning growing up, when I was throwing those dinner parties with my mother, but it was never a conscious thing. Something clicked for me at the Del Rio. With all that concentrated soup base, I knew that there was already plenty of salt, but if the soup was flat, you could add a little acid—lemon juice or lime juice or some fresh tomato—and really bring it back to life. I had so much fun learning to make and taste and fix those soups that, even though they were mostly soup base and only a little bit me, getting "famous" for making really good soups became important to me. To this day I still love making soups.

And then there was the Det Burger. Det Burgers were one of the signature dishes of the Del Rio, a big mover on the menu and a staff favorite. Det burgers were named after a former cook named Detweiler, who got bored making the same old cheeseburgers again and again and decided to improve them.

I remember Neil Lau, one of the other cooks at the Del Rio at the time and a friend of mine ever since those days, teaching me the secrets of the Det Burger with the solemnity and seri-ousness that a French chef might summon up for *pommes Anna* or crêpes suzette, not a jazzed-up cheeseburger named after an itinerant and long-gone cook at a Michigan bar.

But the Det Burger was indeed serious business at the Del Rio. It started with a thawed, preshaped quarter-pound ham-burger patty, fished out from one of the refrigerated drawers in the kitchen and tossed on the hottest spot on the griddle. You cooked the first side until you saw tiny little beads of blood form, then you'd flip it and hit it with a handful of the Det Mix.

The Det Mix was—Are you ready for this?—desiccated green peppers that had been resuscitated in water, sliced black California olives, and canned mushrooms that had been drained and chopped. That handful of Det Mix was topped with a bit of grilled onion from the pile in the corner of the griddle and a slice of American cheese. Then I'd drizzle a little beer right onto the flattop, and as soon it hit, it would hiss and turn to steam. Throw a domed hood over the burger and a couple minutes later, there it was, the Det Burger, steamed in beer. It was one of the best things on the planet. I never got tired of cooking them.

That was partially on account of one of the few rules that the Del Rio actually enforced: no one could work more than three nights a week. Of course, that suited everybody in the college town just fine. Three nights a week and almost no job feels like drudgery.

While I was content slinging Det Burgers, sharing an apartment with my boyfriend and hanging out at the Del Rio on my nights off, back East, my mother could see that I was treading water. I was making sixty dollars a week, living for my man, and doing just about nothing else.

Still, Mom understood that my cooking job was making me happy, so she wrote to Craig Claiborne, who, through his cookbook, had been our stalwart kitchen companion during my teenage years, and asked, "If my daughter wants to be a serious chef, then what should she do?" He wrote back, and I still have the letter. He said if I wanted to be a serious chef—that was my mother's ambition, not mine at the time—I should go to cooking school. He said I should go to the hotel school in Lausanne or the Culinary Institute of America. (And I think, even today, that women need the advantage of a cooking-school degree when they apply for a kitchen job because, although things have improved, it is still the Dark Ages in professional kitchens.)

At my mother's behest and on Craig Claiborne's recommendation, I applied to the CIA. When I was accepted, I was sort of reluctant about going. Even though I was a feminist, I really liked my man and the laidback life we were living. So I said to him, "Oh no, I really don't want to go . . ."

Bill, then my boyfriend, now my husband, said, "You should go. I'd like to see some other women." It was the seventies and he was quite a Casanova. That made my decision easy: I was out the door and on my way to the Culinary Institute. I passed on the secrets of the Det Burger to my replacement at the Del Rio, packed up my car, and drove back East.

The rest is history. To this day, I can't hear Bob Marley without thinking of that bar. I fell in love with making soups there. And though I've updated the recipe—I don't keep desiccated green peppers around the house—I grill up a batch of juicy Det Burgers at home a few times a year in a Proustian salute to the now-departed Del Rio, the place that inspired my career.

Growing Pains
TAMARA MURPHY

Tamara Murphy worked in a number of New York City restaurants before moving to Seattle in 1988, where she worked at Dominique's, then became executive chef at Campagne, near the Pike Place Market. While at Campagne, she was nominated for the James Beard Foundation's Rising Star Chef of the Year award and named one of the best new chefs in the United States by Food & Wine *magazine. In 1993 she became executive chef of Café Campagne, a sister restaurant to Campagne, and in 1995 she was named Best Chef: Pacific Northwest and Hawaii by the James Beard Foundation. In 1999 she partnered with Bryan Hill, the former general manager and wine director of Campagne, to open Brasa, which has been honored by both* Food & Wine *and* Gourmet *magazines as one of Seattle's top tables.*

GREEN BEANS, TOMATOES, cucumbers, corn: we grew a bounty of vegetables out in the North Carolina countryside where I grew up. And on nights when those vegetables made up the bulk of what was for dinner, I reached for the shiny green can, an omnipresent fixture on the dinner table in my memories of childhood meals, and applied the "parmesan" a little more liberally than I did on other nights.

Back then I thought the reason we ate what we grew in our garden was because we couldn't afford the better stuff in the grocery store. I felt the same way about the bread my mother baked: we had it because it was cheaper than the good, sliced stuffed in colorful plastic bags.

Even though it was a betrayal of my covetous feelings for bagged and sliced bread, I liked helping my mom bake. We lived a car ride away from the nearest neighbor's house, and baking gave me something to do other than bother my brothers or poke around out in the yard.

We would start by making a massive amount of dough—it was my job to sift and measure the flour—because on the days when my mother would bake, she would bake enough sandwich loaves to fill the freezer and last the family a few weeks. Kneading the risen dough was my favorite step. I loved the physical act of beating the dough into submission; I loved that comforting aroma of the instant yeast working full-steam ahead. Back then I couldn't resist pinching off a little piece of the fermenting dough and enjoying the malty-doughy-yeasty flavor, and I still can't today.

Maybe it was that obvious pleasure I took in helping my mother bake that led my parents to buy me an Easy-Bake oven for my tenth birthday. (Though I think it is far more likely that it was just what you bought a ten-year-old girl back in the day—*everyone* I knew had one.)

An Easy-Bake oven is kind of like the lowest-powered toaster oven imaginable: it will get warm, not hot. Electric blankets get hotter than Easy-Bake ovens. Even at that age, I had serious doubts about whether I'd be able to bake bread in it. But, as it turns out, the lessons I'd learn from my Easy-Bake oven were far from easy, and had nothing to do with baking.

The first time I used it, it wasn't for bread. See, I was the kid that brought home every living thing that I thought was hurt or needed food or looked lonely. Wounded squirrels, lost turtles, abandoned baby birds, everything was fair game for my wildlife-saving impulses. At the top of my list were frogs.

One day, one of my very large bullfrogs—he lived in a small wooden box out in the garden—was fidgety and shaking a little. I diagnosed him as "cold." I thought cold frog + warm oven = happy, warm frog. I wanted the frog to be happy.

I ushered him into the belly of the Easy-Bake, and after five minutes, under the bright warm light, he began to secrete a gelatinous mass flecked through with black spots. I was freaked. I shrieked for my mother—it must have sounded like I'd discovered a body under my bed—and she came running.

That was my mother's first opportunity to have a birds-and-the-bees discussion with me: it turned out that he was a she, and she was having tadpoles. I was promptly sent outside, through the garden and out to the creek, where I set the frog and her tadpoles free. I was then instructed to keep animals out of the Easy-Bake. Little did I know how dangerously close I had been to my first dish of slow-roasted frog's legs.

The next time I put the oven to use was on a weekend afternoon, when my parents were off in town and my brothers, who were supposed to be watching me, were out getting themselves into trouble (like they usually did.) While sorting through the collateral materials that had come with the oven, I discovered one of the premixed Easy-Bake packets. The options, I believe, were zucchini bread or chocolate bread. But when I tore open the ingredient envelopes and smelled the mixes, they didn't smell like anything—or certainly not like any of the smells and flavors I associated with bread baking. So I figured I'd just whip up a batch of dough like my mom and I made instead. *That* was what bread was supposed to smell like.

I busied myself in the kitchen: I sifted a few cups of flour into a large, stainless-steel mixing bowl. I didn't know how much yeast my mom put in the dough, but when I saw the tiny amount that was in one of the packets, I figured she probably used a bunch of them. I tore open four and shook them into a bowl of warm water. To all this I added a little sugar, my sifted flour, and a pinch of salt. Then I gave the whole thing a good mixing.

After that, it was time to drape a kitchen towel over the dough and put it on the shelf up above the stove. I didn't know what that step did exactly, but it was one of the steps that my mom always followed when we were baking. I got out the step stool, heaved the bowl full of dough onto the shelf, and went off to busy myself—checking in on my menagerie of pets out in the yard, counting clouds—until the dough was ready to be kneaded. I had no idea, of course, when that was, but I figured I had helped my mother bake enough times that I'd be able to tell when the dough was ready.

I was going about the task with such nonchalance—it was just baking, after all—that I was entirely unprepared for the scene in the kitchen upon my return: the dough had spilled over the rim of the bowl, growing so huge and heavy that it had actually pulled the bowl onto its side as it sagged down onto the stove top. It looked like an animal dragging itself out of a trap and clawing its way toward the door.

In a panic—this had never happened when I baked with mom—I grabbed globs of dough by the fistful, mushed them together, and punched them down. The air hissing out sounded like a tire going flat.

No matter how much air I forced out, there was still no way

my tiny Easy-Bake oven could handle all this dough. And I didn't trust the dough anyway: no, there was no saving this creepy concoction. The important thing was to get rid of the mess. I searched the drawers for a plastic garbage bag large enough to stuff the still-expanding dough into, and then stuffed the doughy bag into the kitchen garbage can. I would take it to the large garbage can outside later, I reasoned, after I'd cleaned up the kitchen.

It took me an hour to complete the task. I swept the flour up off the floor, cleaned my bowl, and wiped the gooey dough off the top of the stove. Things looked good, I thought. The only thing now was to remove the dough from the kitchen pail and stuff it under the other garbage in the outside can.

But as I moved toward the can I saw something that my ten-year-old mind had trouble comprehending. The lid of the can— it was one of those old aluminum trashcans with a foot pedal to lift the lid—was being pushed open by this white bloblike substance. I panicked briefly, before I realized that the blob was the dough creeping out and over the trash.

In desperation, I began scooping it out of the trash and on to the linoleum floor that I'd just cleaned. I had to think quickly: my parents would be home soon and, worse still, my brothers would be home sooner, and this was primo bribe material: if they caught me I'd end up taking over their chores for weeks.

I ran and found a big plastic bag from the garage and began shoving the dough into it. I dragged it across the floor and out through the screen door and toward the garden. On my way I grabbed a shovel.

I stopped between the bushbeans and the cucumbers and sunk the tip of the shovel into the loose, black soil. Working diligently in the fading daylight, I dug a grave to hide my failure. I dug with all the swiftness, care, and determination a ten-year-old could have possibly mustered for the strange and grim task. Once I'd dug a sufficiently big hole, I rolled the aborted loaf in, and covered it over as quickly as I could. As I was patting the dirt down with the back of the shovel, trying to make the swell in the garden's landscape less apparent, my brother turned on the outside porch light and called for me.

"Tamara, you better get your butt in here," he yelled out into the dusky sky, not seeing me there, twenty feet away. "Mom will be home soon and you're supposed to be asleep!"

"I'm coming," I yelled back, doing what little I could to throw my voice and not attract his attention to me, crouched over my garden gravesite, shovel in hand.

I ditched the shovel by the back stairs and, moments after I had flipped off the porch light, I saw the light from the high beams on my parents' car illuminating our driveway. I ran upstairs, gave my teeth a once over with my toothbrush, and ducked under the covers of my bed. That's where I was when they peeked in on me a few minutes later, and I took their softly closing my door as a sign that they had no idea what had transpired while they were out.

The house was quiet when I woke up with a start a few hours later. My imagination was working overtime. What was the dough doing now, in a shallow grave in my family's garden under no one's watch? I crept to the window, pressed my face to the screen, and peered out onto the moonlit backyard, nervously scanning the dirt for a flesh-colored bulge pushing up through the soil.

Backseat Chefs and Other Trials of Opening a Restaurant
CHARLES PHAN

Born in Da Lat, Vietnam, in 1962, Charles Phan and his family left after the war in 1975 and relocated to Guam. It was from Guam that the Phans moved to San Francisco in 1977. Being of Chinese descent, the Phans settled in Chinatown. After stints in the garment and software businesses, Phan turned his attention to food. After a failed attempt at opening a crêperie in a hotel in the Tenderloin, Charles set out to open the Slanted Door. Tapping his design background, built a stylish space where he'd serve a menu of ingredient-driven traditional Vietnamese cooking. Phan's formula of showcasing farm-fresh, local products, preparing everything from scratch, and keeping a limited menu has made the Slanted Door one of San Francisco's most popular restaurants for more than a decade.

I F YOU REALLY love to cook and you think you might like to do it in a restaurant of your own someday, here's my advice: Stay home. Have your friends over for dinner and go nuts. But keep out of the restaurant business.

I wouldn't have known to give you that advice thirteen years ago, when I was in the planning stages of opening the Slanted Door. Back then I was considerably more wide-eyed about the biz: I saw a gaping hole in the San Francisco restaurant scene—there was a need, I thought, for a hip, upscale Asian restaurant that served good food made with good ingredients—so why didn't I just open the place that would fill that hole?

It sounded easy enough. But, as I discovered, there is much to learn between the day you sketch out your plan for the perfect restaurant on a cocktail napkin and the night that you've got a wok in one hand and a phone ringing off the hook in the other.

The first lesson you learn is that your restaurant will take roughly twice as long to build as you think it will—and the process will be about four times costlier than your business plan estimated. It doesn't matter how conservative and careful you are. I had studied architecture at the University of California at Berkeley and worked in the building trades as a teenager. None of it helped. You will miss every deadline and soar way over your budget.

But I never became too discouraged, since taking risks was part of my upbringing. I was raised in a family of entrepreneurs. After we emigrated to the United States from Da Lat in Vietnam, leaving behind almost everything we owned, we had to start all over again. For a while my dad was the janitor at an Irish pub and my mother worked in a sewing shop. Once they had saved a little money, they did their best to make it grow: my dad started a beef jerky business (though he knew nothing of the beef jerky business), and my mother started her own sewing shop. From there they made—and lost, and made, and lost—their fortunes. And along the way they taught me the value of persistence.

Or maybe I should say the *necessity* of persistence. Before even building the restaurant, I must have spent months at the buildings department in San Francisco. Every other day I would show up with my architectural drawings, hoping to get approval so I could start construction—and every time there was some problem. This wasn't to spec, that wasn't to code, the ventilation was wrong. Eventually one of the guys got so sick of seeing me that he sat down with my drawings and worked his pencil down to a stub putting in minor details here and there that would bring the design up to code. I brought back a corrected batch of renderings the next week and got the stamp of approval. Finally, I could begin building the restaurant.

Mind you, the approval I was seeking for the original Slanted Door (we've moved twice since then) was not for some daring architectural space. It was a sliver of a restaurant in the Mission district that was lofty, minimalist, and hand built.

And it was largely my hands that built it. Plywood, because it was affordable, played a big part in my design scheme. Still, even with plywood, there were hiccups: I had a plan for a long banquette that would run the length of the space, but when I realized I could only afford to buy eight-foot sheets of plywood, I had to hide how they were joined with metal bands. (I remember an early customer commenting on how cool that detail was . . . If she only knew why it was there.)

Overspending was a constant danger. Even before I'd cost-efficiently tricked out the banquette with metalwork, I had burned through my initial forty thousand dollars. This amount—my life savings plus what I could borrow from the bank—only made it halfway through tiling the kitchen floor. In desperation I had to persuade my brother to get a new credit card for me so that I could max it out and buy the rest of the tiles. And soon I had to go to every one of my cousins with similar requests, for lighting, for stoves, for pots and pans. Pretty much my entire family owned a little piece of the restaurant when it opened. And many of them now work there—I've got twenty-three family members on the payroll today.

The hardest one to get was the first one: my aunt. She is an excellent cook and a hard worker. And after opening night at the restaurant went haywire, I realized that I could not single-handedly cook, serve, and clean. So I went to my aunt and made the case that she should quit her garment industry job—she was working as a seamstress—and come and cook for me. She was not easily persuaded. Come and cook for her nephew who had no idea how to run a restaurant, her nephew who had dragged all of his cousins into debt?

Eventually she agreed, reasoning that I would bankrupt the family if I didn't have someone to help. She said she could give me six months in the kitchen. I browbeat one of my brothers into coming onboard, too, and he and I shared the glamorous dishwasher-cook-server-anything-that-needed-to-be-done role. My team of three ran the restaurant for well into the first year.

The good news at that point was that every night the restaurant was packed. You might think that a built, staffed, and busy restaurant would signal that I had gotten over the hump, but it didn't. That was partially because I had never cooked professionally before. I had cooked for almost as long as I can remember. After my family emigrated to the States, one of my primary responsibilities as a child was to get dinner together for my family every night. As there were ten people in our household—including my aunts and uncles—that meant I had done a fair amount of cooking.

But never having cooked professionally meant that I didn't know how to buy my ingredients like a professional. I was inspired to open the Slanted Door in part by places like Alice Waters's Chez Panisse, and I was determined to get local distributors to let me open a wholesale account with them, but it was tough because my restaurant was so small.

Finally, I persuaded Stanley of Stanley Produce to start doing business with me. But when he asked me what I wanted for the restaurant he'd ask me in some secret marketspeak that I didn't know. For example, when someone asks you for the first time, "How much grass do you want, and do you want it standard or pencil?" and doesn't explain that they're talking about a quantity of either thick or thin asparagus, it can throw you for a loop.

But in time I learned the lingo. And I learned that if I overslept after a hard night at the restaurant—or at the bar—that the farmers would pack up their trucks regardless and leave my day's allotment of produce at the end of the pier in a disgraceful, unattended-to stack. There seemed to be no end to the lessons. Once you get a restaurant up and running, there is a whole new set of skills to learn.

There is so much to be aware of when you run a restaurant. I began to see minor things, like an errant straw wrapper on the floor from across the room, and think, no one was going to walk into my restaurant and notice that instead of the decor or the food or the music. Every detail, every scrap of trash, every mildly disgruntled customer needed my attention.

And I learned that every night brings its own challenges.

Like the time, early in the history of the Slanted Door, when in the middle of service I saw a slight deceleration in the flow of people into the restaurant. I knew that it was going to be my one chance all night to take a restroom break. So I took it. I was out of the kitchen for maybe ninety seconds, and when I came back, I saw a tall, ruddy-faced white guy in a chef's coat barking orders at my aunt and my brother. He was demanding that they get the food out faster. And then he turned and shouted at a guest sitting nearby for some imagined transgression against him, the chef.

Was this a nightmare? And if not—I pinched myself to be sure—then what the hell was going on? There were no white guys working in my restaurant. There was nobody I wasn't related to by blood working in my restaurant. And then it suddenly hit me: He was a cook all right, but not in my place. He must have just gotten fired from another restaurant and, after getting wildly drunk, come here. But none of the back story really mattered. What did was that this guy was yelling at my family and my customers in my kitchen. This guy had to get the fuck out of my restaurant *now*.

I walked over to him and, as calmly as I could, asked him to leave. The second he turned to me, barking something about me getting back in the kitchen—which is where I was headed, though not under his orders—I grabbed him by his starched white chef's jacket and pushed him, stumbling backward, flailing and yelling, out through the door and onto the street.

I slammed the door behind me and made my way to the kitchen, noticing that the guy had nicked my face and I was bleeding a little bit. As I composed myself, wondering how far behind I was because of that jackass's shenanigans, one of the customers sitting nearby asked me, with a touch of surprise in her voice, "Did you fire that guy just like that?"

I smiled at her and considered explaining what had really happened. But I thought better of it. "Yes," I said. Then I turned around, fired up a wok, and got cooking. It's what I had opened the restaurant to do, after all.

The Bad Egg
MICHEL RICHARD

A pioneer in French/California cuisine, Michel Richard's first kitchen job was as an apprentice in a patisserie in the Champagne region of France. His next stop was Gaston Lenôtre's esteemed pastry shop in Paris. In 1975 he moved to Sante Fe, then, in 1977, to Los Angeles, where he opened his own eponymous restaurant. In 1987 he launched Citrus, and in 1988 was inducted into the James Beard Foundation's Who's Who in American Food and Beverage. A year later he opened Citronelle in Santa Barbara, California, followed by Bistro M in San Francisco and two other Citronelles in Baltimore and Philadelphia. In 1994 he opened a Citronelle at the Latham Hotel in Washington, D.C., and four years later, he moved there to man the stoves full time. He has been nominated for the James Beard Foundation's Chef of the Year award five times, most recently in 2006, and was the winner of the Best Chef: California & Hawaii in 1992. Richard is the author of two books: Cooking at Home with a French Accent, *published in 1993, and* Happy in the Kitchen, *published in 2006.*

I STARTED COOKING WHEN I was fourteen, in a farm-country town called Carignan of France. It was a three-year apprenticeship at Patisserie Sauvage (now long gone), under Monsieur Jacques, the chef, who was as brutal with his young charges as the name of his pastry shop.

Monsieur Jacques was stern. There were rules for everything you did in his kitchen. One I would learn very well was to taste and smell every ingredient you cooked with. This wasn't just him being strict; there was a good reason for it. Back in the early sixties everything didn't arrive off a truck clean and refrigerated with spoilage dates, something that we count on today. The eggs, for example, were gathered from the farms in the area, and they'd come in wet with dew, wrapped in newspaper. They were very fresh and very good quality. But we were warned in no un-certain terms to smell every egg, because occasionally one would be off. It was easy to pick out, since it smelled strongly of sulfur. The dangerous egg, however, the egg we lived in fear of in Mon-sieur Jacques's kitchen, was the stealthy *oeuf paille*.

An *oeuf paille* is an egg that has been laying around for a couple days too long on hay that is damp and humid, and it ab-sorbs the aroma and flavor of the moist hay. It imparts a uniquely unpleasant taste to whatever you cook with it. When you break the egg, it will look normal, but will emit a subtly foul smell. You have to be on the lookout for it because, unlike the obvious stench of sulfurous eggs, it is easy to miss an *oeuf paille*. And unfortunately, if you *do* miss it, the rank flavor of just one of these bad eggs will dominate the flavor of a thou-sand good eggs that you are using.

Since we were often working with tremendous quantities of eggs to make batches of pastry cream, we were taught to break five eggs in a small bowl, smell them, then add the eggs to a larger batch. Break five, smell, and transfer to a larger bowl, break five, smell, and transfer, until you have enough eggs for your recipe. You then cook them in four-liter batches, set them aside to cool, and finally add them all together into one large mixer. It was repetitious and tedious, but we were told that if you were not careful to taste and smell everything that you were cooking with, you could ruin a whole batch of pastry.

One day, in the spring, I was making pastry cream to fill twelve hundred cream puffs. The cream puffs were to be assembled into twenty *croquembouches*—those towers of cream puffs, encased in spun sugar, that almost look like Christmas trees—for Sunday. It was the Sunday when the church in town was to have the confirmation ceremony for all the young children, and afterward most of the families were coming to pick up *croquembouches* to help celebrate the occasion.

I started on the pastry and the pastry cream for the cream puffs the night before and worked alone through the night breaking my eggs, making my cream. By morning I had filled the twelve hundred cream puffs from my pastry bag, assembled them into tall *croquembouches*, and wrapped them in spun sugar. They were truly a sight to behold and an accomplishment, I thought, for a fourteen-year-old apprentice.

Shortly after the sun rose, so did my boss. He came in, gruff as usual, and tasted one of my leftover cream puffs. His face quickly reddened and he screamed: "Did you smell the eggs?"

"*Oui*, chef." And I had. I had smelled the eggs. Okay, maybe not every egg. Maybe I missed a few eggs when I was daydreaming in the middle of the night about Brigitte Bardot, but almost every egg.

He grew more furious and shouted, "Did you taste the cream?"

"*Oui*, chef." I had tasted the cream. Or I was fairly sure I had tasted *most* of the cream.

"Liar!" he screamed at me.

Still confident, I popped one of the cream puffs into my mouth . . . and I immediately tasted it: the flavor of an *oeuf paille*. All of my work was for nothing. I could not believe it. I wanted to die.

And in a flash twenty *croquembouches* went into the garbage. The chef could barely look at me; whenever he did, he would start screaming again.

We had to redo everything from scratch, the chef and I. And even with us working from the crack of dawn, it took until the afternoon to remake the twenty giant towers of pastry. Everyone in the village came into the pastry shop merry, their sons or daughters had been confirmed, and grew angry very soon when they found out that it was going to be hours before their *croquembouches* would be ready. Some people remained in the shop for three hours, waiting for us to remake their Sunday cakes. I was certain that my village was ready to hang me, the little pastry chef. I was sure it was the end of my life.

Since then I have smelled every egg I have ever used. I smell eggs when I am making an omelet for myself at home; I smell the eggs we use at Citronelle. Even here, in America, where I haven't seen a bad egg in thirty-two years, I still smell my eggs. That day I learned to taste everything and it was a lesson I have never forgotten.

If you are someone who remembers waiting for your *croquembouche* for three hours after church one Sunday in May

1962, I am the one responsible! I am the one who messed it up. I apologize. And I promise now, like I did to myself over and over that horrible afternoon, that I will never make the same mistake again.

Walking on Eggshells
ERIC RIPERT

In 1995, as executive chef of Le Bernardin, Eric Ripert became one of an elite group of chefs to earn four stars from the New York Times. *In 2006 the restaurant's excellence was reaffirmed when it was one of only four to be awarded three stars in the* Michelin Guide's *first American edition. Prior to arriving at Le Bernardin, Ripert studied at the culinary institute in Perpignan, and worked at some of the world's finest restaurants including La Tour D'Argent and Jamin in Paris, and Jean-Louis at the Watergate Hotel in Washington, D.C. He is the author of two cookbooks:* Le Bernardin Cookbook *and* A Return to Cooking.

M Y FIRST YEAR of culinary school was wrapping up, and summer was on the horizon. Like any fifteen- and sixteen-year-old school kids, (culinary school in France can be like a vocational high school in the States) my classmates and I were excited to get out of the classroom kitchens and get our summers started.

Unlike the way most teenagers spend their summers, however, we were going to be working. Hard. The cooking school arranged summer externships for all of its students, sending them to every corner of France. We didn't choose the externships we wanted, the way kids do today, and so the afternoon that we were scheduled to receive our assignments, the school was abuzz with anticipation. The range of places we could be sent was considerable, and there were famous favorites—and equally infamous nightmares. Everyone was talking animatedly, shouting and laughing, as we learned where we would be spending the next few months.

I had been assigned to a restaurant called Le Sardinal—a sardinal is a boat that goes out for sardines—in Banyuls, not terribly far from Andorra, where I grew up. When I cheerfully volunteered where I was going to the older kids—the restaurant was located near the beach in the South of France, it seemed to me like a pretty good place to spend a summer—they recoiled in disbelief. "Le Sardinal! The chef is *nuts* there! I can't believe you're going to do it."

After I heard the same the thing from a few of my schoolmates, I started to get scared. I had recently had a disastrous turn as the sommelier in the school's restaurant; one afternoon, I dropped a tray full of drinks on a customer, then doused his wife with a glass of wine and, as unimaginable as it is, managed to soak the gentleman a second time with the leftover liquid that had pooled in my waiter's tray. I thought for sure my teachers were sending me to this place out of vengeance for having performed so badly that day.

I brought my concerns up to one of the more sympathetic instructors. "Everybody is telling me this is a terrible place," I told him, "and that the chef is completely crazy."

My teacher dismissed my misgivings with a wave of his hand and reassured me that it was one of the best assignments I could have landed. "It's very hands-on," he told me, "and it's very hard core. The chef is really there cooking in the kitchen. You'll see he has a big mouth—he will scream a lot, but they're all like that. The important thing is that you will be there, beside him, learning firsthand."

He had a point—at some of the really fancy Michelin-starred restaurants you're one of forty guys and you spend months peeling potatoes, chopping onions, and turning carrots. At Le Sardinal at least I'd be cooking, really cooking, not just cleaning vegetables for the entire summer. The kitchen would actually need me, would depend upon me to be successful. With my teacher's encouragement, I got myself excited about the challenge that was ahead of me, which wasn't all that hard, since it was my first chance to work in a restaurant and I had dreamed about becoming a chef since I was a little kid.

A few weeks later, I made my way to Le Sardinal. It was an attractive, well-maintained place with a terrace that overlooked the harbor; whenever the weather was nice, it was jam packed with people. The owner was a friendly man—on weekends he would play his saxophone in the dining room—and his wife worked as the restaurant's cashier.

They both insisted that I have lunch at the restaurant before I started my externship, which was certainly generous of them. It wasn't one-star Michelin food or anything like that, but it was good and well prepared, and I enjoyed my lunch plenty. While I was eating, the owner told me about the chef: he was classically trained, and had worked for a number of years at a casino in Portugal—back when casinos still were considered prestigious—before he'd taken over the kitchen at Le Sardinal. After lunch, I went into the kitchen to meet him.

The chef was, in a word, round. Round belly, round head, meaty round fists—he was round everywhere. He had a bushy mustache and wore a tall white toque atop his head. If you wanted a picture of a "chef" to sell a can of soup or something, this guy was it.

We chatted briefly. He addressed me like I was an adult, which is always flattering to a sixteen-year-old, and explained that there were only going to be three or four of us in the kitchen—and that we'd be serving three hundred guests a night when the season got going. So he wanted me to come back that next day for lunch, observe, and then jump into the action.

I was excited and a little bit puzzled about all the warnings I had received about the guy from my classmates back at school. Maybe they were just giving me a hard time, I thought. I carried my bags up to my room—it was tiny, as the rooms that a restaurant provides its employees unfailingly are—and met the maître d', who would be sharing the room with me. He seemed like a decent guy, friendly enough. The next morning we headed into the restaurant together.

The chef stuck me in a corner to observe lunch service and told me he'd throw me in the mix that night. For now I was just to watch and learn.

The first thing I learned, however, as the orders started coming in from the dining room, was the astonishing speed with which the chef grew agitated. Within minutes, he was fuming—enraged, it seemed, by the simple fact that people wanted food from the kitchen. Soon he progressed into outright fury, yelling and slamming things and threatening everyone, a puzzling Jekyll and Hyde–like change from his calm, thoughtful demeanor just twenty minutes earlier. And then, with absolutely no warning—and no reason that was obvious to me—he grabbed a stack of *torpilleurs*—these silver, ovular platters large enough to serve a whole fish on—raised five or six of them above his head with both hands, and *whack!* He slammed them down on the maître d's head.

The maître d' collapsed on the floor. Waiters scattered. The cooks quieted down. I just stood there, sixteen, silent, and shocked, thinking, What just happened?

The owner rushed in, swept my new roommate off the floor, and sent him off to the hospital. He spewed platitudes, trying to quell the unease in the kitchen as the chef grabbed up his knives, tore off his toque, and stormed out, punctuating his exit with the announcement that he was finished with Le Sardinal. (He wasn't, I'd later learn, he just had an aggravated sense of drama when he pitched his fits.)

By dinner he was back in the kitchen again and the maître d', we were told, was okay. He was spending the night at the hospital, but would return the following day. As a first impression, I'd say the first few hours in the kitchen had not gone so well.

Despite the fact that the chef spent most of his time during service yelling (I comforted myself by thinking, They're all like that, as my instructor at school had told me), he was patient with me when demonstrating dishes or techniques. I considered myself lucky to have his expert attention. And as I began to get the hang of what it actually meant to be part of a kitchen, the chef gave me more responsibilities. Day by day the pressure increased, but I was handling it well. As a consequence, he and I developed a decent working relationship—at least during the times when he wasn't screaming for another order of grilled fish. I even forgave him for knocking out the maître d', who had made it a habit to return to our room at the crack of dawn every night, blind drunk, where he would throw up in the corner before passing out on the floor.

Much of the work I was responsible for during the first

month at Le Sardinal was reinforcing and stocking the restaurant's larder. We did as much as we could in advance, so that when the really busy summer weeks arrived, we could churn the food out. It's a very old fashioned way of running a restaurant—you receive mushrooms one day, tons of mushrooms, and for the next three days you clean them, cook them, put them in containers, freeze them, and so on. Then, when you're slammed in the middle of service in the summer, you've got the mushrooms prepared and ready to use.

One morning I came into work and there were ducks everywhere, hundreds of ducks. The place was covered in ducks. The chef told me, "Eric, your duty today is to butcher these ducks. Turn the legs into confit and freeze the breast meat."

So I got down to business: cutting up ducks and ducks and yet more ducks. I tossed leg after leg into a container where I'd eventually salt and season them, and begin the curing process to turn them into duck confit. As for the breasts, I placed them into giant freezer bags that I'd seal once they were nearly bursting with meat, and then carry the huge, twenty-five-pound bags down to the walk-in freezer. I made fast work of the task and was pleased with myself. I thought I really had the hang of this cooking thing down.

Fast forward to July, the height of the summer season, when the restaurant was really busy, doing a couple of hundred covers a day. In the middle of lunch, we started running low on supplies for a duck dish we were serving, and the chef told me to run downstairs and pull out five duck breasts from the freezer so that we could make it through service.

I dutifully sprinted downstairs to my stash of duck breasts to fulfill his wishes. Except, since I hadn't given much thought to why I was doing what I was doing when I was butchering those ducks, it was impossible for me to return upstairs to the chef with five duck breasts. Or ten duck breasts. Or even twenty duck breasts. What I had—what the restaurant had—were five giant plastic-wrapped boulders of frozen duck breasts, fifty or more to a frozen bundle. I knew I had fucked up. And although I was plenty afraid of the chef, what could I do? There was nowhere to run. So I went back upstairs with one of the massive bags in my arms and said, "Chef, we have a problem: all the breasts are stuck together."

He visibly reddened. There was an uncharacteristic silence for a second—and then he erupted. He hurled every epithet in his repertory toward me as he rushed me with his chef's knife. I dropped the frozen boulder of duck in his path and ran. Luckily, since I was a skinny young kid and he was a fat old chef, I escaped. Later on that afternoon, while I was hiding out downstairs in the prep area, he sent one of the cooks as a peacemaker to find me and tell me he wanted to talk.

I tried to keep a few feet between us when I went upstairs to meet with him, just in case he pulled out that knife again, but he was remarkably calm. "I'm going to forgive you, Eric," he said. "But that was a big mistake. You should have thought about it logically. Why didn't you wrap them one by one? What kitchen could ever need this?" He gestured disapprovingly toward my thawing boulder of duck breasts, "You've got to be focused. You just did it like you were a machine, you didn't *think*. You have to use your head in the kitchen."

I was appropriately contrite, and then we got to my punishment: "This afternoon you are going to clean the salamander."

Salamanders are the high-powered cousins of broilers that restaurants use—and they get a *lot* of use. By the looks of it, the one at Le Sardinal had never been cleaned. It was disgusting, full of blackened grease and old charred fat. I didn't know what I was going to do: cleaning it would be impossible. The chef, however, managed to make the task even more Herculean when he instructed, "Use only steel wool and rags to scrub it clean. No soap. Certainly no water. Until it's spotless, you are not leaving this kitchen."

The chef left for his afternoon break and, after about thirty seconds of fruitless scrubbing, I knew I was either going to spend the next week slaving away on this crusted-over piece of filth or I was going to have to get creative before the chef returned. I opted for the latter option.

I mixed up a cleaning-fluid cocktail from the bottles and jars and jugs stashed under the dishwasher's sink that would probably melt flesh from the bone. I doused the salamander with it and went downstairs to do some prep work, and also to escape from the overpowering smell of my concoction. The chef usually took an hour-long break, so I figured I'd give the stuff thirty minutes to work whatever magic it could and then finish the rest by hand.

After half an hour I went back upstairs, grabbed the spray attachment on the dishwasher's sink and hosed the salamander down from five feet away. To my amazement, as the foamy grime disappeared in the stream of steaming hot water, I saw that my potion worked better than I could have ever imagined: the thing was sparkling clean. It looked brand new. I toweled it off, patted myself on the back for figuring a way out of the jam I'd gotten myself into, and went back to prepping.

When the chef returned from his break, he walked into the kitchen, suspiciously eyed me not cleaning the salamander, and then went over to the machine to inspect my work. He circled around it, hands behind his back, one eyebrow raised. But there were no two ways about it. The thing was clean.

"Excellent," he said. "You got it cleaned. And fast! You've learned." Then he began to lecture me on how important it is to learn discipline and to learn hardship and so on and so on.

I started to drift off a little as he went on with the chefly prattle . . . That is, until he said, "You didn't use water on it, right?"

"No." I had, of course. I had soaked the thing. And now I realized why I was supposed to use elbow grease alone: it was an electric salamander. My throat tightened.

"You're sure you didn't?" He was being coy and maybe even playful at this point—he might have been impressed with himself for scaring his young charge into working so diligently and quickly.

"No, chef." I couldn't help myself. I couldn't tell him the truth.

So he reached over and flipped the salamander on and—zzzzzzz—the current started running through his hand. Worse still, he couldn't get his hand out or away—he was stuck to thing, stuck getting shocked. With me standing there right in front of him, paralyzed with fear and responsible for it.

Luckily, the sous chef had the presence of mind to run and throw the jumper, cutting off all the electricity to the kitchen. As soon as he hit it, the chef collapsed to the floor like a sack of potatoes.

I was waiting for him to regain his strength and come after me full force—and I was ready to take it. I deserved it. But he didn't: he just lifted himself up, gave me the most piercing, dirty look that's ever been directed my way, and silently hobbled off to regain his composure. That was the end of it. We didn't talk about it. I was never punished, reprimanded, or confronted about the incident.

But for as much as the other cooks and I privately laughed about it—and you did need something to laugh about with a chef like this—I felt terrible. Because what I did was stupid, dishonest, and unprofessional. Even as a sixteen-year-old I knew that. And perhaps because the chef didn't slap me with a pan or hurl a mountain of soup bowls at me, I didn't have anywhere to displace my feelings: I had to confront how I'd behaved and change the way I worked in the kitchen.

The incident with the salamander didn't stop the chef from giving us hell—I'm sure nothing could actually have stopped that—but he never singled me out again. I'd like to say it was because he was afraid of me, but I know that wasn't the case: he could have broken me in two. It's probably because I did a lot of growing up in that one afternoon, and for the rest of the summer I worked hard to show him that I could hack it.

And as to whether or not I was sent to Le Sardinal to get discipline beaten into me or just because it's the lot I happened to draw, I'll never know.

Christmas in Paris
MICHEL ROUX

A native of England, and son of legendary chef Albert Roux, Michel Roux worked in a number of kitchens in France, London, and Hong Kong before becoming chef of Roux Restaurants, London, in 1985, a position in which he oversaw the kitchens of Roux Patisserie, Roux Lamartine, Le Poulbot, and Le Gamin. In 1991 he became chef de cuisine of Le Gavroche, which was founded by his father and uncle, Michel, in 1967. Under his auspices, Le Gavroche has received numerous honors, including the Award of Excellence of the Carlton London Restaurant Awards, the Restaurateurs' Restaurant of the Year award, and the Moët & Chandon London Restaurant Award for Outstanding Front of the House. (Le Gavroche was also the first UK restaurant to be awarded one, two, and three Michelin stars.) Roux has been a business columnist, and has authored four books, Le Gavroche Cookbook, The Marathon Chef, Matching Food & Wine, and Vin de Constance.

T O B E B O R N into a family of chefs is to never be left wanting for advice. My father and my uncle both believed that the best way to begin a career in the kitchen is to immerse yourself in the world of pastry, because its necessarily intense and exacting focus on technique fosters a discipline that will benefit any and all cooking you do for the rest of your life.

So it was that in 1976, at the age of sixteen, I left school in London to travel to Paris and work in a pastry shop. Not just any pastry shop: it was the best in all of France, and as such perhaps the best in the world at the time. (Appropriately enough, the space that once housed the shop is now home to the shop of another pastry luminary, Pierre Hermé.)

The shop was in the Fifteenth Arrondissement on Rue Vaugirard. It was the very model of a Parisian pastry shop, a scrupulously clean, romantically lit, marbled shrine to the art of baking and the pleasure of sweets.

The chef, *maître patissier* Hellegouarche, was a big, strong, massive bear of a man, about six feet tall, balding, with a loud, bellowing voice, which he rarely raised. He didn't have to: he had the respect of all of us because he led by stellar, unwavering example. He was a true master who could perform any task in the kitchen at the drop of a hat; a truth proved over and over because of his penchant for filling in personally for sick or vacationing employees, doing their jobs with joy and passion.

In short, M. Hellegouarche was larger than life, a person we thought of as you might a character in a play, or from a film, an impression heightened by his broad smile that revealed numerous silver-crowned teeth, probably acquired from working in such a sugar-rich environment.

The chef's wife was petite and always immaculate, exuding the glamour, style, refinement, and femininity typical of French Parisienne women. She ran the front of the house, and she was just as strict as her husband: in the morning, before we opened for business, her brigade of counter girls, all dressed up in their frilly little uniforms, lined up for inspection whereupon Mme Hellegouarche would pass by them like a general to ensure they were just as neat and lovely as the orderly lines of pastries that filled our windows and shelves.

I learned a lot from M. Hellegouarche. Obviously, I gleaned all the promised knowledge that a pastry education was to confer upon me. Not just the technique, but also the organization of the kitchen: located in the back of the store, it had stainless-steel work surfaces everywhere, big baking ovens with long, pull-down doors, and a separate ice-cream-making area. There was also a cellar for stored items, such as flour, sugar, and fifty-kilo sacks of almonds that, as you'll soon learn, can be used to teach more than cooking.

But there are other, less predictable lessons one learns in two years' time in a kitchen like that.

For instance, all culinary students have it drilled into their heads not to be wasteful. It's one thing to be told this in a classroom and quite another to see it applied in the real world.

I had a dramatic illustration of this ideal one Christmas when the kitchen had produced an enormous amount of pear cream—about one hundred liters I'd say—in preparation for making charlottes. Two cooks were carrying the unwieldy stainless-steel vat of cream into the main walk-in refrigerator. They disappeared inside, then we heard a loud clanging, banging sound ring out through the kitchen, the kind of noise after which any caring soul would ask, "Is everything all right?"

We all looked over with concern just in time to see M. Hellegouarche emerge from the walk-in, covered from head to toe in pear cream.

I'm not quite sure where he was standing to produce this

result—perhaps the cooks were trying to set the vat on an inadvisably high shelf—but it was so incongruous in the otherwise perfect kitchen that we all burst out laughing.

But not M. Hellegouarche. Ever the professional, he kept calm, and in his firm commander's voice, spoke from beneath the glop that encased him: "Quickly, quickly, let's save the cream."

Following his instructions, we each took a plastic scraper in one hand and a small bowl in the other, scraping the cream off M. Hellegouarche and into the bowls, then passing it through a sieve into one large bowl and transferring it to a clean stainless-steel vat.

Under M. Hellegouarche I also learned that being a truly strong leader means working at least as hard as your troops.

That same Christmas season, we worked a grueling schedule. The week leading up to Christmas Day was pandemonium, we only slept four or five hours on any given night, so the entire brigade became more and more sleep-deprived as the twenty-fifth drew closer.

On Christmas Eve, we all worked straight through until eleven o'clock in the evening, preparing pastries for one of the busiest days of the year.

When eleven o'clock rolled around, M. Hellegouarche announced: "All right, lads, I've prepared you a meal."

We were in disbelief. He was always there, right alongside us. How had he managed to prepare a dinner as well?

We stepped out into the public area of the shop and, amazingly, he and his wife had laid a beautiful table. I remember it as though it were yesterday: there was roast beef, potatoes, vegetables glistening with butter, and several bottles of wine, already uncorked and ready to be poured.

We all sat down and ate like I imagine soldiers eat—with an

intensity born of fatigue and stress—pouring and drinking an ungodly amount of wine, unabashedly helping ourselves to seconds of *everything*, and laughing hard at even the most meager joke.

The meal only took about forty-five minutes, but it was such a pleasure to be nurtured like this. We were exhausted, but now we were ready for the onslaught of Christmas Day.

We were also ready to go home to our flats for our daily ration of sleep, but M. Hellegouarche hit us with a surprise.

"Okay, lads. Fifteen minutes' break, and I'll see you all back in the kitchen."

I was shocked, but only for a moment. Because if M. Hellegouarche needed me, then I was there for him—we all were—especially since we all knew that he would work with us right though to sunrise.

I had a cigarette, changed into some clean whites, and baked my way into Christmas morning. The shop opened at seven, and closed at midday. I went to visit some family in Paris, and I was a zombie.

I don't remember the family visit at all, except for one detail: I didn't stay long.

Because I had to be back at work at six in the morning on the twenty-sixth.

Although M. Hellegouarche preferred to lead by example, when the example didn't produce the desired behavior, he could also be quite the stern taskmaster. Nothing coaxed out the disciplinarian in him more than tardiness. He simply couldn't countenance lateness, by anyone, or for any reason, and this is why I've never forgotten those gargantuan sacks of almonds.

Now, I've always considered myself responsible, even at the young age at which I arrived in Paris. But I was also a typical seventeen-year-old boy.

Each year the shop took on two apprentices, so my primary social circle consisted of myself and my contemporary, plus the two eighteen-year-olds who had been there since the previous year. The four of us lived in a flat just five minutes by foot from the shop. When we weren't immersed in pastry, we were enjoying the sheer bliss of being in a wonderful, vibrant city like Paris. We were out every night and often didn't come home at all. In fact, there was a local bar, frequented by "ladies of the night," where we often ended our evenings, having one last drink before running off for a quick coffee en route to the shop.

You can live like that when you're seventeen and get away with it.

Most of the time.

The first time you were late in M. Hellegouarche's shop, you got a warning. The second time, you got another warning.

If you were late a third time, then you would hear him bellow the dreaded words, "That's it: The bag of almonds tonight is yours."

He was referring to what was a legendary corrective measure at his shop, remembered painfully, I'm sure, by anyone who ever worked for him: your punishment was to peel an entire fifty-kilo bag, and to do so *after* working a full day in the kitchen.

On two separate occasions, after late nights on the town, when I lingered too long over my morning coffee, I came running into the shop to find that the minute hand on the wall clock had cleared the hour mark. There was no point in even *hoping* that

M. Hellegouarche wasn't there, because *he* was always on time.

My employer would look up from his work and matter-of-factly inform me to consider myself warned.

The third time I was late—for the same reason of course—I earned my first night with the almonds. There was no getting around it. Because M. Hellegouarche would stay there with you to the bitter end, a logical and, I must say, admirable extension of his work ethic.

Peeling almonds is a real bastard of a job: the only way to do it is to blanch them for a few seconds in boiling water, drain them, and while they're still warm, squeeze them between your thumb and forefinger until the fleshy almond pops out of the rough brown skin.

Peeling fifty kilos of almonds takes quite a toll: after the first twenty-five kilos, your thumb and forefinger get raw and so numb that you need to watch your every movement, trusting your eyes in place of your diminished sense of touch.

At thirty-five kilos, you begin to curse yourself, because whatever it was that made you late could not possibly have been worth this torture. Had I really needed one more drink? Could I not have survived the day without my beloved sunrise coffee? How foolish!

At about forty kilos, your fingers—and I'm not exaggerating here—begin to bleed.

By the fiftieth kilo, you are left with real mental and physical scars.

Most people are never late after a night with the almonds, but—seventeen-year-old that I was—I was late one more time.

So I peeled a total of one hundred kilos.

And I did so without a word, or thought, of complaint.

I've never forgotten M. Hellegouarche. His impressive bearing, the respect he commanded, or those almonds.

I don't use the same punishment in my kitchen. If somebody requires discipline, I'll make them stay late and clean the stove, or something like that.

But I'm never tardy myself, even though I'm running the show, so to speak. If I even begin to suspect that I might get to the restaurant later than I'm expected there, I feel a tingling sensation in my thumb and forefinger, and pick up the pace as thoughts of peeling almonds come freshly to mind all over again.

Catching the Wave
CHRIS SCHLESINGER

Chris Schlesinger was born and raised in Virginia, where he first developed his love for barbecue, spicy food, and live-fire cooking. He opened his first restaurant, East Coast Grill, in 1985, and tripled the ever-popular spot's size (and shifted its focus from barbecue to seafood) in 1996, the year he was named Best Chef: Northeast by the James Beard Foundation. He is the coauthor with John Willoughby of several cookbooks including the James Beard Cookbook Award–winning The Thrill of the Grill *and, most recently,* Let the Flames Begin.

D URING THE SUMMER after I dropped out of college, my sister came home one afternoon and told me that all the cooks at the restaurant where she waited tables had walked out.

She said that if I wanted a job cooking she was pretty sure they couldn't turn me down. I said I wasn't interested—I had things to do, like catching Red Sox games on television and surfing—but my grandmother, who we were staying with down in Virginia Beach, overheard the exchange. After a few stern words from her, I was off the couch and on the way to the restaurant.

It didn't go exactly as my sister predicted: they didn't hire me as a cook, not immediately. Instead, the chef pointed me toward the dish room, a closetlike area with a sink stacked full of soiled plates and grimy silverware. He told me to grab a beer and clean the dishes. So I did, and I had a blast; it was an unexpected rush bringing order to the chaos. And it was even more fun afterward, when the shifts were over, and the nighttime waitresses and ragtag kitchen crew and I sat around putting back beers.

It wasn't more than a few weeks before I'd graduated from dishwasher to cook. I hadn't been the most focused kid in school, but when I found the kitchen, I found the place I knew I wanted to be. It was hot and hectic during service, but when you were in the groove, it didn't matter, it was a constant buzz. Back in those Virginia Beach days, no one got mad when you drank beer all through service, and having a job where I could surf in the morning and then work and sip on beers at night seemed perfect to me.

With my dad's encouragement, I got a little more serious and made my way from that restaurant on the beach to the Culinary Institute of America. Back then the CIA wasn't like it is now: it was a trade school, even if it was a distinguished trade school. It took guys like me and molded them into efficient and eminently hirable cooking machines.

I parlayed my degree into some decent work down at a couple of hotels in Florida—hotels that just so happened to be near good surfing spots. I took my chef status seriously, sure, but surfing and hanging out were still important to me. I was a much more peripatetic guy at the time, though it's not unusual for people in this profession to travel around a lot: the skills are portable. After Florida, I made my way to Cambridge, Massachusetts. My sister lived up there—done with waitressing, she was in graduate school at Tufts studying city planning—and it was where my dad grew up, but I wasn't looking to put down roots. I was just passing through. We went out to dinner one night, and that was the night I stumbled onto Harvest.

Harvest had been open for about four or five years when I started cooking there in 1980. It was different than any of the other places I had worked: it wasn't tied to classic sauces and staid French cuisine. The owner, Ben Thompson, wanted it to be a very cutting edge, esoteric restaurant. He backed up that demand by making sure the kitchen could cook anything. Jim Burke, the chef, would place a phone call to France and buy whatever the guys on the other end of the line were selling. A cook would be dispatched to the airport to pick the stuff up and haul it back into the kitchen, where we'd open up the boxes and try to figure out how to use it. This was anything but normal in American kitchens of that era. At that time, kitchens were bastions for macho men who took a workingman's pride in what they did. The temperamental, artistic side of cooking had no place in them.

Harvest was the first kitchen—and remains one of the only ones—where I've worked where cooks would make trips to the library to find out more about what they were cooking with and how they might cook it. We played around with roe scallops and all kinds of great seafood, plus a bunch of ingredients that sound incredibly common today—haricots verts, baby vegetables, kiwi fruit—but at that time were considered exotic, the very building blocks of nouvelle cuisine in this country.

Not wanting to be left behind, I started spending more time with cookbooks and reading about food. I wanted to be able to keep up with the conversations the other cooks were having while we were prepping. It was the first place I'd worked where the cooks talked more about the food they were cooking than about which one of the waitresses they wanted to sleep with. I was eschewing morning trips to the shore to surf because I'd been up late with my co-workers eating and talking, coming up with crazy new things to try in the kitchen.

And it wasn't just the cooks in the back of the house—the waiters and bartenders and managers were all just as enthusiastic about what the restaurant was doing. Our collective enthusiasm for food spilled over into out personal lives: we cooked for each other in our apartments; we ate at other cutting-edge restaurants together. There was a palpable sense among the people who I worked with at Harvest that we were ushering in a new age in American restaurants.

I remember never having seen or even heard of a premeal briefing before Harvest. A premeal briefing, as I discovered, happens right before guests arrive: it's when the chef goes over the menu for the night, explaining the dishes and the specials to the waitstaff, and maybe offering a taste from the wine list so that they are well-prepared when a customer asks about it. That's standard practice at any good restaurant today, but it was initiated back then during the creative boom of the early eighties.

Since the sous chef at Harvest at the time was slightly uncomfortable talking in front of people, he asked me to take on the premeal. I am, as anyone who knows me can attest, a natural ham. And at that time I hadn't been up in the North very long and everyone thought my southern accent was hilarious. So I would get out there and ham it up, really mangling the French names of the cheeses and having a good time with it.

Those good times carried over into the kitchen, where we

cooked a lot of very good food. We butchered all our own meat, made our own pickles, stocks, and patés; if there was an ingredient that we were curious about—head-on chickens, for example—we had it available the next day. It was a cook's paradise in that way. The repetitious drudgery of most kitchens, where there was always a veal chop done this way and tenderloin with some overly buttery French sauce, was entirely absent.

There was a new challenge every week if not every day at Harvest, and a host of new dishes and techniques to learn and master. Much of what we cooked was simple and light and delicious—and some of the best food I've ever had a hand in making—but we were also the perpetrators of many culinary atrocities in the name of nouvelle cuisine: smoked scallops with strawberry sauce, smoked kiwi beurre blanc, raspberry quiche. It went with the territory; the boundaries of nouvelle cuisine were still being mapped out.

And we were always pushing those boundaries. One night we'd gotten in a whole wild boar from West Germany, a fierce-looking critter shipped to us with a full head of hair and plenty on its haunches, too. It was a spectacle to behold—fatty, meaty, and feral—and we treated it as such: we decided to cook it on a spit outdoors, out on the deck, in front of the guests. They were not as pleased as we were, however. Customers would come up and stare, their faces barely hiding their revulsion. The outdoor cooking station was my domain at the time, so I was the one who had to hear, again and again, "You shouldn't be cooking that *thing.*"

I was undeterred by their reactions, even egged on a little bit. That is, until we got busy and I turned away from the spit for a minute. It was probably less than a minute. However brief the interruption, when I turned back I saw that the spit had stopped turning and some of the boar's hair had caught on fire. And it didn't take any time for the fire to ignite the fat that was dripping off the animal; in an instant the spit-roasted wild boar had turned into a conflagration of skin and meat and hair. I stepped away in horror as huge red flames crackled and sizzled around the animal. One of the cooks raced for the fire extinguisher and put it out, right there, in front of the guests. Oh, was that humiliating.

But those were the sort of disasters we were courting—we were constantly pushing the limits of what we knew. Sometimes you'd go down in flames. More often, though, we were cooking excellent and exciting food.

I had been at Harvest for two years when I got an offer to go and cook at a Marriott in Hawaii. Two years was a long time for me to stay in one place back then, but I wasn't itching to leave. I liked my co-workers, whom I saw as peers instead of fellow hooligans for the first time in my career. I liked the progressive and professional environment in the kitchen at Harvest. And they liked me. In fact, they liked me enough to offer me a better position and a raise.

But I was torn. I had always wanted to surf in Hawaii. The hotel was on Maui, and for the first few nights after the offer came in, I drifted off to sleep at night with visions of the best surf spots on the island dancing in my head. With one of these phone-it-in cook's jobs at a corporate hotel, I'd be able to surf as much as someone who has to earn a living could.

I called my dad and asked him his opinion. Without a moment's hesitation, he replied, "Go to Hawaii." It was out of character for him to say so, but if he thought me going to surf and screw around in Hawaii was the right thing, I was behind it.

My friends at Harvest sent me off warmly, and I headed to

Hawaii, to what I thought was going to be paradise for a surfer chef like myself.

But after a couple of great mornings of surfing, dismal days in that horrible hotel kitchen, and empty nights of mai tai swilling, I was miserable. Harvest had changed me: food was important. Doing a good job—not just doing what was acceptable—was important. I had stumbled into a community of creative, thinking cooks and waiters at Harvest, and it was a community that I needed to be a part of. Every restaurant on the planet had beer and waitresses. They weren't the draw anymore. And the surfing up in Massachusetts wasn't all that bad when I got around to it.

As for my father, he gave me the perfect advice: if I hadn't tried Hawaii out, I probably would have felt like I was missing out on something. But now I knew for sure where I needed to be. A few months later, once I'd saved up enough for the airfare, that's just where I went.

Six Little Words
BRUCE SHERMAN

Bruce Sherman owned and operated a catering company in Washington, D.C., before moving to New Delhi, where he acted as consultant to a pair of family owned palace hotels in Jaipur, teaching the local Rajasthani cooks how to prepare Western food for locals as well as the visiting tourists. In 1996 Sherman enrolled at the École Supérieure de Cuisine Française in Paris and followed up his studies there with stints in the kitchens of a number of France's best restaurants. He returned to his hometown of Chicago the following year, and in 1999 accepted the chef's position at North Pond. In 2003 he was named one of Food & Wine *magazine's best new chefs. He currently holds a position on the national board of Chefs Collaborative, an organization that promotes sustainable cuisine, and is a founding member of Chicago's Green City Market.*

I T ' S   A   D E C I S I O N any ambitious cook has to make at some point in their career: when to jump off the cliff and see if they can fly—when to try their hand at being the chef.

And it's funny how there are those memorable phrases throughout life that let you know you've arrived—like the six little words one of my cooks uttered on my second day at North Pond. Six words that let me know I was the chef.

I had always been a cook, a member of the brigade, until I took the chef's gig at North Pond in the late nineties. At the time, I had been cooking professionally for fifteen-plus years and was working the line at the restaurant at The Dining Room at the Ritz-Carlton in Chicago. I was a little burned out and I decided to get away from the kitchen for a while. My wife and I had just bought a house, and we thought we'd take some time off to fix it up.

Trying to be somewhat pragmatic about my employment situation—a lingering symptom of the fiscal discipline I picked up during the time I spent studying economics at U. Penn and the London School of Economics, before I realized that what I really wanted to do was cook—I thought I should keep an eye on what was out there jobwise during my sabbatical.

My wife and I were barely three weeks into rehabbing the house when I saw an ad for an executive chef's position in the *Chicago Tribune*. It was anonymous, meaning that I didn't know the name of the restaurant I'd be faxing my résumé off to, and though I wasn't planning on looking for a gig, I thought there was no harm in keeping my toes in the water.

Much to my surprise, I got a call back in a matter of days from the owner of North Pond. I didn't know much about the place because I didn't really go out at the time—I had always worked nights, and had a four-year-old, so my schedule was pretty full.

I was asked to come in and do a tasting, a standard if nerve-racking audition that potential chefs everywhere go through: walk into a kitchen you've never seen before and cook what you hope is an impressive meal for your potential future employers.

I came, I cooked, I conquered. They told me they wanted me in the kitchen. Better still, they embraced my vision for the restaurant; to change it from a café in a park to a fine-dining restaurant that served as a showcase for the exceptional local ingredients available from the farmland around Chicago. The kind of restaurant, in other words, where I'd really want to be chef.

Certainly there were challenges: The restaurant didn't stock the level of product that I had gotten used to working with at the Ritz or in France. Much in the kitchen was preserved or powdered or purchased; there were few stocks and little was made from scratch. The kitchen wasn't in great shape, and the staff wasn't either.

The place did have charm, however. It is uniquely situated in an arts-and-crafts-style building on a pond in the middle of a major Chicago park, wonderfully disconnected from the hustle and bustle of the city just beyond the trees. Despite the fact that the original chef had largely been in absentia over the most recent six months, it was a location destination, a century-old warming house at the end of dark nighttime stroll through the park.

So I decided to give it a shot. A couple of days before I was to start, the owner—now my business partner—set up a meeting between myself and the sous chef, the guy who was running the kitchen at the time. This guy, my staff's ostensible leader, was going to be critical to my success or failure. And as his new boss, I'd be critical to his.

On the following Sunday, I made my way to the restaurant early, grabbed a coffee, and got ready for the initial meeting. The appointed time came and went. I sat there, shaking my head in disbelief: here I was waiting around at the restaurant on what was my day off, one of only a few I knew I'd have over the next six months, when I could have been home with my family.

Finally, just as I was about to leave, the sous chef showed up. I was annoyed, but I decided to cut him some slack. After all, I figured he had to be a little nervous about coming in on *his* day off to meet a new boss who surely had all these plans about how he wants to change the restaurant. I could see how that would be nerve-racking. That's when I noticed something: he was drunk. The kind of drunk you can *smell*—at noon, on a Sunday.

I tried to take it in stride, but it was hardly an encouraging sign. Inheriting a kitchen staff, I knew, is akin to inheriting crazy in-laws. There was going to be an inevitable transitional period for me as I learned to run the kitchen and drive these guys, and for them, too, there was the adjustment of learning new recipes and techniques—as well as a whole new methodology of cooking. So during the beginning of my tenure, with all these long-term changes in mind, I simply had to accept—for now—what was on the menu and who was in the kitchen.

I went in later that week for my official first day. I didn't intend to change anything off the bat—I just wanted to get to know the place and its rhythms. Day one went fine. We got the food out; we made it through the night.

Day two progressed similarly, I came in and the dishwasher was making pierogi for the menu in the morning. (I made a mental note to put a stop to that as soon as possible.) The kitchen hummed along calmly all afternoon.

Around five thirty, I was going to do my line check: standard chef stuff, casually supervising the mise en place, the prep work, to make sure that everyone was ready for service. But one thing I immediately noticed was off. There were only two guys in the kitchen: the dishwasher standing by the sink, and one cook—out of five—fussing with something on the range. That was it.

I looked for the rest of the guys in the walk-in refrigerator, a not-uncommon refuge from the heat of the kitchen for cooks. No luck. I looked out back behind the restaurant to see if they were taking a cigarette break together and came up empty again. Eventually I checked the restroom and, oddly enough, the single stall with four pairs of feet in it. And then I heard sloshing liquid, a bottle being passed, muffled laughter.

Now, I'm not that much of a confrontational guy. It's not really in my nature to bust in on a situation like that. So I quietly left and leaned against the wall, waiting for them in the vestibule outside the restrooms with as much casual confidence as I could muster at that point.

After a while they sauntered out. They were clearly busted. My arms crossed, I stared them down sternly. Three of them averted their eyes and slinked off toward the kitchen. The fourth, the obvious ringleader, had no problem staring back. "What the fuck is your problem?" he asked me.

It caught me off guard. I shook my head and said, "I don't have a problem." Thinking, *Boy oh boy do I have a problem. This* is my staff?

I knew that for as much shit as I could give these guys, I was the one in really deep. So after a minute or two spent composing myself, I followed them into the kitchen to try to put the pieces back together. Maybe we'd just gotten off on the wrong foot. We could fix this! . . . That's when I noticed that they were all changing out of their chef's clothes, stripping down to muscle shirts and putting on jeans, ready to go on their merry way. They were leaving—no one needed to spell it out for me.

So I retreated into my shoebox of a chef's office, sat down, and lay my head face first on the desk. I was more dazed than angry. *What I have I gotten myself into here?* I thought. I sat up, rubbing my eyes, and tried to digest everything that had just transpired, tried to figure out what my next move should be.

And just then the ringleader burst into the office. He stalked over, leaning in close so that we were practically face-to-face, his breath ripe with the smell of tequila, and said, "I am gonna fuckin' kill you." And, as if his meaning had been obscured—somehow—that first time around, he said again, "I am gonna fuckin' kill you."

His hands were shaking. His eyes were bulbous and bloodshot. He stood there for a moment, glaring at me with pure hatred, and then he stormed out.

That's when I fully understood the burden of being a chef. There's plenty of other stuff to worry about—uncertainties about skills and talent and leadership and creative vision—and then there's a situation like the one I was in that night, when despite everything that was going on—down four guys on my second night, a hundred guests about to arrive, not to mention a freshly delivered and highly convincing death threat—it is up to the chef to make it work.

And we did, my two remaining cooks, my dishwasher, and me. Afterward, I had to fill out a police report—form D610317 for assault, for which I reserve a special place in my office—and the cops insisted that they accompany me from the restaurant to my car that night. Not that I minded—the quaint trails through Lincoln Park to our "moonlit cabin in the woods" no longer seemed so quaint now that line cooks with murder on their minds could lurk undetected.

The next morning, after dropping my daughter off at preschool, I was less than excited about going in and trying to put the place back together. I was trying hard not to regret having taken the job.

But there was no turning back. Seven years later, we've renamed the restaurant North Pond, and it's a place—menu, staff, and everything—that I proudly lay claim to. It turned out that the death threat and the walkout were just the first of a number of speed bumps on the road to getting the restaurant where it is today. Every once in a while I look back at the time it has taken to get the restaurant to this point or remember those nights of scurrying through the park, always looking over my shoulder, and I think, Would I do this all over again? But once you've jumped off the cliff, there's no turning back, no matter how badly you would like to have finished fixing up your house before you made the leap. I know the answer is yes.

The Living Proof
NANCY SILVERTON

Nancy Silverton cofounded La Brea Bakery and the restaurant Campanile with Mark Peel and Manfred Krankl in the late 1980s. Nearly two decades later, Campanile retains its status as one of Los Angeles's best restaurants and the bakery has become the most widely recognized artisan bakery in North America. Nancy has written successful cookbooks on her own, Desserts *and* Nancy Silverton's Breads from the La Brea Bakery, *and coauthored two more with Mark Peel:* The Food of Campanile *and* Mark Peel and Nancy Silverton at Home: Two Chefs Cook for Family and Friends. *In 2006, she and Mario Batali plan to open a restaurant together in Los Angeles.*

WHEN MARK PEEL, Manfred Krankl, and I were in the planning stages of opening Campanile back in 1988, we sat down and wrote up a list of what we felt we needed to open the best restaurant we possibly could.

We would need a great wine list, which Manfred knew how to put together, a great chef, which Mark is, and great desserts, which were my responsibility. Then we got to talking about how much more complete the restaurant would be if we had great bread, too. But except for a couple small bakeries, there *was* no good bread in Los Angeles in the late eighties.

Eventually we reached the conclusion that if we wanted truly great bread—consistently and cost-efficiently—we were going to have to make it ourselves. After a long hunt, we found a space that was large enough to house both our fine-dining restaurant and a commercial bakery that could supply the restaurant—and the city at large—with good artisanal bread. Our investors were dubious about the venture: there was no precedent—no successful fancy restaurant and commercial bakery combination. Ultimately, though, they went along with it.

How naïve I was back then! I didn't know how to make anything more than the most basic of breads when we decided we would be opening La Brea Bakery. I had done a little baking at Wolfgang Puck's behest when I was the pastry chef at Spago, an olive bread and a multigrain bread from a mix, but that was about the extent of it.

All I had going for me was that I knew the excuses that had been thrown around for there being no good bread in the States—that we don't have the right flour, we don't have the right water, that you just had to go to Europe for good bread and silently suffer what we had available to us here—were just that: excuses. When I was in college, I'd eaten enough of Steve Sullivan's incredible breads at Acme Bread Company in Berkeley to know that at least one person on this side of the Atlantic was making excellent sourdough breads. And I figured that if he could do it then I could do it, too. Why not?

I enrolled in a weeklong baking class at Lenôtre's cooking school in France. I had taken a few of the school's classes in pastry making and found them incredibly beneficial to what I did back in the States. I figured the bread-baking class would work the same way and that after five days, I would come back to Los Angeles with a handful of recipes and that Campanile would have the best bread in the city.

The class turned out to be very hard for me, not because I didn't speak French, the language the classes were taught in, but because I didn't speak the language of bread. The pastry classes had been a breeze, because I knew the language of pastry making: if I saw someone adding the flour before the sugar and the end product was fantastic then I knew that was what I needed to do. Bread baking is its own discipline, however, its own science, and it has its own vernacular. I struggled through the week trying to keep up.

But eventually I did, and I came back from France with a book of recipes and high hopes. A friend who had a catering company let me experiment in her ovens while La Brea Bakery was being built. She didn't have steam-injected ovens, which are the ovens of choice for professional bread bakers—the additional moisture is critical in the formation of a good crust—but they would work. When I was making my first loaf of bread, directly from the pages of that little recipe book, in the same manner as I had the week before in that town outside of Paris, everything seemed right about it. The dough felt right. I took great care in shaping and scoring it. I was ready to pull it out of the oven, yell "eureka!" and get on with the rest of the work we had ahead of us in order to get the bakery and the restaurant open.

As soon as I slid my peel under the baked loaf, however, I knew something was amiss. You can tell a properly crafted loaf of bread immediately. There is a solidness to a good loaf, yet, when you take it in your hands, it feels slightly lighter than its appearance would lead you to imagine. My loaf was heavy.

A beautiful sourdough loaf, burnished brown on the outside, has a solid but not impenetrable crust, subtly blistered with tiny fermentation bubbles. My loaf was dull.

And though it makes a certain amount of sense to assume that if you bake a loaf of bread long enough at a high enough temperature, it's going to be golden brown and beautiful, that's not the case at all. As soon as a loaf made with under- or over-fermented dough begins to cool, it takes on a very ill pallor, almost a yellowy, mustardy color. Guess what color my loaf was?

Yes, I had all three of those problems right off the bat. Those initial loaves were just terrible. They went straight into the trash. Consequently, I was a wreck. I couldn't get my mind around what was wrong. In pastry, you learn each of the steps in a preparation, and it may take time to master these elements, but once you've made a chocolate cake properly once, it's not hard to do it a hundred or a thousand more times. I had made this same loaf not a week before in France and it had been perfect. It was nothing like the flavorless, uninspired lump I had just stuffed in the trash.

I didn't quite know what to do next or how to handle what seemed like certain failure. There was big money riding on my ability to produce great bread. I diligently followed the recipe a couple more times with the same result: terrible, flavorless bread. I couldn't figure it out—the dough looked beautiful and felt beautiful. I shaped the loaves just the way I had been taught to shape them. I waited the appropriate amount of time for the yeast to work its magic. And yet the bread was no good at all.

That's when I decided I had to start again from the very beginning. I would raise a sourdough starter of my own. I would find a new flour. I would experiment and search for the perfect combination of ingredients and techniques. Looking back on it now, I think that my success, if I've had any, is that I didn't know what I was doing. I didn't stop at anything and I didn't not try anything.

First, I needed a sourdough starter. I had read that Steve Sullivan made a starter with flour and grapes. In France, I was taught to make a starter with flour and raisins. Unsure of what would yield the best result, I made a number of different batches with different combinations of ingredients and varying ratios of flour to water. Then I waited and watched. After ten days I chose the one that looked the healthiest. It was survival of the fittest: everything else went down the drain.

It's funny to think that four gallons of this haphazard concoction made in the construction site that was going to be Campanile has now yielded hundreds of thousands of gallons that we use for La Brea breads every day. Honestly, after I published the recipe for it—which is essentially one bunch of grapes, some water, flour, and two weeks of patience—in *Breads from the La Brea Bakery*, I was waiting for someone with a much more thorough and scientific comprehension of the workings of wild yeasts and cultures to tell me I was full of crap, that I waited two weeks for the starter but you really only need twenty-four hours or something. But it hasn't happened yet.

Next, I needed to pick a flour. I formulated a baguette recipe and even though I knew that what I was going to make was not going to be my ideal bread, it would be a way to compare apples to apples, even if I wasn't happy with any of the apples. I ordered flours from ten different companies and baked loaves with each of the products before I settled on one I liked enough to push ahead with.

The flour and starter culture selection process took about a month, which left me with just a few more months to figure out how to get those two ingredients to work together before we were scheduled to open the bakery.

I decided I was going to come up with seven varieties of bread: sourdough, baguette, white loaf, whole wheat, rye, olive, and rosemary. With these seven breads, I told myself, I could open my bakery. The first one I wanted to master was the baguette. Because what's a bakery without a good baguette?

But baguettes are tough. Really tough. That's because with a baguette you're talking flour, water, salt, and leavening (in my case, the wild yeast starter) and that's it. There's no room for disguise. There are lots of breads that you can make with chocolate or cherries that taste good but—though no one would suspect it—don't pass muster on a structural level. I made dozens and dozens of batches of baguettes, batches that took twenty-four hours from start to finish, before I settled on one that I felt was decent. Along the way I was learning that with bread, you can't just follow the formula. If it's hot one day and cold the next, there are a dozen variables I'd need to pay attention to. I wasn't consistently happy with my bread because my bread wasn't consistent. But it was getting better. The other recipes took time to develop, but getting the baguette right was the toughest challenge.

We opened the bakery and then, according to plan, had six months to perfect the bread until Campanile would be ready. It's good we had that extra time, because it took a while to adapt to the baker's life. In the beginning, we had few accounts, so I didn't have to do the all-night shift; I would get up at two or four in the morning, and that was early enough to start that day's bake and prepare for the next day's production. But as the bread grew more popular—and I was managing the pasty program at the restaurant—I began working an eleven p.m. to eight a.m. shift. Baking, I discovered, is unlike any other kind of cooking job in more ways than one.

The biggest difference is that you're constantly living at least a day or two in the future. Besides the continually disorienting fact that you start work just when everyone else stops, you're planning and preparing dough that's going to take twenty-four or more hours to go from scratch to loaf. (Additionally, and I've talked to a lot of other bakers about it, when you're waking up at four o'clock in the afternoon after working all night, your dreams are screwy.)

On top of coping with my new vampire's hours, I had plenty of bread disasters in the early days of the bakery. I would make the dough, shape the loaves, and bake them, but when the bread came out it was missing something. It was just unsatisfying. So I'd walk over to the door, turn my open sign to closed, pull down the shades and start over—dreading the call from one of my partners, who would be frantically wondering what happened and why we weren't open.

It was at some point during the six-month stretch between opening the bakery and opening Campanile that I finally had what turned out to be my eureka moment in sourdough-bread baking, though it was less of a sudden revelation and more of a dawning awareness, a reluctant acceptance on my part.

It was in the middle of the night, during one of the peaceful, undisturbed stretches that make a baker's hours tolerable and when the lack of distractions from the world beyond the bakery door allows you to really develop a relationship with your bread.

I realized that I couldn't think about bread the way I thought about pastry or pasta or any other typical culinary undertaking. Bread is alive. Minor inconsistencies are a fact of life, not a mark of failure. The tiny variation in the loaves from day to day made them unique, not imperfect. And the relationship of a baker to her bread is like any kind of serious relationship you have with anybody in life. It's never perfect. It takes so much work. And every time you think that you've mastered it, the next day you're brought back to reality and it needs some more work.

Once I accepted that bread was alive and inconsistent and temperamental, it was easier for me to anticipate its wants and needs, to nudge it in the direction I wanted it to go. Accepting all that didn't improve my bread overnight, but I was ready to work with the bread. I was, finally, a baker.

Clothes Make the Man
JACQUES TORRES

Jacques Torres is one of the world's most celebrated pastry chefs. He moved to the United States in 1988 and soon after signed on as the pastry chef at Le Cirque in New York City, where his fantastic creations were enjoyed by presidents, kings, celebrities, and even Pope John Paul II. *In 1998 Jacques released a fifty-two-episode public television series,* Dessert Circus with Jacques Torres, *along with two companion cookbooks,* Dessert Circus: Extraordinary Desserts You Can Make at Home, *which earned a 1999 James Beard Foundation Award nomination, and* Dessert Circus at Home. *Jacques Torres left Le Cirque in January 2000 to pursue his lifelong dream of becoming a chocolatier. Jacques Torres Chocolate opened that December in a renovated warehouse along a cobblestone street in the DUMBO neighborhood of Brooklyn. In December 2004 Torres opened Jacques Torres Chocolate Haven, a state-of-the-art eight-thousand-square-foot chocolate factory and retail shop, in downtown Manhattan.*

I AM A VERY lucky chef, a chef with luck on my side. I've worked hard for all of my career, but I think there are lots of chefs with talent who work hard who didn't get the luck that I got.

Take the story of how I got my first real kitchen job: it was 1980 and I had just finished my military service. Back then, military service was required in France, and I had just finished a miserable twelve-month stint in the Alps—me, a boy from sunny Provence, up in the mountains, out in the cold, walking in the snow all day and sleeping in igloos at night. So I was happy to be in Nice afterward, where I was sleeping on the warm, sunlit floor of my then-girlfriend's tiny dorm room.

As a teenager, I had apprenticed in a pastry shop in a town near Bandol, which may sound romantic now that everybody wants to go to culinary school and become a chef, but back then it was like trade school—rigorous and ordinary. Still, I did well, finishing first in my department.

While I had an interest in food by the time I got to Nice, mostly it was an interest in eating it. I didn't know what a Michelin star was back then, I didn't know what the Meilleur Ouvrier de France was, I didn't know what a "gourmet" dish was. I knew about the food that my mom made and that I learned about in my village. But I knew nothing about the bigger culinary world that was out there.

One afternoon, my girlfriend and I were walking around town and we passed the Hotel Negresco, the famous hotel in Nice on the Promenade des Anglais with that huge pink dome. Since I was fresh out of military service, I had a little money saved up but I didn't have a job. So as we were passing in front of this palace of a hotel, I turned to my girlfriend and made a bet that I could walk into the Negresco and walk out with a job.

It's important to understand that when you're a kid from the

South of France like me, who grew up with no money, you pass in front of those hotels and you know that you don't go in there. They are for rich people, not for you. These places are for rich tourists *only*. Especially the Negresco. It was a ridiculous boast to tell her that I was gutsy enough to walk into *that* hotel and ask for a job.

Gazing up at the famously luxurious façade of the Negresco, my girlfriend laughed and dared me to try. So I went for it: marching right up the stairs and into the lobby, where I told the first employee I encountered that I was looking for a job in the kitchen. The gentleman kindly turned me around and sent me back outside, down the stairs, and around to the back of the building.

It turns out that workers, potential or otherwise, don't enter a hotel like the Negresco through the main entrance. Lesson learned. I headed around back to find the staff door. A minor setback, but no one saw it, so I kept my head high. I went in and talked with the guy we'd call the human resources guy today and told him I was looking for a kitchen job. He told me they "might be looking for someone" and to follow him. I did, down a flight of stairs and into the kitchen of Canteclair at the Negresco.

Believe it or not, I'd never seen a real kitchen before. My apprenticeship was in a pastry shop in town, a simple place, nothing like a Michelin-starred restaurant kitchen. That was my first time in a professional kitchen and it was, I'd later learn, one of the finest in France. As brash as I was, I was a little bit impressed by the sight: everybody in white, all the copper pots polished and hanging, nobody talking, everything shiny. We wound our way through the kitchen and the man showed me into a tiny office no bigger than a closet, where only one person can sit down and one person can stand up. The three of us crammed in there: me, him, and some guy smoking a cigarette wearing a button-down shirt that's open almost to his waist.

This guy, I thought, whoever he is, really doesn't present himself well.

The man who brought me to the office explained, "This young man is looking for a job."

The guy with the cigarette looked me over with a fair bit of disinterest and asked, "What do you do?"

"I'm a pastry cook," I told him, with all the wide-eyed pride a twenty-year-old can muster when he doesn't know he's talking to Jacques Maximin, one of the most celebrated chefs in France. In the early eighties, Jacques Maximin was huge, one of the biggest young chefs in the country, with two Michelin stars.

He said, "I have thirty people working in my kitchen," and he gestured toward the gleaming kitchen just beyond his office door, cigarette smoke trailing his hand as he did, "and there's no space for losers."

I was stunned. Why was he implying I was a loser? Who was this slob, I thought to myself. He couldn't be the chef—he wasn't wearing a chef's jacket, right? He was barely wearing a shirt, for that matter.

While I was standing there wondering what to say, he lit a fresh cigarette off his previous one and said, "Listen—you're good and I'll keep you." Drag. "If you're bad, you go."

I gathered myself up and thought: No problem. I can take abuse from some middle manager like this. "Fine," I said.

After another drag off the cigarette, he said, "Come back in an hour with your chef pants and jacket." That was his interview. And suddenly I was out of the tiny office, hurrying back through the kitchen, and around to the front of the hotel to where my girlfriend was waiting for me.

I finally exhaled. "Holy shit!" I shouted, "I think I just got a job! But I have to be back in an hour with pants and a chef's jacket."

It was like a starter pistol had gone off. The race was *on*.

One hour in Nice is barely enough time to get anywhere and back—it's a resort town, not a place where things are zooming by—and I had to run all the way across town. Luckily my girlfriend had a car, a little red Yugo, so we hopped in and went off careening through the Mercedes-crammed streets. I anxiously tapped at the dashboard when we got stuck in traffic, first on the Promenade des Anglais, then in then Place Massena. When we finally made it to Le Roi du Bleue, I ran inside and shouted hysterically, "pants!" A salesman wandered over with a calm, amused expression on his face and then, just as leisurely, strolled off to find my size.

As I waited—endlessly—for him to return, I began to *really* worry. At the time, buying a jacket and pants cost real money, at least to me. What if it didn't work out with the hotel? What was I going to do with this costume?

Fear of wasting money only compounded my fear of being late. I wanted to make the most professional impression, and having just come out of the military, where following orders was important, I really wanted to be back before an hour. The truth is that while the chef had given me an hour, he probably would have just as easily given me two. In fact, I doubt that he even remembered our little talk. Still, not knowing this at the time, I was so stressed out about making the deadline that I could barely breathe. My girlfriend kept putting her hand on my back and rubbing softly to try to relax me.

Finally, I got the pants. I got the jacket. I handed over what little money I had and jumped back into the red Yugo and moments later, across town, I burst into the kitchen. I was ready for my new job, on time—not only on time but early; it had been *less* than sixty minutes!

Of course, nothing happened. No one was waiting around with a stopwatch. Eventually someone noticed that I was back and told me to change—right there in the kitchen, in front of everyone more or less—and I was pointed in the direction of the pastry shop.

And that was I how I got my start working in professional kitchens. Right then and there, less than an hour after I took my first step inside the Hotel Negresco. Two months later I was the pastry chef.

I stayed with Maximin for eight years. He taught me everything, introduced me to everyone—Bocuse, Ducasse, Lenôtre—and he sent me to work and to travel and learn all over France. Me, a kid coming out of military service with no experience who walked in off the street and asked for a job.

Maximin pushed me hard enough when I was twenty that I still feel the momentum today. I was good, so I stayed, I guess. Or I was lucky, because I showed up at the exact right time. Regardless, I was on my way.

Under My Thumb
MING TSAI

Ming Tsai grew up cooking alongside his parents at their family owned restaurant, Mandarin Kitchen. While pursuing a degree in mechanical engineering from Yale University, Ming spent a summer at Le Cordon Bleu in France. After graduating, he studied in kitchens around the globe, training in Paris under pastry chef Pierre Hermé and in Osaka, Japan, with sushi master Kobayashi. A graduate of Cornell University's Master's program in Hotel Administration and Hospitality Marketing, Ming has held positions in both front and back of the house at restaurants across the United States. In 1998, Ming and Polly Tsai opened Blue Ginger in Wellesley, Massachusetts, to immediate acclaim. An Emmy Award–winning host and executive producer, Ming can be seen on Public Television's Simply Ming, *as well as* Ming's Quest *on the Fine Living Network. He has authored three cookbooks and created a line of foodstuffs for Target.*

IN 1986 I graduated from Yale with a mechanical engineering degree and promptly hopped the next flight to Paris. While I had worked hard to earn my degree, my true love had always been food, and I was ecstatic to immerse myself in the culinary scene and show the world how much I knew. Or, as it turned out, how little I knew. Pierre Hermé, the world-renowned pastry chef, was kind enough to let me work for him at Fauchon, the famous *traiteur*, where you can find everything from terrines to stuffed ducks, foie gras and more foie gras, and desserts and pastries like you wouldn't believe. Pierre was the youngest executive chef ever at Fauchon. He made the best croissants, the best chocolate cake, the best macaroons, the best everything in France. (They sold at twice the price, and were worth it.)

Pierre Hermé was a perfectionist. For example, in the kitchen, he had what he called the pastry box, and into the box went all the pastries that didn't live up to Pierre's obscenely high standards. If a croissant had a tiny flake off the top of it, if the *chausson aux pommes* had the slightest flaw—into the box. Pierre's rule was that the kitchen staff could eat as much as they wanted out of the pastry box; and considering how incredible these "imperfect" discards were, it seemed like paradise to me. That is, of course, until a few weeks had gone by, by which time I had eaten so many *pain au chocolat* that I couldn't bear even *thinking* about another one. Before I got to that point, however, I made my first stupid mistake at Fauchon. When I saw Pierre reach into the box, grab a croissant, and take a huge bite of it, I immediately followed by grabbing a chausson aux pommes. Unfortunately, *my* pastry had just come from the oven. As I bit into it, the volcanically hot filling flooded my mouth. It was probably about ninety-eight degrees centigrade. I stood there in agony, literally burning the roof of my mouth off. Of course, I didn't even wince in front of the chef.

Aside from the molten breakfast pastry incident, I was doing okay—learning quickly (or so I thought) and taking on any task assigned to me. One day, Pierre challenged me to scale up a ganache recipe. I still can't decide if he did this because he thought I could handle it or because he thought I couldn't. Involved were about two thousand dollars' worth of deluxe chocolate, cream, and a thirty-gallon, 220-volt electric kettle. Considering that I had a mechanical engineering degree, and that I had come from a family of engineers, one would think this was a no-brainer for me. I eagerly started the task, ready to make Pierre proud not only of my culinary abilities, but also of my superior calculating skills.

Hours later, chocolaty cream was sloshing around in the giant three-foot-deep kettle. It didn't even *slightly* resemble ganache. Instead, it was like very expensive hot chocolate. Bewildered, I went back over the recipe and realized—unbelievably—that I had miscalculated the amount of cream. When Pierre looked at my calculations—all the cooks were required to write them out—he informed me that I was off by a factor of ten.

Even though I had added ten times the amount of cream required, I couldn't just let all those ingredients go to waste. It simply wasn't an option. First, because Pierre would never allow it, but second, it was a matter of pride and determination. I needed to right my wrong. I could not let that kettle of murky cream be the downfall of my culinary career.

Pierre himself got the proper amount of chocolate and dumped it into the kettle of cream, admonishing me not to burn it. He was keeping his famous temper in check at this point, but I think scorched chocolate would definitely have been the last straw. By this time, every pastry chef in the kitchen was watching me. Once you start the process of making ganache, you can't stop. I started stirring, and I had to be especially careful using this electric kettle, because it heated not only on the bottom, but also on the sides, which meant I had to continuously stir or the chocolate *would* scorch. That kettle had never seen so much ganache at once. It was filled to the very, very rim. Pierre was not amused—I was amazed at his restraint, actually. He stood back and let me finish my task.

I stirred that ganache for a full, continuous forty-five minutes. As I was stirring, the chocolate kept splashing around me and getting on my hands. I started wiping them on my apron, but very quickly I ran out of clean places on my apron. So I started licking my hands. By the time I was done, there was chocolate everywhere. I had chocolate not only on my hands and forearms, but also all over my face, on my apron, and behind my apron on my pants. There was chocolate in my hair and in my ears. And my workspace looked just as bad— chocolate splatters all over the floor.

When I went to the locker room to change at the end of my shift—totally wired on chocolate, I'd literally OD'd on it—my arms and shoulders were aching from rescuing that sorry batch of ganache. I thought I'd cleaned myself up pretty well, but I couldn't believe it, there was chocolate in my clogs and even in my socks! To this day, I still half-expect to find chocolate on some forgotten part of me.

A few things happened that day I saved the ganache. Though Pierre was far from pleased, I ended up making about a two-week supply of it. I earned the nickname Monsieur Chocolat at Fauchon. And I ruined myself for chocolate for the rest of my life—I still don't really enjoy it. Being wired on the caffeine and sugar from it for two days and basically bathing yourself in it will do that to you.

Fast forward to two months later, I did something that's

probably even worse than my miscalculation with the ganache.

Pierre Hermé is known for his absolutely beautiful, virtuosic work with blown sugar. One of Pierre's many talents is his ability to take a regular photograph and, from that, recreate an exact likeness of his subject in sugar. During the time that France was courting the Walt Disney Company to bring EuroDisney to the country, Pierre decided to make a sugar work of Mickey Mouse to display in the front window.

He worked on Mickey for one full week, which is the longest I ever saw him work on a piece. When he was done, there stood a three-foot-tall replica of Mickey Mouse. It was perfect. From the shape of the ears to the buttons on his shorts to the little black slashes on his gloves. Absolutely perfect. Nothing was unaccounted for. Mickey was left in the back room to dry, as it took a creation of that size about two days to do so. The back room was also where the freezer was, which meant all the kitchen staff was constantly in and out of that area.

Well one day, as I was going to the freezer, I stopped and looked at Mickey. I remember just marveling at him. I don't know what prompted me to, but I took my thumb and gently touched him on his belly. When I took my thumb away, I'd left a huge, clear-as-day thumbprint. I ran.

For days, I woke up in a cold sweat, just waiting for the morning that Pierre would line us all up and demand to compare our thumbs with the thumbprint. I honestly thought about burning my thumbs or maybe getting a cut there to try to obliterate my thumbprint. I decided that was probably a bit over the top, and obvious, at that. Instead, I just went to work in fear, waiting to be summoned.

Fortunately for me, Mickey was displayed in the front window before any of my nightmares could come true. And, also fortunately for me, when you looked at him through the window, you couldn't see the thumbprint. He looked just as he should have.

I honestly have no idea if Pierre ever saw the thumbprint. Maybe he did and thought it wasn't productive to try to pursue it. Maybe he thought it was his own—though I can't imagine Pierre's technique ever allowing for that. I don't know, because I've never, ever told him what I did. I truly hope he does not read this book.

My time at Fauchon was an invaluable education. I was lucky enough to learn technique from one of the masters. And in France—a culinary capital. But Pierre's perfectionism also helped me understand how to be a perfectionist while still being able to adapt to what's happening around me. I use Pierre as a barometer for my own behavior—I think, if Pierre Hermé could have dealt with me when I was that young and foolish, I can do whatever task is before me with at least half as much aplomb. The fact that Pierre did not explode at me over the chocolate is amazing. But every man has his limits. If I had burned it, that would have been another story. I would not have wanted to see that wrath and, thank goodness he never saw the thumbprint, because I'm not sure I'd be here to tell the story!

Hawaii High
NORMAN VAN AKEN

*Norman Van Aken founded a visionary way of cooking called
New World cuisine. Presenting an approach that embodies the
essence of this country and its dynamic ethnic mix, he melds the
exotic ingredients and rich cultural heritages of Latin America,
the Caribbean, the southern United States and even touches of
Asia. In addition to being an award-winning chef—he is the
only Floridian to have ever won entrance into the James Beard
Foundation Who's Who—Van Aken is highly regarded as a culinary educator, television celebrity, and cookbook author. He
shares his passion for cooking by teaching classes at Norman's,
his renowned Miami restaurant, as well as culinary schools
across the country. He is the author of four cookbooks:* Feast of
Sunlight, The Great Exotic Fruit Book, Norman's New World
Cuisine, *and* New World Kitchen.

I WAS FROZEN MY first winter of college: intellectually,
spiritually, nearly sexually (not by choice), and, most
painfully, *physically.* My most vivid memory of that unbearable

time in 1970 was of walking in my thin and shabby Salvation Army retrieved coat along the snowy streets of Dekalb, Illinois. Merciless winds only a Wright brother might wish for tore across blinding white cornfields, now desolate and buried under icy powder, and right through me. Head bowed ineffectually, I trudged on wondering why, in the name of anything holy, or even profane, I was there. Before spring came and could cause me to forget, I forged my resolve to follow the path of my older sister, Jane, and head west to Hawaii, to the university in Honolulu.

By some miraculous exchange of savings, luck, and a gift from an elderly friend of my mother's, I was able to afford the dream, and off to Oahu I went in the late summer of 1971, arriving with my two buddies from Mundelein High days, Joel and Ralph. The first week there we crashed at the YMCA. It was a bad start for Ralph. The Y only allowed two persons per room, and Joel and I drew the straws that put us together. Ralph slept alone . . . that is until around two a.m. when the cockroaches began to wake him. While Joel and I somehow got a room without the goliath-sized insects native to Hawaii, Ralph spent a horrified and sleepless night smashing as many as he could with the Gideon's Bible provided so thoughtfully in each of the Spartan rooms. In the morning he looked like he was ready to take the next flight home or get booked into a padded cell. He had a large, intelligent face and the vein that ran across his forehead throbbed like a telegraph wire sending an SOS from his bug-deluged brain.

But we soon found a nice little place to live on the ground floor of a fifteen-story building at 2440 Date Street just off University Avenue, near the school. We enrolled and then we went looking for dope. Days went by and no weed was ours to find. In the meantime we drank the local beer—which we also broke the law to do, as we were only nineteen and the legal drinking age was twenty-one, *eons* away. And then one afternoon I went for a dip in the tiny apartment-complex pool at the end of the cracked black asphalt driveway. There was a guy there reading the *Honolulu Star Bulletin* and after a minute he said, "Get high?" I wasn't sure what he meant, what with his white oxford shirt and Beatle bangs. Trying not to sound desperate, I said, "Um, high?" and he beamed back, *"Reefer?"*

About ten minutes later we were cruising in this guy's jazzy red convertible down the Ala Wai Boulevard toward glitzy Waikiki, past towering palms and a cerulean sky that God in heaven would envy. All of the windows were rolled up and the top was up too, as we smoked a joint the size of Mauna Kea, containing some pot that had a strength my midwestern medulla oblongata had never known. We turned around near the Diamond Head Crater and looped back toward the Manoa Valley. The nearly ever-present rainbow that hung over the hills seemed to contain a few extra bands of color I had never noted before. Roy G. Biv . . . meet Fuchsia and Periwinkle. My new friend fronted me some "j's" and dropped me off back at our apartment.

I walked in the front door and Joel and Ralph glanced up from their reading, Joel with Nietzsche—while humming something by Jesse Colin Young—and Ralph with a Fabulous Furry Freak Brothers comic book. After a mere moment both of them leaped to their feet, rushed straight at me, peered into my manhole-sized irises, and shouted in unison, "You're fucking *stoned*!!"

Well, no shit, boys! They were so pissed, so *white hot* pissed, that they started circling the dilapidated dining room table in animal exasperation until I spread the five masterfully rolled joints the "friendly stranger" had just laid on me in front of their dope-bereft straight-ass faces.

As quickly as you could strike a wooden blue-tipped match our little apartment filled with the thick cloud of cannabis that was such a part of my sophomore year at the University of Hawaii that we came to call it the University of "High-Why-We." It was our mission statement, our raison d être.

Despite the immense cost of school, apartment, groceries, anything—or maybe in some aberrant way *due* to it—we decided that college was much less important than bodysurfing. So after the initial weeks of the UH indoctrination and seeing what kind of female talent might be in the mix of our classes, we slowly but most assuredly began to explore the heaven on earth beaches of Hawaii. It was the seventies, and hitchhiking was not yet considered dangerous—and we had no car anyway—so hitching to Makapu'u and Sandy's Beach became a part of our everyday life. We were as white as Oreo cream with a little baby fat when we arrived, but after a few weeks the tropical sun burnished us into "bronzed gods" by our own account and hard-bodied young men by anyone's. The downside was that with all of the energy it took to bodysurf and the hunger cravings inevitable with the ingestion of "dope-a-wana" we were almost perpetually crazy with hunger.

We didn't cook and we really couldn't afford to go out and eat. Breakfast food was the only way to go, so we lived on cereal: Rice Krispy critters and Sugar Smack daddies.

After one afternoon at Sandy's Beach (renowned for dumping your ass facedown at the end of an amazing aqua-borne roller-coaster ride), we hitched back into town. We were, as ever, ravenous. We'd have knocked down a hottie in a miniskirt if she'd been standing between us and a plate of fried chicken.

We decided to get a loaf of bread and some bologna at the grocery store down the street from our place. As we roamed the aisles we stared like perps at a peep show at the big pineapple-draped honey-glazed hams, thick T-bones, barbecued chickens, whole "Luau pigs," Italian sausages, golden wheels of imported cheeses ... Hell, the fucking cottage cheese looked like a miracle on ice, so pure, so white, so—all important—*filling*! At that age we weren't sated until we were "full," and "full" equaled "laid" (algebra 101, male version).

As we headed toward the checkout line I looked up and to my great surprise noticed a guy I had last seen back in Illinois six thousand miles away. His name was Jeff Hagel, and he was a near legendary badass from our town. He'd quit or gotten kicked out of our high school, joined the Marines, and gone to 'Nam back in '67 or so. Myths surrounded him. Not quite Colonel Kurtz but an early adapter of gonzo, no doubt. I had come to know him during my frozen year in Dekalb through my sister Jane. He'd just gotten out of the Marines and we would drive down to college drinking an entire case of beer between the two of us as Jane handled the wheel. He turned me on to a bunch of books, and we'd get into all kinds of sloshy philosophical raps, which usually devolved to the point of us hanging our heads out of the speeding Mustang.

Now he was standing there wearing a Don Ho red and white flowered shirt. He had one lime in his hand as he waited for the checkout lady. We had our bread and cold cuts, and once we got past the head shaking and the-world-is-a-small-place observations, we caught up with the where he lived and where we lived stuff, moving through the line until it was Hagel's turn. The checkout lady turned to him and said, "That's it, big fella? One lime?"

Hagel had eyes that were as blue as sapphires. His championship-wrestler's build held an electric fluidity that caused the tattoos on his lower forearm to pulse a little as he squeezed the lime. He stared at the woman. She looked down to avert his molten gaze and that's when she saw his bulging wet trunks and the blood running down his legs. We watched her expression turn to horror and followed her gaze to see its cause. Small rivulets of watery red switched back and forth across Hagel's bare legs, dribbling toward his bamboo flip-flops. He shifted his stance and painfully limped a few steps forward, pulling at a now-deadened appendage. We looked away, trying not to gag. She did, too, and rang up his lime. He dropped a quarter on the rubber conveyor belt and hobbled out into the Hawaiian sunlight. We paid our bill and hustled out after him.

I said, "Hey buddy, you okay?"

"Yeah, fine. Let's get down the road a block." And he now broke into a very healthy stride.

Once we had gotten a good distance from the store he let out a yowl. "Fuck! I nearly froze my *nuts off* in there!"

Huh?

And then he pulled a two-pound package of frozen burger meat from under his trunks, once masked by the blousy, rococo flowered shirt, the blood now dripping directly onto his hands. We laughed like lunatics and went to his place and fried up the meat on an electric hot plate barely waiting for it to thaw, slathering it with plenty of ketchup, salt, and pepper and mashing some of the white sandwich bread we'd bought in the drippings in the skillet to get everything and anything that meat could give us.

Over the next few days, Jeff introduced us to some of the folks he was living with at the time, and folks that simply hung out for marathon parties involving unbelievable amounts of all manner of drugs. Hawaii was a scene back then that was not capable of surviving for very long. But her mad flower was as vivid as an orchid thriving in Oahu. Haight-Ashbury expats, Vietnam vets, disenfranchised intellectuals from New York clutching books on Zen by Alan Watts or copies of *Howl* covered with margin notes and roach ashes, surfers who went from beach to beach and party to party, Navy cats who looked like they belonged on a box of Cracker Jack but got as high as Sufis—they all converged on Jeff's place. One guy ate absolutely nothing but papayas he'd steal from people's trees. He claimed that his shit was pure white as a result! We were the youngest in the crowd so we sort of sat back, kept quiet, and dug in. We'd go there to hang out, to ponder the sacred Dharma as riffed on by Jack Kerouac, and to listen to some of the older hippies talk about actually partying with Neal Cassady, flipping his trusty hammer back in the early sixties Frisco days . . . There were three older men who almost looked like triplets . . . if the triplets were a cross between Allen Ginsberg and Mahatma Gandhi. They lived seemingly eternally connected to a huge hookah. I never saw them get up to pee or eat. They all had thick glasses, and they sat cross-legged in little more than their cotton underwear. I'm not sure who even reloaded that pipe or went out and got them the dope. They spoke of Vedic scriptures and Krishna and the Tao, occasionally taking the time to play a little music on the bongos and flutes near their forever-parked asses. We called them "The Three Hookahs" . . . but we meant no disrespect. We really thought it was cool to have such old cats hanging out and being part of this scene. It made it hipper and so far beyond what our friends back in Illinois could be doing. One guy Jeff knew from back home was there. His name was Grover. He was a slim, boyish person with long chestnut-colored hair he pulled behind his ears. He was known to do prodigious, scary amounts of acid. And he'd talk to you and somehow still be able to make sense. Even above the roar of

"I'm Your Captain," the Grand Funk Railroad song that he *never* stopped playing.

> I can feel the hand, of a stranger,
> And it's tightening, around my throat.
> Heaven help me, heaven help me,
> Take this stranger from my boat . . .
>
> I'm your captain, yeah, yeah, yeah . . .

But he was just too much. Even for us back then. He might have been *somebody's* captain, but not ours. *No one* did hundreds of hits (truly, *hundreds*!) of Stanley Owlsey's lysergic shit for long and not expect to pay with their mind. The last time I saw him he was walking down the center of Kalanianaole Highway at midnight in the pitch dark—*willing the cars to drive around me, boys!*—cars screeching and veering to avoid wasting the stoned soldier.

But our hunger kept us mortal.

Hagel led us to a place one night not far from his apartment called King's Bakery. It was an open-all-night café and bakery. For three bucks you could get a thick stack of buttermilk pancakes and two farm-fresh eggs *and* thick-cut bacon with a big glass of whole milk (none of this 2 percent, man). It became our place many nights that winter of 1971 to '72.

It was at King's Bakery that I think I began my odyssey of learning how to cook. There was a guy there who worked the all-night shift. I never spoke to him, or he to me. But somewhere in the midst of all of those nights at King's his body language began to cut though the hallucinogens and other odd and sundry psychotropic substances that tempted my buddies and me back then. Somehow the smells and the flavors of food were hitting me in a way that spelled long-term salvation. He moved with a dancer's liquid grace and a juggler's love of handling disparate objects. Each motion was a purposeful, tai chi waltz that put eggs—click, crack—softly into pans, whisked cream into high voluminous peaks, ladled perfect orbs of zaftig pancake batter onto gleaming hot griddles, and flipped and impaled rashers of bacon and slabs of ham with spatulas twisting like Samurai swords. The aromas of that bacon fat, of caramelizing onions, of soy-and-ginger flank steaks charring on a wood grill filled the space with a haze of smoke more alluring than any joint's, hitting some erogenous zone deep inside that made me practically quiver. The cook seemed to hum and smile just a little at the edges of his mouth; a Buddha of Breakfast, the Guru of the Graveyard Shift. When his plates went down on the Formica counter at four o'clock in the morning on a humid Honolulu late night we shut up and we ate. We ate slowly, with contemplation, wordless and dreamy as the empty, aching sacks that were our stomachs filled with this cheap and wonderful food.

I grew up in a family that loved good food. My mom was a waitress-hostess-cashier in a variety of restaurants during the sixties as well as a Girl Scout leader for part of that time. We did a lot of cooking back home in northern Illinois and Mama taught my two sisters, Jane and Bet, (the younger one) and me to can produce harvested from our neighbors' amazing garden. We'd also go along with her to midwestern farm stands that stood right next to prospering fields, getting just-picked corn, green beans, and strawberries from farm daughters, mothers, aunts, and children. My mother would reach into her purse and pull out the few dollars it took and off we'd go back to our kitchen to transform some items into dinner and preserve others for some future meal. Our basement was lined with knotty pine shelves holding mason jars of tomatoes and home-made pickles. Mama was not a fancy cook but she was dedicated to our happiness. We spent many hours in those sweet years at home together doing something with food.

One night back in Honolulu we were at Hagel's place partying with all of the stoners and about six of us got the munchies and headed to King's for a late-night fix. The counter where the open kitchen stood and my cooking hero produced his magic held about ten stools. One of the guys in the group came from a wealthy family in the book publishing business in Chicago, and Hagel told me that Cromie was paying and we might as well take advantage. So we ordered up an array of burgers, pancakes, omelets, pies, and coffees, whatever each of us craved. We talked and feasted for an hour or more. Cromie had just arrived and was new to the Honolulu scene and seemed to be digging King's as much as we all did, chowing down on one of the teriyaki burgers. Finally we'd reached our max and Hagel said, "Let's go fellas . . . Cromie's gone to pay the cashier."

So we strolled out as nonchalant as fat cats, pausing in the parking lot under the fluorescent lights of the restaurant's front door, waiting for our new benefactor to join us. A few minutes later, Cromie came out and said, "Where'd you guys go?"

One of the stoners said, "Waitin' for you boss. Thanks for the meal. I haven't eaten like that in a month!"

Cromie said, "Why are you thanking *me*?"

Hagel was now walking at a rather brisk clip toward the street.

"I was in the can," Cromie noted.

Through the large plate-glass windows we could see the cashier and my culinary guru pointing at us. A security guard was fondling his holster, getting the info, and swiveling his gaze to find us. We suddenly realized *no one* had paid . . . and since no one *could* pay that whole bill we took off in a five-man dash down the street. As we sprinted back to Hagel's place, we could hear him laughing a block ahead of us, rousing the barking dogs of the kennel down the darkened section of Beretania Street.

Our culinary oasis was now going to be off limits to us. We'd been eighty-sixed. They couldn't catch us but they knew what we looked like and now we'd never sit on my cooking hero's counter stools again.

That's when I decided to become the cook of our bachelor's apartment.

It wasn't the easiest start. We were typically broke college students, feeling out this newfound freedom of living away from home and making our way in the world. We'd fuss over who did the dishes, whose turn it was to vacuum the rug, who drank all the milk. We'd celebrate our flowering decorative strengths with a freshly purchased set of three candles or a milk crate bookshelf. We'd go to the store and argue about how to spend our precious pooled resources. We could only afford meat once a week, so there would be a huge debate on not only what we could afford but also what we had the skills to prepare. To our nineteen-year-old bodies beef was the trump card of meat. Steaks . . . ah sure . . . yes, of course, but who could do more than dream as they were priced in the stratosphere. In fact, *everything* in Hawaii was ungodly expensive because it had to be shipped in from such faraway places. We all loved roast beef, so one afternoon we agreed on a small tip roast for our one-night-a-week feast. We got baking potatoes and some corn (things I'd cooked back home). I asked the landlord's wife, who had grown to practically despise us due to our taste and volume in music, how to cook the beef, and she was so

disarmed by my requesting her help that she made us a blue-
berry pie for dessert, bringing it by just before we got loaded.
Domesticity was looking up. I followed her directions to fire up
the oven to 350 degrees and put the beef in a frying pan with
some salt and pepper and let it cook. I forgot to ask her how
long so we let it roast until we couldn't wait any longer. When
it came out, the world was suddenly a new place and I was its
happy new owner. My pals Joel and Ralph had to admit . . . I
was now the chef of our Date Street bungalow.

It became our Saturday night fever. We went on like this for
about two months. One day Hagel asked me if I felt up to
cooking one of my famous roasts at his place. He'd been sup-
plying the party for the past months and maybe—he hinted—
we should do a little payback. I knew he was right but
countered, "Jesus, man . . . there's always like fifteen folks partying at your place. How are we supposed to afford feeding all
of them?"

He laughed and said, "Hey, most of those lunatics don't eat,
maybe a little peyote but not much else. Don't worry about
them. We'll set up a table on my patio and just go there, get
high as loons, listen to some music, and when it's done chow
down like freaking rajas—just the four of us."

I had no comeback, so we planned it for the following week.

When the night arrived, Ralph and Joel and I set up our little
traveling cooking plan. Since we only had about four ingredients it wasn't hard. We walked down Date Street, turned on
University and then over to Beretania with the treasured goods
and my now-trusty black iron skillet, tromping up the wooden
stairs and into Hagel's kitchen as the dogs launched into an immediate howl. Hagel's place was pretty big, and cheap, for a
Hawaii apartment, but part of the reason it was affordable was
that it was right behind that goddamn dog kennel.

We set down our groceries and tried to figure out how to turn on his oven. It seemed no one had done that for some time. Once we finally got the pilot lit and the heat began to build, a situation arose that we hadn't imagined. *Thousands* of cockroaches marched out from behind the oven wall!

Joel, always the most pragmatic of us, grabbed the precious meat and stashed it in the rickety fridge and away from the massing insect army now traversing the ceiling. Some of the hippies in the living room got wind of the insect invasion, and whether they were worried about hallucinations or simply amazed at the durability of these creatures was unclear. They stood in the doorway passing a joint and a bottle of wine. One of them was a fifty-year-old stoner who'd changed his name to Harmony when he'd left Long Island in '66. His folks owned a deli, and he saw the prep that we had started.

"Making dinner, guys?" he asked—Einstein in a tie-dye shirt and cut-off blue jean shorts.

"Uh, yeah . . . we owed Jeff a favor . . . so a little roast is all."

"Meat?" he replied. "No can do." He leaned against the wall, apparently oblivious to the shroud of cockroaches tramping along the ceiling above him. "Do you have a dessert plan?"

We admitted that we didn't. In truth we'd spent all the money that we had.

"I have the perfect dessert!" he offered. "It's a mix of powdered mescaline and Hershey's cocoa. You just snort it. All you need is a straw! Killer . . . It melts in your mind, not on your tongue!" and he let out a spacey howl.

The bugs proceeded down the far wall and toward the kennel. The Huns had less formation than those tick-tock syncopated aliens.

As the afternoon went on we prepared our palates with some

pot that Hagel called "Breath of God." Afterward, we went out on the patio and looked at the flickering lights of Honolulu spread out around us. We set up a table on the porch with a garage sale tablecloth and candles. I placed the baked potatoes and corn in the center and went back to the stove to get the meat. I was rip-roaring stoned and yet primed to eat this meat and show these boys that I was truly learning to cook.

I pulled down the oven door. The beef was a perfect shade and the smell was enough to give a vegan pause. I blushed with pride and grabbed the pot handle. But I had forgotten to use a potholder. The red hot metal stung my naked hand with the jolt of a thousand vipers. I wheeled around but the pot was stuck to my flesh. As I circled in a dazed 360-degree spin the meat suddenly launched out of the pan and shot up, airborne . . .

Hagel, Joel, and Ralph stopped nodding their heads to the music now. They watched in horror as the roast kept going . . . up, up, and *over* the fence . . . and down to the kennel cages below.

There were no roofs on those cyclone fence canine cubicles. The pan crashed horribly to the stone pavement and the meat thudded with a sickening smack in the middle of the compound. A dozen dogs used every ounce of strength they had and leaped over their units and fell upon the hot prize. The growling and ripping sound brought the stoners back off the couches and beanbag chairs. Aghast they watched the power struggle below them play out. The noise was awful. Ralph, Joel, Hagel and I watched, too. All that meat . . . all that money . . .

I've never taken a pot or a pan out of the oven again without a side towel in my hand.

Acknowledgments

Thank you to Karen Rinaldi for gallantly leading the effort; Panio Gianopoulos for your skilled editing and gentle nudging when we needed it; Maya Baran for always aiming high; and Sabrina Farber for your watchful eye. This book would not have come together without Eleanor Jackson, David Forrer, and Alexis Hurley, who once again have helped in every way imaginable; and for the time, effort and support you've shared: Annemarie Ahearn, Beth Aretsky, Suzanne Baldwin, Dan Barber, April Bloomfield, Anthony Bourdain, Dana Bowen, Sophie Braithwaite, Georgina Capel, Juli at El Bulli, John Carlin, Caroline Cook, Courtney Cook, Mel Davis, Annie DiGregorio, Paula Disbrowe, Courtney Jo Drasner, Georgette Farkas, Abi Fellows, Jen Fite, Mark Fitzgerald, Johnanna Frenz, Andrew Friedman, Jennifer Galdes, Irene Hamburger, Gabrielle Hamilton, Victor Hazan, Sarah M. Hearn, Robin Insley, Jessica Kingsland, Mark Lawless, Pamela Lewy, Ellen Malloy, Louise Miller, Mary Morris, Marion Oputa, Mandy Oser, Leanda Pearman, Neil Perry, Alexandra Pringle, Leah Ross, Felicity Rubinstein, Lori Silverbush, Belinda Smith, Arabella Stirling,

Mark Stone, Sarah Swanson, Chiaki Takada, Laura Trevino, Jean-Georges Vongerichten, Zoe Waldie, and Roisin Wesley.

—K.W. and P.F.M.

My thanks, as ever, to all of my colleagues at Inkwell for supporting these adventures, and to Peter Meehan for his talent, dedication, and good humor. I am also very grateful to Mhelicia Sarmiento, who knows how to cook and so much more. Above all, much love and thanks to my family, without whom no book would be worth creating.

—K.W.

To try and whittle down how essential Eleanor Jackson and Panio Gianopoulos were to anything that is good about this book to just a few words is beyond me. In the months to come, I will have to learn to stop myself from instinctively reaching for the phone to dial Eleanor whenever I hit a spot of trouble or Panio when I'm mired in a directionless story. I will miss working with them both.

I owe thanks to my coeditor, Kim, for inviting me to be part of this project and taking a chance on working with a writer she'd never worked with. Additional thanks go to Mark Fitzgerald for his hard work and quick turnarounds. And, though I can't thank her enough for it, to Hannah for putting up with me.

—P.F.M.

A NOTE ON THE EDITORS

Kimberly Witherspoon is a founding partner at Inkwell Management, a literary agency based in Manhattan, and the coeditor of *Don't Try This at Home: Culinary Catastrophes from the World's Greatest Chefs.* She is very proud to represent six of the chefs in this anthology: Anthony Bourdain, Tamasin Day-Lewis, Gabrielle Hamilton, Fergus Henderson, Masaharu Morimoto, and Norman Van Aken. She lives with her family in North Salem, New York.

Peter Meehan writes about food and drink. He contributes regularly to the *New York Times.*

A NOTE ON THE TYPE

The text of this book is set in Linotype Sabon, named after the type founder Jacques Sabon. It was designed by Jan Tschichold and jointly developed by Linotype, Monotype, and Stempel in response to a need for a typeface to be available in identical form for mechanical hot metal composition and hand composition using foundry type.

Tschichold based his design for Sabon roman on a font engraved by Garamond, and Sabon italic on a font by Granjon. It was first used in 1966 and has proved an enduring modern classic.

7